THE HIMALAYAN LETTERS
OF GYPSY DAVY & LADY BA

THE
HIMALAYAN LETTERS
OF GYPSY DAVY
AND LADY BA

Written on pilgrimage to the
high quiet places among the
simple people of an old folk tale

With Maps

Decorations
by the Ballad Singer

BOOK FAITH INDIA

ISBN : 81-7303-031-6

Published by:

BOOK FAITH INDIA
416, EXPRESS TOWER
AZADPUR COMMERCIAL COMPLEX
DELHI-110033 (INDIA)

Printed at:
Rama Printograph
Delhi - 110 051

INTRODUCTORY LETTER

Dear WINIFRED,

Gypsies don't write books. But a promise is a promise, even after many years. One of those journeys has been recorded at last,—a safar in the Himalaya, a pilgrimage, revisiting, in some state this time, the high quiet places, letting my lady live in the old folk-tale that life still is among those mountain people. Here's your book.

We found it quite as impossible to write the tale for strangers who might not care to hear it, as to tell it properly anywhere but at a fireside with the family sitting round us on the floor. So we have written letters to particular firesides where the families listen that way.

We have signed them, as the matter or the correspondent moved us, now with one and now with another of the names we have at various times been dubbed. But the names we like the best are those we had of Dorothy, Cynthia and Rosalind, in that rapturous week of gypsying among Cornish hills, singing the old ballads with the country people, dancing the old dances on village greens. Didn't this "Lady Ba" "put off her silk-finished gown and put on hose of leather O" and "go with the Gypsy Davy"? Haven't we gone on from year to year, kidnapping likely boys? Haven't we told fortunes truly? Aren't we always trading horses or asses? It's mountain gypsies we are, though, never quite at home save among mountains, with a caravan of ponies or a string of asses at our backs.

We are camped, or rather bivouacked, in this high place, because the making of this book seems worth while here. We have gone over copies of our letters to grown-ups and boys and girls, kept by the Lady Ba in lieu of diary, and some of the letters which the boys we kidnapped for one or another year of the safar wrote home and wrote us. We have kept the best, written new ones here and there, and borrowed from the boys.

The little russet-backed hawk polices the air while we work. The raven crosses at his peril; a harried flight, full of side slips and quick dodges and nose-dives. Morico stands near

the fire, pointing his long ears at us.   Juan has just unloaded
the water barrels, a loaf of bread, a jug of goat's milk.   Juan
and his ass have climbed a long way up from Vilaflor, through
cloud, among dripping pines, to these dry lava crags, broom-
spotted.

There's tumbled cloud below us, on the one side, to the
round horizon, hiding the sea and the villages.   On the other,
El Teide blots out much sky, beyond a loud abyss,—austere
pile of cinders and writhing lava flows.   The winds rush
down El Teide's slopes, and roar up the pinnacled precipice
at our feet,—a dozen steps from our fireside to the brink.
The swallows toss like blown leaves there.

Juan has paved a little open space among the rocks with
broken bits of lava, for our living-room, and one, adjoining,
for our kitchen, and he has roofed a narrow cleft in the lava
for our larder, with pine boughs and dead pine needles brought
up by Morico from the forest far below, and he has piled more
needles deep for our beds.   We burn the broom.   The sky's
our roof.

Gypsy Davy

Roque del Almendro,
    Tenerife,
       Las Islas Afortunadas.
    June, 1926.

P.S.—A proper cartographer has put together a good flat
map for us, from the latest sources, which you will find in a
pocket in the back of the book.   He has also made several
smaller maps which you will find scattered through.   Among
other things he has marked to the nearest thousand the heights
of most of the mountains that they know the heights of, over
the proper places of their tips on the map.   He has also marked
all the heights he could find on the rivers.   Between these
two sets of figures, you can get some idea of the relief, though
heights unfortunately are scarcest where you most need them.
But we are ultimately depending on legends for our topography
as symbols have the effect on us of exhibiting a country through
the wrong end of a telescope, which we particularly don't want
to do, in this case.   We have other legends to enlighten you
on other matters of moment.   You will have little difficulty
in finding your way about, if you follow our trail, noting camp
numbers as you travel.

I have erased a lot of the cartographer's little streams and
things, that crowded the map confusingly, and don't matter
to this book of yours.   A ballad-singer has done further mischief

letting loose dragons where his glaciers were. The glaciers of the Kara-koram do somewhat resemble English dragons, though in no such balance in the matter of claw and wing, and not so ponderously, considering the scale of the map, as she would have you believe. I must admit, though, that no amount of exaggeration could begin to give you any idea of the real magnitude of these monsters. You will have to bear in mind that much of the blank paper between dragons, in the track of her devastating eraser, stands not for bare mountains, but for snow and ice with only an occasional precipice or sharp arête too steep for snow to lie on, showing through. She has set the map about with Tibetan dragons blowing wind and fire, and with other Tibetan monsters and Buddhist symbols, linked the five bats of luck in the title-frame, and set thunder-bolts in the corners.

No map can show the country so vividly as sticks and books piled on the floor before the fire while the tale's in the telling, but I think this one has its good points.

We are indebted to Dr. Francke, of course, as everybody who meddles with Ladakh must be, and to Dr. De Filippi, and Col. Waddell and Drew and Miss Duncan, and very deeply to our Forbes dictionary.

Yours,
G. D.

London,
October, 1926

THE TABLE OF THE MAPS

THE TABLE OF THE LETTERS

PAGE

PART III—SUMMER AND AUTUMN ON THE TRAIL AGAIN

PART I
SUMMER AND AUTUMN ON THE TRAIL

SUMMER AND AUTUMN ON THE TRAIL

Lady Ba   CAMP 4
                                                   DRAS
                                           August 23

Dear HARLAN,

Mountains and mountains and mountains!

You know the feeling when you've climbed up from the big valley to the crest of the Sierras. You look ahead west, and up north, and down south, and you see and you see and you see—mountains; and, looking back beyond the wide valley, more mountains. The distances you are to measure in burro paces seem very great.

Up on that crest you're out of the net of roads and railways, but the gap in the net is very narrow, and they're working fast to close it. I could barely forget the net, and Gypsy Davy couldn't. That's why we're here.

Here there's nothing to forget. Gypsy Davy says it's months and months hard riding to any road,—the roughest road for the rudest cart.

The great mountains at last! Ever since I "went with the Gypsy Davy," I've wanted to know what the great mountains are like, that are always in the back of his mind. Now at last I'm in them.

For all they're so huge, they don't seem huge. We may have to stay years perhaps before I begin to appreciate them rightly. Everything is on such a colossal scale that nothing seems particularly big. I suppose the skyline I'm looking at is a mile higher than any I've ever seen, but I'm not realizing it. I must, somehow. There are skylines a mile higher than this, ahead.

Our caravan is very different from that compact little outfit of your first Sierran experience,—four of us and a dozen donkeys, wasn't it? Now we've twenty or more ponies for the sahib log, eight menservants, a lot of coolies carrying loads from one village to the next, and always a village headman or two escorting us.

3

Rasul collected the caravan at Leh and sent it a ten days' journey to meet us at Sonamarg,—it barely escaped being overwhelmed by a mud flood at Kargil on the way. Rasul himself is eating his heart out because he can't leave his post in Leh as Aqsaqal (supervisor of traders) in the busy season. He has been looking forward to rejoining his "ponpo" master ever since they parted twenty years ago, after two years' travel together. And now we have come at an impossible moment. However, he has made all the band-o-basts (a most useful word which I mean to adopt into my English). He chose Ibrahim, a young man on that long ago expedition of the Sahib's through here, for caravan bashi. Ibrahim had set up shop in Leh, but he sold out to come. Khalik, the butcher's son, had taken over his father's business, but he shut up his shop and came too. Rasul says he is "very good for put shoes to horses one man." And Ahmat, who was dismissed for foolish conduct, begged Rasul to let him rein-state himself, serving without pay. Rasul says: "I have pardoned to him." "That old cook" who went all the way to China is dead, but his son Sultan represents him.

It's more like a home-coming than like a foreign journey, you see. The other men are new, but they all know the traditions, fostered in Leh by Rasul through two decades. They know the Sahib's objections to villages, his predilection for hilltops. "Which every man liking more villages than deserts, but this sahib going always from top hills to hillstops. His travelling are more different than any man's." I can't think about Rasul without using his "breaking English." Ibrahim tells me that Rasul's Sahib is known in Ladakhi as "Ri Sahib" which I translate "Lord Hilltop," and Sahib himself "Tophills Esq."

This caravan is a thing of colour. We gave Rasul carte blanche in fitting it out, but I think he might have taken it anyway to express his feelings as to the importance of the occasion. I, if you please, ride a snow-white steed, fresh from the Wazir Wazarat's stables, harness covered with silver balls and crosses, stirrups inlaid with silver, a saddle of wood (from Andijan) painted in delicate designs of red and yellow, with ivory along the edges, and a birch bark lining. And a long blue runner out over the tail, fit for a knight's charger, and under the saddle, over a white felt embroidered in yellow, just peeping out, the most beautiful little blue and gold rug from Lhasa, another handsome red one, a gift from Ibrahim, on top—I'm getting all mixed up in the order of my descriptions! How do you suppose they ever get them all on him, and me besides? Lord Hilltop's stout little grey Nun Chun, which Iba bought for him here at Dras for two hundred and five rupees, has equipment quite as splendid, harness blue enamelled, and a whip of ebony inlaid with silver from Lhasa, Iba's present. O, and Khalik brought us little wooden drinking bowls, lined with beaten silver.

Chot has a black horse with sufficiently gorgeous trappings. "Chot" is short for Chhota Sahib, which struck our fancy when we first heard it applied to Roger, as the only meaning we knew for it then was "little," and Roger, as you remember, overtops even the Bara Sahib's six feet two inches. We now know that it means "younger" or " minor " as well. I am the Khush Qismat Mem-Sahib, the " good luck lady." And they call all of us "Huzur" when they address us, which means nothing less than "The Presence."

Harlan, my dear, I daren't write more, lest you give up college and join us—why don't you?

Yours,

THE KHUSH QISMAT MEM-SAHIB

Every horse has a sweetly tinkling bell!

Lady Ba   CAMP 8
                                              TANG
                                        SHINGO VALLEY
                                         August 29

Dear JANET,

That was a versatile animal you were riding by the fire when we last visited you at Killam's Point, the horse Alexander made you. I suppose he carries you to the tilting yard or the round-up or in hunting pink over hedges and ditches any day. But I'll wager you haven't had the experience with him that I had today with Tomar.

I was climbing a steep high bluff on Tomar, up toward a tiny village. The caravan was strung out behind me, descending the opposite bluff and crossing the little torrent in the bottom. On the mud walls of the village above me were a lot of sullen-looking women in black homespun gowns, all looking down at me. Suddenly Tomar stumbled and fell. I was off and on him again very quickly, of course, so that he shouldn't think I distrusted him, but I was surprised, for he had never stumbled with me before.   Iba looked worried.

I wanted to loiter in the tiny alley-ways of streets, and smile at the funny babies, and look at the women as curiously as they looked at me, but Iba hurried me along, unsmiling.

When we were well outside the village, he plucked a wild rose and brought it to me, saying under his breath: "It wasn't Tomar's fault.   It was the Evil Eye."

That gave me a start, I can tell you.   Ibrahim really believes it.   And why shouldn't it be true? Suppose you were working yourself to the bone in a dreary valley—even the mountains mud-colour—trying to collect enough barley and black-eyed peas, and sheep's wool to keep your family alive over the winter, and you suddenly looked down the hill and saw another woman on a milk-white steed, silver and scarlet harness, and a long line of coolies and ponies carrying loads behind her. Don't you think you might be tempted to cast an evil spell over her horse or her if you knew the secret?

I was afraid Ibrahim might want to make Tomar wear shabby harness, or smear him with soot and grease, to protect him, but he hasn't so far suggested it.

I wish you would ride your horse into the Shingo valley some day, after the harvest, at the head of a caravan loaded with bales of cloth, every kind of colour, red, blue, green, yellow, orange, violet, purple, magenta, pink, lavender, mauve, crimson and scarlet.   When you reach the village where Tomar stumbled, have your headman call all the women and children together, and distribute your loads, a gorgeous long strip of cloth to every one, long enough for a dress.   And then ride on up the valley till the brown mountains and the ploughed fields by the grey river seem to swarm with Brazilian butterflies.

You'd better bring a band along, too.   I wonder if you could get them dancing.

Yours,

Lady Ba

P.S.—Roger has just been having supper in the men's tent. He likes the way they do things—pouring water over their hands before they eat, eating with their fingers from one big bowl, a prayer afterward, then making toothpicks, and taking turns at a huqa.   He says to-night they are all very solemn, and their talk appears to be all about the "kharab ankh,"— the evil eye.

Gypsy Davy   CAMP 13
                 ON THE HIGH PLAINS OF THE DEOSAI

September 8

Dear MALCOLM,

We have seen you only once. You ran a race with me, holding a crocus in your hand. We have never had a letter from you: perhaps you never write them. I don't think you have ever had one from us, but we often think of you.

This morning we specially missed you. Lady Ba and I— that reminds me, perhaps you never knew our real names: Gypsy Davy and Lady Ba. We are gypsies. We live in a green Arab tent with red knobs on top. We are always travelling on mountain trails, winter and summer, with our caravan. Shaggy little ponies carry a good many of our loads, and dark men, ragged and barefoot, carry the rest. A flock of goats give us our milk. You should have seen one of them fight with the marmots who live here. Nobody else does live here!—Now you know who we are, I can go on where I left off. Lady Ba was riding her beautiful white pony, Tomar, very gaily caparisoned, and I my little iron-grey Nun Chun. We were a long way ahead of the caravan, miles and miles. Of a sudden we topped a rise, and there at our feet lay a bright sapphire lake, and behind it, looking across the lake and across a little pass, we saw a great snow mountain, gleaming white with the morning sun full on it, and behind the mountain there was deep blue sky. We thought it must surely be the highest and most beautiful mountain in the world.

The sun rose higher behind us, and lit the lake and the grassy slopes about it,—and they were all blue with tall dark larkspur.

There's monk's-hood higher up, all hairy, here where rough winds blow. Ibrahim says the roots of it and the roots of the larkspur are used for medicine in Lhasa. Ibrahim knows all about medicine. He carries a pouch at his belt, in which he keeps a lot of little folded packets of soft Chinese paper, each with some kind of medicine in it, and none of them labelled. There's a pinhead bit of black stuff in one of them, from the stomach of a unicorn in Tibet. It will cure all pain forever. And poisonous snakes fall into a deep sleep when Iba passes, and cannot harm him.

Yours,

GYPSY DAVY

Lady Ba   CAMP 13

Just over the northern edge of the
barren Deosai on a wide ledge from
which precipitous spurs plunge down
into dense coniferous forest far below

Dearest ROSLYN,

We have been seeing Nanga Parbat from various points of
view, and at different times of day. The first sight of it was
at dawn from our first high camp, about a thousand feet above
Marpo La, which itself is in the neighbourhood of sixteen
thousand. The main caravan camped under the La, but the
Sahib, Roger and I, with the cook and another man spent the
night away up at the snout of a little cliff glacier. Our tiny
forester's tents were pitched at the very edge of a precipice,
down which rocks rattled from time to time during the night.
We didn't sleep much, and regretted the time we did spend
sleeping. We could see mists floating up and down and north
and south and east and west. The full moon came up over the
glacier, and broke through the mist for a minute—luckily we
weren't dozing then. We had little hope of seeing Nanga,
for the clouds in that quarter were thickest of all and she was
a long way off. I'm stealing a paragraph from Gypsy Davy's
note-book to give you that dawn:—

"A sharp little white peak came pricking through, and
suddenly lighted up, above all the miles and miles of swirling
mist and driving snow and heavy cloud that lay between us
and it, to all intents and purposes vertical miles. Infinitely
high, it rode majestically up across the rosy halo of Earth's
shadow into the full glare of the sun. And then it was gently
covered for the day, lest some less patient watcher might see
it without prayer and fasting."

The Sahib and the Chhota Sahib (Roger) spent the next
night on a spur above our valley-bottom camp (Camp 8A).
Chot's note-book for that:—

"Woke several times during the night and saw the dim
bulk of Nanga Parbat, greyish white in the north-west.

"Woke finally at four and watched the transformation as
the light grew stronger. Old faces took new shapes, and
new ones appeared. Finally the opaque blue under the twilight
arch descended behind the mountain and the sun's rays first
touched and tinted the little pyramid on top, a deep purplish
red. This quickly travelled down the mountain, leaving behind
varying degrees of red, orange, then yellow-gold, and finally,

when the lower part was in the purple, the peak had a white-gold colour. All the time new angles and new faces came into view, and shadows helped to show the tremendous size of the most beautiful mountain that can be.

"In a few more minutes it was all white, but a whiteness that put the clouds to shame and made them seem grey-black."

Attempt the third was not so successful according to the note-books:

"Chot and I camped high above the Hunter's Pass (Kara-polensa La) our gateway to that glacial dump, the Deosai, in wind and snow and driving mist. We had a glimpse of the tip of the peak at sunset and saw a bit of the dark face through a low rift in the cloud.

"Bulla and Khalik served us piping hot meals in spite of the storm god's efforts to thwart them. And in the morning when the caravan hove in sight, slowly climbing from below, they took our packs on their backs and went leaping down steep talus, singing 'Ha *dam* ma *la*' to which the climbing caravan replied: 'Ha *dam* zer!'

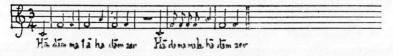

On our way to this camp above Charchur La: "We lifted the great mountain radiant in a clear noonday sky; dwarfing everything about it, though not of that fabulous height of the earlier day: a pure, holy, untouched thing."

Yesterday my lord spent the entire day high above the pass on a ridge to the north. We could just make him out up there, and when we saw that he was surely going to stay for sunset, Khalik saddled his pony and took some food and went off to meet him. He was tired enough! But the sunset was worth waiting for:—

"The mountain seems to rise—a delicate radiant fringe of mist on all its edges—becomes translucent, dim, golden. The crest rises and rises until it seems as if the vast translucent face would cover half the darkening sky."

Yours,

THE KHUSH-QISMAT MEM-SAHIB

Gypsy Davy   CAMP 15
                                                 DEOSAI
                                          September 10

Dear NED,

We were making ready to camp this afternoon near the northern edge of the Deosai, when we met a thirteenth-century page in sober grey stooping under a big basket of melons and grapes and apples and apricots, a dali for us from Mohammed Shah, out of friendliness to Rasul.

The man must have toiled at least two long arduous days up from the sunny gardens and orchards of Skardu, over the Burji La, sleeping out two bitter nights, with no knowledge of how many more days he might have to travel in this bleak place to find us.

Our wizened little bakri-wala is begging to be let start back with his twenty goats to his home in the Shingo "before the storm which follows the harvest." You would think that goatherd would be tempted by this beckoning of the promised land. Probably he has never seen Skardu or any fruit-tree. But no, he will be hastening back to his lugubrious valley. It is a long bleak way ahead of him. No villages but marmot villages. No wood—we had to bring ours. No shelter. A high pass at the end, and lowering skies. Many a man has died on this Deosai. I doubt if any one ever ventures here so late with goats.

He will save his goats one cruel pass by turning back before the Burji La. We shall have the temerity to-morrow to camp right on that pass.

Yours,

P.S.—How's ⨪ for a signature? "Ri" in Roman. They call me "Ri Sahib" because I camp high, always,—on the top of something if I can get there. This hieroglyph means literally "mountain," and would have to be supplemented with another hieroglyph to make "hilltop," but it serves our men for that, alone.

Lady Ba
CAMP 16
BURJI LA
September 11

Dearest ROSLYN,

Here camped on the very pass, I am copying for you some more bits from Gypsy Davy's note-book. We have climbed up out of the Deosai, and I have a little camp here on the top of the pass, while Iba and the caravan are in a more reasonable place below, and the Sahib and Roger are still higher up on a peak to the right of the pass—have been there since long before dawn.

As I can't climb so high, I am recalling all the views we have had of Nanga Parbat, which I shall not see again. My men will see her today and also look ahead to the great peaks of the Kara-koram range.

Here is a dawn from that camp above Charchur La, from which I wrote you last.

"The arch that frames the shadow sinks down far below the summit, behind the mountain, before anything more than a gradual brightening of the surface takes place. A curious dull whiteness all the time. Then, as the peak emerges from the shadow, it turns violet for an instant, then burning gold, then white gold, then radiant white. My lord the Sun runs his colours in waves down the mountain's face.

"A buttressing arête in the lee of this flood of colour and light lies late in shadow, but at last one crag glows white, then another and another and another."

And a sunset from the same place:

"The mountain rode up dark into the twilight, and grew huger and huger and huger as the darkness deepened. We thought the sun well set, but suddenly a shaft of light shot through an unsuspected cleft in snowy ridges, and, for a moment burned the great dark hazy face golden translucent. Just before the shaft of sunlight was snuffed out, it lit a delicate halo of mist and blowing snow along the crest. The hazy darkness deepened as the mountain rode on up into the night, until we lost it. We thought we saw stars shining where we had last seen it. Toward morning a pale old moon rose over an eastern peak in the arms of a golden crescent, and ever so faintly lighted Nanga."

With the keenest wish that you might be seeing all this with me

Yours,
THE LUCKY LADY

P.S. *Next Day.*—Chot says I may copy part of his letter to his mother about his tremendous yesterday. I got a fair view of the Kara-koram myself from my pass camp, three peaks suddenly lighted up and distinguished from the mass of innumerable peaks and ridges filling all space out there. But what a contemptible day mine was! A cautious climb up a few hundred feet; sketching a furry-leaved larkspur; sending Bulla up with food for the climbers; petting Yellow Dog Hamra; mending a little—while Roger was doing this:—

"This morning early—hours before we should be turned toward the sun—we (Sahib and I) got up and climbed a peak above the Burji La in the southern wall of the Indus valley.

"We reached the top while all was yet dark and could see tremendous blocks of shadow around us—everywhere: huge mountains and wondrous peaks which, as the heavens became lighter in acknowledgment of the sun, took on a cold life. Then, as the light became stronger and finally the sun rose, the mountains, peaks and ridges became translucent, airy and colourful in succession. It was such an expanse of immensity as I have hardly imagined. Godwin Austen (K^2) sixty miles to the north-east of us, and Nanga Parbat sixty miles to the south-west, were within the circle of our horizon; and between, around and beyond them were mountains, valleys and mountains.

"Sahib really communed with the universe up there and I felt as if I could—in my smaller way—also do it. He was gloriously happy, really living. He stood up, his head raised, his nostrils dilated, inhaling it all fiercely.

"It seems you cannot talk in a matter-of-fact way in a place like that. It is with an awed voice that you speak of the tremendous blocks and pyramids rising around you as far as you can see, and at their edge passing you on to the heavens, the solar system and the universe so that in the end they seem at once tremendous and infinitesimal—and still I don't believe they ever do seem really small, no matter with what I compare them.

"When the sun rose we could really see the curvature of the earth, for the eastern down-sweeping horizon brought K^2 into the sun's rays several minutes before Nanga Parbat to the west got any light.

"I thought the Sierras were large, but here, where we could see three or four score miles north, south, east and west, and see only mountains, and most of them above twenty thousand feet, the Sierras seem like sand dunes—and yet they are wonderful sand dunes.

"We sketched, talked, looked and thought—and so went a day—*the* day. We stayed up until the stars came out, and in the evening saw the folding up of what was unfolded for us in the morning.

"I must turn in. Tomorrow we start down the Burji toward Skardu in the Indus Valley. We had a glimpse of it today and I am eager to see it at closer range."

Gypsy Davy   Camp 16
                                        Burji La
                                 September 12

Dear Dick,

Chot and I got some sense of height and depth hereabout yesterday. We sat all day from starlight to starlight on the northern battlements of the Deosai, above the Indus at, I suppose, about seventeen thousand feet.

So long as it was dark, there was no height or depth, only a vague dark planetary surface with vague limits betrayed from time to time by the sudden disappearance of stars to westward and the sudden flashing into sight of other stars to eastward.

As Chot agreed, we did not feel height until long after our horizon had been clearly defined in the morning light and had uncovered the sun. Then we began to feel it.

There is an array of peaks along the stretch from Nanga Parbat round through Hunza to K² and beyond, of proportions so immense that watching them in many changing lights a long day through broke the spell that binds the lowlander to see things low, in terms of trees and steeples, and set us free to see them high and big. I suppose the watching had as much hand in the release as the peaks themselves.

When the sun lit the great valley yawning beneath our battlements, we thought we felt something of its depth. We could even surmise the magnitude of the gorge below Gilgit (denied us this time) with which they say no other gorge in the world is comparable.

We tried to picture the Indus valley from where the river spouts from the lion's mouth in Tibet, on down to where it breaks through the mountains and flows out across the Punjab to the sea. But it was a feeble business. We may have got some vague ideas of height and depth, but distance is still an enigma to us.

The people, by the way seem to make little effort to think

of the river beyond what they can see of it at their doors.   It
bears various local names along its course through the mountains,
as if they thought of it only in sections.   Rasul thinks further
than most of his fellows, but the Indus is too long even for him.
He has travelled over much of the country between Hunza
and the Tibetan border, been within a week's march of Lhasa
with Littledale, and seen the Brahmaputra there.   He has
seen all the big rivers of the Punjab, and travelled on the Hwang
Ho and the Yangtze-kiang, but he said to me one day of the
Indus: "I thinking, sir.   Here come Shyok from Depsang.
Joining to it Nubra.   Then Kargil river.   Then Hunza river.
Getting very big.   Going,—I not know where going."

Yours,

Lady Ba   CAMP 17

SKARDU

September 16

Marjorie dear, we're not in India! I hate to have you think
of us along with "the Taj Mahal and pearl mosques and bullock
carts and women in pastel-hued saris" as you say in your letter.
(What fun it was to get letters here! Mail-day postponed for
six weeks becomes a festival.)

I know you had to put "India" on your letter to reach me,
and the stamps Iba will stick on this letter to you will be Indian.
But suppose Mexico were to annex Southern California, would
you turn Spanish?

These mountain countries are part of the Tibetan highland,
really, and were called Tibet until about the time of the California
gold rush. Then a fighting Raja down on the borders of
British India began to look about for country to conquer.
Every time he looked south, I imagine, the lion's mane bristled
with bayonets.   So he took an army across the high mountains
to the north, and conquered two countries up here, Baltistan,
where we are now, and Ladakh, where we are going.   If you
should see the simple little forts they had, you'd not think it
much of a trick! The conquering General ventured too deep
into Tibet and never came back—which is some comfort.
His Maharajah's son now rules Baltistan and Ladakh as provinces
of Kashmir, a "British protected state"—which accounts for

postage-stamps and rupees and addresses and Hindu officials
serving time on the frontier.

But India is a long way off, and foreign, really foreign.   What
is that in the first sentences of Caesar, about the Belgae and
the Aquitani and somebody else? "Inter se differunt, moribus,
institutis et lingua?"

I'll answer the rest of your letter later. • I'm due this minute
to go to call on the enclosed ladies of a Mohammedan maulvi.
What will they think of my knickers? I've no skirts within
two months' journey.

Love all around.   And keep writing.

Lady Ba

There's a man at Iba's tent with a falcon on his wrist!

Lady Ba   Camp 17
Skardu
September 16

Dear Colony,

We've been visiting school.

The Headmaster called on us in our guest-tent yesterday,
along with the Next-to-the-headmaster, and the one next to
that, O very formally, having sent a servant before him to ask
whether we could receive him.

It was a busy day socially, for the Raja was calling too,
wearing a pink silk robe, gold-embroidered, and yellow army
boots. He couldn't speak a word of English. My Urdu
is still at the stammering stage and Roger's is worse, so it was
a relief when he left and the schoolmasters arrived desiring
to talk their English.

We were so cheered up that we promised to visit the school
next day. The Head told us school was supposed to open
at ten, but that he could not be sure of all the pupils being
on hand before twelve.   (That made me gasp a little, remembering how my heart used to thump when the last bell began
to ring while I was crossing the Park!)

A servant arrived next day a little before noon, and led
us by narrow paths under fruit-trees, along the edges of irri-
gating ditches (little streams of clear running water—pretty
things!) past wooden houses with loggias and lattices, past
a small stone mill grinding away without a miller, past the
stone dung-towers, the pride of Skardu's sanitary department,

and up a steep hill to the schoolhouse. "A.V. Middle School" we read over the door as the Headmaster came out to meet us. "Anglo-Vernacular," he explained. The children all learn English as well as their own Balti, and of course they learn Urdu. Imagine three languages before you are ready for High School! A little arithmetic and a course in General Information is all there is time for besides.

In the school courtyard some boys performed for us on parallel bars. One was very good indeed, but he had a lot of trouble because his big purple pagri dropped off every time he lowered his head.

The little tots were in a dirt-floored room with one window. They all sat on the floor and sang us a song, one of them singing so very lustily that Gypsy Davy said he would grow up to be a muezzin and call the people to prayer.

In the next room the pupils were up off the floor on a bench. There was a wall-map of their own country and a blackboard. And on the blackboard was written: "A Verb is the name of a person, place or thing." When we read that, we looked away politely, but the Head had seen it and he looked like a thundercloud. "Who wrote that?" he demanded, and all the children turned and stared at the poor Next-to-the-bottom-master who said humbly: "I did." And the Head marched to the board and rubbed out "verb" and wrote "noun" very big and plain, and told us it was a hopeless business trying to teach when you had only nincompoops to help you.

He had the next teacher show us some English letters the boys had written. They were much neater and more correctly spelled than some letters I get, but there wasn't much sense in them. The Head said that they only wanted the pupils to be able to speak and write "with fluency." They didn't care what they said or wrote!

In the highest class the boys sat on chairs. The Master had a very handsome chair in each room. I think one of the reasons why people want their children to learn English is that they may have a chance to sit in chairs. (I am sure they think we gypsies are very strange because, though we own chairs, we prefer to sit on the ground.)

After we had visited all the rooms, the whole school marched out to a big parade ground, and all who had uniforms drilled for us to the music of a fife and a drum with a hole in the head. Those who couldn't afford uniforms hid, and peeked at us. We gave the Head some money to get uniforms for them. It's a free school, but you have to furnish your own books, and usually you have to coax your father to let you go. And when it comes to buying uniforms!

Do you remember what Rasul said about learning to read?

"I said my friends: 'I will come for reading at padre school.' They said: 'You must come. There we find books without prices and teaching very good.' My mother not liked the reading business. She said: 'That is not our business. Reading business is for rich man.' My sister told Mother: 'Let Rasul go. If not, will make very sorry because those his friends go, and he not go.' Then Mother said: 'Yes, you may go.' I went to the school. The Padre Sahib gave me one primer. I reading that primer in ten days, because I had reading it before with my friends. When finished, the Padre Sahib gave me first reader. That finished very soon. God helped me to going ahead my friends. Now come spring. My mother bade me go mountains for bushwood. I went mountains, but what I reading, that I never forget."

I wondered if any of those little urchins would ever grow up to write a book in English, as Rasul did. I don't believe they will. Rasul never tried to talk fast in any language. He had a lot to say and often had to draw on several languages in order to say all he wanted to. Very different from Kim's munshi. Rasul says: "My English is like crooked spoon. Not very good, but can take food."

After the drill, when they had played "God save the King," and saluted King George—queer little row of "British protected persons" ten thousand miles from England—they all sat down, and the Head said to us: "We have Mohammedans here who have always hated and persecuted Hindus. And we have Sikhs here who have always hated and persecuted Mohammedans. And we have Hindus here who have always thought that to touch anyone not of their own religion is to become impure. But here they all sit, side by side, and what is more, they pray together."

Then he gave a signal and they all began to chant a long, long prayer. He gave us his translation of it, and I'll put part of it here to end my letter:

"Almighty, do not allow Thy humble devotee to bow his head at any threshold other than Thine.

"I crave spiritual enlightenment. I am dazzled with Thy glory.

"There is a great fluttering in the atmosphere of Thy rose-garden. But alas! The bird, whose feet are tied with a cord, feels choked in a cage.

"Our days pass away. The swift-footed hours of life pass.

"I would that the plain of life were more spacious.

"I wander as a supplicant, measuring the skirts of the wilderness.

"Seekers after Thee inquire from one and all: Where is He Whose manifestation is the universe?

"O God, we bring our desires to Thee. Do Thou consider them and show us their value."

Do you sing hymns in your school?

Yours,

LADY BA

Gypsy Davy   RIGHT BANK OF THE INDUS
AT THE FERRY
September 21

Dear DONALD,

We've crossed the Indus in an old scow.

When we got to the appointed place on the bank, we saw the old thing a long way down stream balking at the far end of a long grass cable. Her ragged crew at the other end were straining, or pretending to, with all their might, but she gave no heed. As soon as we were unpacked, Chot hurried off with a squad of our men to help. They got her up where they wanted her eventually. We jumped some ponies in. Dog Hamra had to be carried in, he was so scared.

They gave her a violent push from the shore. The current seized her. The crew began rowing furiously with three huge oars, any one of them big enough to outweigh all the oars of the Cornell 'Varsity boat Chot rowed in this summer.

We had our hands full with the ponies. Nun Chun was set on jumping out. It was a wide, exciting crossing. Struck shallow water in the nick of time, it seemed to me. Things down stream looked nasty.

The crew leaped out with the cable, and as many of our men as were not busy with the ponies followed. The long frayed grass thing held. We swung round violently and came to shore. The ponies were out in a twinkling and stood about pointing their ears at the old tub.

All hands leaned against the cable, singing "*Ha* dam ma la *Ha* dam lay," and the scow moved off very slowly upstream, It is now dashing across for another load.

Is the violin beginning to mind you?

GYPSY DAVY

Lady Ba   PAKORE
                                        BRALDOH VALLEY
Dear ELIZABETH,

How would you like to cross a bridge, a suspension bridge, made of nothing but braided birch twigs?

I've crossed two, and have another tomorrow.

The first was a badly frayed one. Many of its up-and-down cords were broken and hung dangling. I didn't need to cross it, but I knew that later on I should have to cross one or two up here, with a lot of people watching, so a month ago down in the Shingo Valley I practised on that broken one privately with Roger. It took me a deal of time to get started. I tried it first with shoes, then without, then with again, while I was getting up my courage. Roger went across twice, the second time backwards. He even walked a little way without taking hold with his hands. I didn't feel at all acrobatic. I stepped along as cautiously as my old donkey in the Sierras. Coming back was easier—at least it was necessary.

Today I was glad I'd had that practice. The bridge we've just got over is very long and very high, and the water far down below looks savage. The men thought Mem-Sahib was bahadur. They aren't used to such things themselves. Iba prayed all the way over. He made the bridge-tender walk backward in front of him, and gave him bakhshish at both ends. (Iba's rather economical about bakhshish.)

The most awful places are where you have to climb over the sticks that hold the hand-ropes apart. If Gypsy Davy hadn't helped me there, I'd have disgraced myself.

I suppose Donald would have hung from the foot-cable and swung himself across like a monkey.

Yours,
LADY BA

Gypsy Davy   CAMP 32
                                          ASKOLE
Dear DAVE,   *October* 10

You hear of tigers down in India now and then, mauling men.

There are no tigers here, but there are ice-dragons which maul the valleys.

This valley was mauled by one, not so long since. The old fellow was incredibly long and fat. His tails lay on high passes far to the east, and his horrid snout, far down the Shigar, vomited gravel and grey water into the Indus. His many feet clawed the very mountain tops, and his wings covered the mountains. For spines he had ice pinnacles. There were dark markings on his back, long ridges of moraine. His belly was spiked with sharp hard rocks.

His tails stayed on those high passes, while he stretched his body very slowly, longer and longer, as a worm does. He might have reached the plains of India with the help he had, if the warm dry airs of the Indus had not thawed him back.

He's asleep now, at the head of the Braldoh, shrunk to a mere thirty miles. And his helpers sleep up side nalas.

We saw him there three days ago, vomiting grey water, and we heard him groan.

He left many of his feet behind him, or rather in front of him, as he shrank back, withering, but still clawing at the mountain tops.

How he has messed this valley up from top to bottom! Once long rocky spurs reached down on every hand, and bathed their feet in a clear torrent. They were so steep that you and I could never have scrambled over them. They overlapped so far that we could never have seen farther up valley than from the foot of one to the foot of the next. The torrent had to travel farther from side to side than it travelled ahead. It came tumbling down in long cascades and now and then fell sheer in waterfalls. No one would have picked the valley to travel in in those days, let alone to live in.

The dragon changed all that. That rock-spiked armoured belly of his ground and tore away the feet of the spurs and smoothed the rough bottom out until it had made a deep gorge with sides that went straight up. He polished everything with fine rock-flour before he left. He continued to vomit gravel and grey water, all the while he was shrinking back, till he had filled the gorge with it. Each of those abandoned feet of his kept on clawing more stuff down the valley sides to pile up in little piles on the gravel in the gorge.

Now that the old dragon is asleep, the water has stopped filling in and set to work, digging. The big stream from his mouth has cut a winding canyon down through the deep smooth gravel, and the little streams from his withered feet have cut straight ones through the piles.

There's a trail now in the valley, dangerous enough I think you'd call it. And there are some little villages. But as I told you, the dragon is not dead. He's only sleeping.

Yours,
GYPSY DAVY

Gypsy Davy.   BRALDOH VALLEY
                                          October 13

Dear FAY,

This is a wild valley for men to be farming, even if the men be black, bobbed-haired fellows, barefoot and strangely clothed in grey, dingy homespun wool, folds and folds and festoons of it.

Deep, incredibly deep the valley. The mountain crests on either hand are hid for the most part from the valley bottom by steep slopes and towering walls of old rock; walls shattered by frost and rent by earthquake; huge, sinister masses poised, ready to come crashing down, no man knows when, in avalanche; fresh scars above, and ruin below, through which we must laboriously pick our way. But now and then there's a glimpse of some tall spire or tower or great cathedral roof dividing the snowy mantles the crests wear.

The valley would be quite uninhabitable, had it not been for an immense old glacier, thousands of feet thick, that once ploughed through it.

A fearful engine of destruction this, the feeders of it yet to be seen, scouring the upper reaches. One, the Baltoro, we saw thirty miles of, still hundreds of feet thick. Dirty ice, so thickly covered with silt and sand and gravel and huge boulders fallen from the cliffs about, that you would think it no glacier, but some huge avalanche track. The old glacier when it was intact must have been resistless. Armed below with almost as many rocks frozen in as appeared above, it ground its way down, turning a wild, intricately sinuous, quite impassable valley into a wide, flat-floored gorge, with every jagged spur ground off. It was abetted by a host of smaller glaciers, now shrunken back, lying hidden in deep valleys, and in corries under the crests on either hand, but once sprawling widely, grinding their way down to meet the master glacier.

And then there came a time when the ice began to melt back faster than it came on, dumping its heavy load, choking the valley with it. And the loads the corrie glaciers had been carrying came pouring down steep slopes and over cliffs, heaping up in steep piles and gently sloping piles, piles lying at all angles. This stuff is still coming down, not infrequently on people's heads. It has killed seven men within the last year or two on a particularly bad stretch of trail we had to travel yesterday.

This shrinking of the ice seems to have happened in a long

dry spell. (It was drought that made the ice shrink back, not heat—lack of fresh snow on the snowfields.) Sand blew then, and silt blew and a fine rock-flour as fine as Portland cement that glaciers are famous for the milling of, this fine flour blew everywhere, even high up the steepest slopes, and one or other or all of these, sand, silt and rock-flour, accumulated in thin beds and thick beds, on jagged spurs and smooth slippery slopes, on ledges and on gravelly boul dery flats and piles. A certain amount of water helped the wind till, between the grinding by the ice and the cloaking by the wind and water, the valley became in a manner of speaking, passable —at any rate, in cold weather when there wasn't much water running.

Later on the filling-in stopped and the main stream and all the side streams began gorging and terracing the gravels. I suppose the water had less load to carry then and was freer to cut, or perhaps the mountains rose higher and a steeper grade gave the water more power.

So well mixed were the materials that the streams cut into, and so evenly were the various cements, rock-flour and lime and iron and others, distributed through the mass, that coarse gravel walls, hundreds of feet high, now stand up as vertical as any wall of granite you ever saw, and when they fall, fall off in great slices or slump in masses, acres in extent. The effect of this sawing by the main stream and the side streams has been to leave a block between each pair of tributaries, projecting from the valley sides, some of them little, and some, miles across. The block-tops slope at all angles. Some are smooth with cloaks of silt or rock-flour, and some very rough, with pebbles and big fallen masses and big boulders left by the ice all over them.

The trail laboriously and dangerously picks its way, up over one block, down into a difficult gorge and up over another block, or out upon a lower terrace, along the base of the bluff of a higher, or among tremendous boulders close to the edge of the main stream. Where the main stream nips the rock wall of the valley, the trail goes straight up by ladders, or precarious footholds in the rock, perhaps straight up a thousand feet to where a narrow crooked ledge supplemented by unsteady scaffolds traverses the cliff, and then straight down again. Here and there it crosses the main stream itself by a spider web bridge, two or three hundred feet long, of braided birch twigs, swung at a dizzy height above the torrent; a few strands for your feet, a few for either hand. Some of our loaded men funked these, and some of the unloaded looked pretty tense, halfway across.

Men have come in here on such a trail, and in some way have got goats and sheep and dzo and yak in with them, how, I don't know, perhaps in the egg. There is no horse nor any relative of his in the valley that I know of.

To pasture their stock, the men have made trails days long, up difficult side nalas, up dangerous slopes in the main valley, zigzagging laboriously up to where rich grass grows at the snow's edge. If you were to come up the main valley trail in early September you would see practically no stock anywhere.

To cultivate they must lead on water, that raging, destructive grey water. They catch it in the colt stage in small side streams, where it comes tearing down in horrible little gorges, and lead it in ditches, beautifully engineered without instruments, along vertical gravel walls and steep cliff faces, across wicked little fans where the ditch is continually demolished, to the gentler slopes. There, by patient labour, they have built up an intricate series of little terraces, irrigable by clever distribution of the water. The ditches themselves have a considerable hand in filling in behind terrace walls, for the water carries a heavy load of very fine silt. They catch a lot of this in small ponds—for mud plaster, I suppose.

They have led the water, not only where there was already a crust of something that might become soil, on the gravel, but also where a thousand years spent in hauling off big and little boulders would only make matters worse. They have transformed such coarse, bare, gravel slopes into long flights of smooth, gently sloping terraces. And they have dunged them with human dung, and with goat and sheep dung, brought down from the high pastures in tall baskets, on men's backs. (Dzo dung, I believe, is too valuable as fuel to be all wasted on fields.) And they have planted them with wheat and barley and buckwheat and millet and a kind of pea, and apples and apricots, and mulberries and walnuts, and even, in rare little patches, with tobacco.

They have planted Lombardy poplars in the lanes of their villages. They use the poplar for the tall ladders and props they need in bad places on the trails, and also for general timber, for the supporting frames of their mud-and-pebble houses, door frames and doors and many another purpose. A little crooked poplar grows wild, I think, and there is wild birch for the rope bridges. (Imagine a very long suspension bridge of braided birch and nothing else, every year renewed!) There is wild birch for tines for pitchforks and dung-forks, and for hooks and rings. There is wild willow for baskets and lattices, and all these woods are used in making the full tale of tools. Almost the only iron they have is the adze and the tiny point on the ploughshare, (if you can call a knee a share!) and the little saw-toothed sickle.

The villages at harvest time are very lovely, perched at various levels. At a little distance they look like low piles of big flat-topped boulders, among tall Lombardy poplars and spreading fruit-trees, all exquisite shades of autumn. Terraces about them, yellow with ripe grain, step down to the very edge of precipitous bluffs, and up to slopes too hopelessly steep,—always a willow-bordered ditch, leading from the gorge to the village.

The mud roofs now at harvest time are piled high with stacks of threshed buckwheat, or millet unthreshed, or are golden with drying apricots. And always we see groups of men, women and children working on the roofs, stopping to watch us pass. And up through a hatchway in every roof sticks a ladder-end.

In the midst of each huddle of houses with crooked six-foot alley-ways for streets, there is a little mosque, a porch merely, where men go sometimes to pray, and whence the muezzin at daybreak and at nightfall and at noon calls a long ringing call, bidding men, wherever they may be and whatever they may be about, to face toward Mecca and bow down and pray.

Up and down the yellow terraces there are dingy grey bundles of men and rusty black bundles of women squatting, reaping with those sickles, taking a handful of grain in one hand, cutting a few stalks, uprooting the rest, laying it down flat, much as a scythe would. They never bind it, except with the pack-ropes, when they carry it off to the threshing-floor on their backs in huge bundles.

And after the reaper, the gleaner, a solitary, utterly ragged woman at twilight, crouching beside a pyramidal basket, carefully gathering each stray stalk the reapers have left lying. The more prosperous or generous farmers see to it that there are gleanings to be had.

When the grain is all cut, and the last stalk gleaned, the cattle come down from the high pastures, and range the terraces, the clumsier of them after stubble or leaves knocked down for them on the ground, the goats in the trees.

Teams of lumbering dzo and yak, three, five, six abreast, are harnessed by the necks to birchen rings on solid posts set in the centre of hard-beaten threshing-floors. Six or eight

neat little stacks of grain stand around each threshing-floor.
A man on one of them keeps his team half buried in grain until
he thinks he has pitched down as much as can be tramped out
in a day. The team plods slowly round and round, with
many stops, and much painful tail-twitching and much beating
and yelling by the boy behind it, all day long. And all the
dung is quickly gathered if not actually caught as it falls.

The buckwheat they cure very thoroughly, roots up, then
heads up, and thresh with long forked sticks by hand, and then
stack the stalks on roofs and guard them from intruding cattle
by abatises of thorn-bush. Wild rose is good for that.

And now to mill, for the water is falling, and soon day-to-day
grinding will be out of the question. The streams and larger
ditches are lined with tiny mills, one close above another, often.
You might think them boulders at a glance. Rude little wooden
turbines, on to which water is shot from steep troughs a dozen
feet long; small gneiss boulders roughly dressed on one side,
for mill-stones; a pyramidal basket for hopper with a joggler
riding round on the undressed surface of the revolving boulder
to keep a slow feed working; a hard earth floor for the mill
to spray its flour out upon; a brushwood broom and a coarse
wool swab for gathering the mixture of grain-flour and rock-
flour and earth-dust—a profitable business for the miller if he
charges by weight, but there are so many mills I think each
farm must own one. The miller fills the hopper, starts the
mill, fastens the tiny door with a wooden lock, and lets it grind.
They grind the grain both raw and roasted.

What, beside these various grains, they eat I don't know.
We never caught them eating anything else. Men carried
all our luggage on their backs, and the only food they had was
coarse meal of roasted grain, eaten with water. No tea, nothing
to smoke but dried rhubarb leaves, no cigarettes, no pipe but
an improvised tube moulded in wet sand or clay by the trail-
side, with live coals in the bowl. They had to lie down and
put their mouths to a hole in the ground to get a whiff from
this thing along with a good choke and a mouthful of sand.
These men find themselves ordinarily. Another time I would
furnish mutton, if it could be had, and tobacco.

Everything that is carried in this valley is carried on a human
back. Our goats rode thus at fords, slung in their owner's
shawl,—icy water, grey and turbulent, hiding big slippery
boulders. The goats' heads overtopped the man's. We had
twenty milch goats and a number of little sheep for mutton,
and an odd willow crate full of chickens, when we went on

up the valley a long way beyond its highest village. The chickens rode all the way, but the sheep had to walk.

Carrying loads is a regular occupation. A man hires out his back as you farmers hire out your horses or automobiles. They regularly carry dried fruit a hundred miles to sell, and stout strips of yak-hair cloth, and wool ropes, too. Some of their freight they carry thus, hundreds of miles.

There are said to be more people than the land can support, but we heard of little permanent emigration. The more adventurous peddle their apricots all the way down to Hindustan, getting a job there, coming back a year or two later with brass and copper, aluminium and enamel vessels for return freight. The next year or two I suppose they stay at home and lie at ease, eating what they can get in exchange for the vessels. The well-to-do, or those in need of vessels, doubtless share their takings much more liberally in exchange for the fellow's labour in the indirect form of copper pots.

The people are all poor enough and shockingly dirty. Perhaps some of it is shamming. Rapacious tax-collectors breed men who can act the poor man's part wonderfully well in any country. Every one has strong white teeth from eating coarse bread and meal, and they have rosy cheeks like all mountain folk. There is rich crimson in even the blackest cheeks. Many have fine features, but the dirt dims their beauty. In three weeks in the valley I have seen but one washing: a man tramping out a woollen garment in a little wooden trough, by the trail-side, using cold water and no soap.

None of the terraces are quite safe from avalanche. Those on the higher benches are safe enough from flood, but there are whole networks of them on the lower benches which are not safe. The side streams run near the surface on the lower benches, and in time of flood they, so to speak, stampede the terraces down there. In spite of the transitory nature of things within range of the guns of these little devils of streams, there are low buildings so exposed, for storing the short straw and chaff from the threshing-floors, and there are mills in plenty.

We crossed two little gorges on our way up valley, below Askole, half choked with freshly dried mud. These gorges belch liquid mud suddenly with very little warning, in great quantities. They are rather dangerous to cross, as you have to climb down into them and up out of them. But there are no people living near.

They say there are lots of red bear in the valley. I didn't see any. Lots of wild sheep, too, at twelve or thirteen thousand.

I surprised a band of ibex at close quarters, fifteen strong, stocky, bearded fellows, rather greyer and shorter-legged than a wapiti, whitish rump, short chunky black tail, long fluted horns, unbranched, curving up and back. They fled up precipices where I had no mind to follow them. I heard them still climbing above me after I got up to seventeen thousand, with thousands of feet of rosy cliff above them still to climb and much snow and ice.

There are big eagles in the high places, or perhaps they are lammergeiers. The village ravens are tremendous fellows. The crows are as numerous and noisy as yours. The pigeons continually hurry back and forth across the valley in big flocks. They start on some gentle slope high up the valley side, and suddenly find themselves miles deep in air. There are wild ducks on the river, resting on a most arduous journey south.

But lest you forget what sort of valley this is, let me remind you that we found that old glacier growling in his lair up valley. Old Appo Mahmat told us that he has seen it rooting down over grass and jungle.

It snowed on us up there in our camp, close to the old grey monster's snout. Rough winds shook our tent. The ground and the monster were all white in the morning. We had hit the trail by daylight, I can tell you, flying down valley through the storm as fast as we could travel.

Yours,

BA

Gypsy Davy
CAMP 37
TISAR
Where the Braldoh and the Basha join
to make the Shigar

October 16

Dear HAL,

That big boulder by the river-bank near your house, you know, was brought there when they were using glacial ploughs in the corn belt.

There was a lot of ice in this part of the world then, too. It has left its mark everywhere, high and low. It isn't all gone yet. We find the tail ends of great glaciers in every valley we go up.

We built some cairns, several hundred yards in front of the snout of one of them the other day—the Baltoro—and made a little compass map, with directions and distances and the date, and hid it in one of the cairns, so that the next comer may know how far the old boar travels down or backs up between our time and his.

We had about fifty coolies with us, any one of whom might be counted on to steal the tin match-box in which the map was hidden. So Iba pronounced a dreadful curse in the presence of them all, which should fall on their villages, should anyone lay hands on the box: drought and flood and pestilence, and I don't know what besides.

Our salams to your family.

Gypsy Davy

Gypsy Davy   Camp 40
Shigar
Last of October

Dear Roland,

We are camped in a most lovely spot, just level with the tops of the highest of the apricots, dripping blood, looking down over a forest of delicately shaded crimson and gold and grey and green, across a cold grey Shigar, over drifting sand, over the long brown sweep of a barren fan, to brown facets and steep snow-powdered slopes, and glaciers and snow-fields, and sharp arêtes beyond the Indus, " entermingling along with the skie."

We made all haste up out of the Sind, to save the Aqsaqal's magnificent outfit from the poison grass, came to Dras, and set about preparing to stalk Nanga Parbat from there.

We had our first glimpse from a cold snowy windy camp, high above the Shingo La* (east of the Marpo on the French army map) above sixteen thousand, at the foot of a little cliff glacier, warmly snuggled in our blankets, warmed inside with piping hot soup, hot vegetable stew, hot pilav, hot chapatis, hot apricot sauce, hot goat's milk chocolate, all deliciously cooked by Bulla, how, on that wind-swept arête, without a vertical foot of shelter anywhere, I know not. Our intrepid Goanese Pinto who had insisted on accompanying us, to all intents and purposes a frozen corpse by four p.m. A waste of words for some, all this about hot soup, but not for a well-favoured man, sitting by a comfortable wood fire on a cold January night.

---

* The symbol for this pass and its name were both omitted from the Map by an oversight, and Camp 6 was placed exactly where the symbol should be, instead of up to the right at the lower edge of a small glacier, which was also omitted.

A welter of mists, now delicate wisps, now heavy banks, filling the great cirques below us, blowing a dozen ways at once, now hiding, now revealing, arête beyond arête to the north-westward. Flurriés of snow, fierce gusts of wind, wide patches of blue overhead.

The western rim of the world rode steadily up, regardless of all this, and put the sun down in such an agony of colour as never was on earth before. The eastern rim rode down as steadily, and we lifted the moon.

We slept and waked and slept and waked again, all through an unforgettable night, too holy to bespatter with words. But there was no sleeping after the first glimpse of dawn. Of a sudden there shone clear, just pricking through a sea of swirling mist, high, incredibly high, a violet pyramid tip, tip of a baseless pyramid, an ethereal thing,—shone for a moment and vanished.

A week later, from another wind-swept arête in another storm, this time above the Karapolensa La (between the Shingo and the Nagpo Chu, shown on the new two-mile sheets) at seventeen thousand, we saw it at sunset, the top of the peak, and miles below, through a rift in the clouds, dark cliffs.

Another week, and the Mem-Sahib riding her gay Tomar and I my spirited little iron-grey Nun Chun, far ahead of the caravan, far out of sight and sound, approaching a sapphire lake, set in the yellow green of September grass, and the dark blue of high mountain larkspur, at the foot of a low pass, the Charchur La (Sarsingar on the French map) tawny with withered grass, tawny cliff and grassy ledge on the one side, tawny cliff and long scree on the other,—in such a frame we lifted the mountain, radiant white against an azure sky.

Of course we pitched our tents on a grassy ledge just over the pass, and we lay there for days, and bathed our souls in the beauty. Our eyes ranged from the dark fir forest deep down in the upper Astor valley, to the snow peak high above us. We knew how low the Indus runs on the far side of Nanga where the mountain rises clear twenty-three thousand feet above the water. We knew a few days' march would bring us there, through clouds of dust (twelve thousand pony-loads of grain on the trail to replenish depleted stocks, we hear, not to mention trade traffic) in sweltering heat, among hosts of embattled microbes and crowds of black, inhospitable, lousy men. We were keen to go on any terms, but the Agent wrote us he could not make exception to his rule in our case.

I suppose there must be some rare camp site high up the right bank, that commands the river and the peak.

It is our pilgrimage to Mecca, this Himalayan journey. We go about in a sort of rapture. It may be years before we get back.

Roger and Ahmat are out foraging for money. I expect they will be a long time on the trail.

We are always thinking of you and wishing you were with us,

Yours,

BA

Gypsy Davy   CAMP 40
                                                   SHIGAR

                                                    October

Dear RAY,

A ball for a ball. A Baltistan polo game for that Exeter-Andover football match of yours.

The game here's polo. "Polo" means "ball." Kids begin at five, on foot, and their elders play on pony-back until old age incapacitates them. It is odd that the game should be played so well, where the mounts are so few and so poor. Most of the travelling in the country is done on foot, and apparently all the packing is done on men's backs. Our caravan of twenty odd ponies is an anomaly, and the Caravan Bashi has had his troubles, getting feed enough for them. In fact, if he had not had the luck to find favour with a big Maulvi dwelling near the mouth of the Braldoh we might have had to quit these parts sooner than we wished. We feel uncomfortable about the ponies eating the dzo's winter stores. But the people may live better for it, not that they can eat our silver, but that they can afford to eat some of their own apricots which otherwise they would have had to carry on their backs all the way to Srinagar or to Leh or further.

These fellows are feeble load carriers, when they are working for a sahib. (I suspect they can carry heavy loads of their own!) But chicken-hearted though they appear under a sahib's load, there is nothing chicken-hearted about them on the polo field.

Given the men and the ponies, space for running has to be found. There are very few of these villages in which you would think to find it. The villages are built on little terraces in the midst of broad flights of little terraces, thousands of them, few at the same level, terraces much too little for a polo

field, built by the labour of generations, quite literally by hand.
Yet many a village has an ample polo field.

The game is said to have come in from the north with the
Moguls, the English learning it from the Baltis.

The Raja of Shigar had a game played in our honour the other
day on a grassy stone-walled field, about three hundred yards
long and sixty wide, with low stone goal-posts and low centre-
line posts. The Raja and the young prince (in arms) came
on in some state, huge trumpets braying before them: trumpets
so long that boys had to hold up the far ends, brays louder than
any Three-Corner Round donkey's and as uncontrollable. And
there were pipes and drums as well, all hard at it, not paying
much attention to each other, and none at all to the trumpets.
There were three camp-chairs placed for the sahib log on a
fine rug on raised ground. Chot gave his to the .togaed old
Raja who accepted it, but found some difficulty in handling
his huqa at that elevation.

The players came on without their mounts and squatted in
a circle on the ground at our feet, twenty of them, every man
with an aster or a zinnia behind his ear. The grey rabble
closed in about the circle in a thick solid wall, every man of
them likewise with an aster or a zinnia behind his ear. The
Mem-Sahib in her turquoise-blue postin was the only woman
on the field, but outside, under a great pale yellow chinar
tree, was a bank of purple and black-clad women watching.
Up the slope behind the chinar, orchards flaming with autumn
colour, and behind them, brown crags towering, dusted with
fresh snow.

The players all drank water from a silver goblet. Then
the Zildar, a fine-looking fellow, wearing a big white pagri,
baggy white trousers, a billowy white blouse, and red rubber
boots, took all the players' whips and laid them in pairs at
the Raja's feet. A little boy stepped out, and seemed to me
to be interfering with the arrangement at random. I thought
the idea was to choose sides by chance, but Chot, who had
read Drew's old book *Jummoo and Kashmir*, thought the boy
was acting in response to nods from some judge who knew
the merits of the players, and was trying to make equal teams.
They seem to have no teams as we understand them. The
men of one side were handed mallets of one shape and those
of the other, mallets of another.

These preliminaries over (preliminaries rather older than
Andover and Exeter!) the players jumped up, the rabble scattered
to the side lines, the small boys who had been knocking balls

about all the while, last off the field, of course. The ponies
came on, the players mounted, and all assembled at our end.

The mounts were shaggy little ponies, not much bigger
than Buster. The Zildar had a beautiful little chestnut,
faster and finer than any of the others. They all had gay saddles
and trappings. The players wore all kinds of clothes. Some
were rich and some were poor. The Raja's brother was among
them and so was the Raja's cook. The brother, father of the
little prince in yellow silk, was a tall handsome sophisticated-
looking fellow, as white as any white man. I have a notion
he powdered if he didn't paint. All the rest were good and
black.

The band struck up. The Zildar was off at a mad gallop,
leading the rout. Midway of the field he threw the ball and
caught it on his mallet and sent it nearly to the farther end.

We failed to make head or tail of the game. The rules are
different from American polo, but as we don't know anything
about that it didn't matter much to us. It all seemed to
be one side. Sticks broke, heads flew off, ponies' shins were
whacked, caddies ran out with new sticks. The ponies, by
the way, were badly trained, even the Zildar's chestnut. There
was very little wheeling at critical points, and no stopping
them until they ran into something.

Every now and then the Zildar would skim out ahead of
the others, driving the ball before him right between the goal-
posts—the faster he rode the better his aim seemed to be—
and then he would have to dismount and pick up the ball before
it could be reckoned a goal. And the band would flourish
and the rabble would shout. The music varied with the
goings-on, speeding up or slowing down, according as the
game went.

After a while the players dismounted and squatted in their
circle again, sang a bit of a song, drank more water from the
silver goblet, and passed the huqa, the rabble closing in around
them as before. Then the raggedest among them got up
and did a Gilgiti dance.

The Raja asked the Lady Ba whether she wished to see more
polo, and when she seemed about to ask enthusiastically for
more, he told her that polo was very hard work; and she changed
her answer. Ibrahim distributed largesse to the players and
the band and the dancer, and then every one moved off to the
centre of the field where a mound of dobe had sprung up,
on which Ibrahim planted a silver rupee.

Then half a dozen of the players, including the cook and

the Zildar, mounted and rode off to the far end of the field, with bows in their hands and quivers at their backs: bows of ibex horn, handed down from times as remote as those which saw the making of the great trumpets. Then one after another, each rode furiously at the target, dropped rein as he came opposite, and let fly a shaft. The cook shot worst for a while, but he finally pinned the rupee, and they all did him honour. The Zildar was a very vain fellow, but a rattling good sport for all that. He took defeat as gracefully as he had taken victory.

Hamra, a big yellow Yarkandi dog, who adopted our caravan when it left Leh to meet us, followed our men to the show, and got right into the game. We had a fearful time getting him out.

The Lady Ba wishes me to state that we were escorted to and from the field by the Zildar himself. Everybody we met bowed low, not to our honours, nor yet to his high office, but to a great polo player.

She also bids me advise you that she is sending you a flint-and-steel pouch such as our servants carry at their belts. When your canoe tips over, and your matches are soaked, it may come in handy, if you have an eye for good tinder.

Yours,

GYPSY DAVY

Lady Ba   CAMP 40
                                          SHIGAR
                                        October 23

Dearest MOTHER,

I can see you sitting at the bare dining-table in the evening pointing out with your knitting-needle the intricacies of "ich hätte geliebt worden sein" and "wir werden geliebt werden," though you couldn't read them yourself. Or persuading the Methodist parson to read the Greek Testament with me, using a trot. Or launching me in Latin when a New York teacher came to town for six weeks once. And I can see myself on the attic stairs picking out "Renard et le Corbeau" with the help of a vocabulary in an old book of yours.

But all that linguistic history, irregular as it was, is reaching its climax here and now in Urdu. At least, I suppose it's Urdu. The people who talk to me in it say so, but the

D

text-book I bought in London calls it Hindustani, and if you want to get quite labyrinthically involved, I refer you to the *Encyclopaedia Britannica* on the subject.

You see, Rasul,. who learned his "breaking English" from his sahib and my rom, couldn't get off to serve us, and Ibrahim, who came in his stead, knows only one word of English: "Oyes." The Sahib has forgotten the Turki he learned twenty years back, and the only means of communication between us and the outer world, besides signs and grimaces, is my Urdu.

The aforesaid text-book was written in 1859 and is chiefly grammar. On the way up to the mountains I fell in with a kind old Mussulman who gave me a tattered officers' manual and a little *New Testament* in Urdu printed in Roman characters.

I had great hopes of taking naturally to the tongue, partly because I've such gypsy tastes and the real gypsies speak a corrupt Hindi, and also because "Urdu" means "the language of the camp." But alas! it was the conqueror's camp, and the conqueror was a great Mogul, with power to flay folk who didn't understand him or weren't intelligible. Ours will be a conqueror's camp indeed, the day I feel sure of Urdu!

Iba is a marvel at understanding me. He watches my lips in the long pauses in which I grope for words or constructions, and makes most helpful suggestions. He acts out little plays to explain his own words to me. The Sahib is a marvel at understanding Iba. I'm sure it is only mind-reading, for he doesn't know half the words I do, but whether it's legitimate or not, it often saves the day. Chot is becoming helpful, too, —got on really well with the Raja yesterday in a discussion of polo, asking questions he knew the answers to beforehand, having crammed Drew for an hour.

In fact, Chot knows enough now to be annoying. When he heard me try to say to the cook whose head was tied up in flannel: "What a pity your ear aches!" he was so brutal as to account for a blank expression between the flannel folds by telling me that I had really said: "What a pity you have a tooth in your thigh!"

When we want a word we have to try to recall some text containing it in English. I broke my mirror the first week out, and longing to see how tanned I was by the time we reached Skardu, I looked up that verse in *Corinthians* and sent Iba to the bazar for the kind of glass in which the young St. Paul saw darkly. The cook understood me at once when I told him to do to the chickens what Herod did to the innocents.

And I got a patch put on the Presence's trousers by referring to the new cloth and old garment passage.

I've started making a card catalogue dictionary of *The Gospel according to Matthew*, which I carry about with me in a pasteboard shoe-box. The greatest nuisance about the language is the number of synonyms in it. You see when the Moguls conquered Persia on their way to India, they learned Persian, which was already full of Arabic words left in it by some previous Mohammedan conquest. Then they grafted this Perso-Arabic scion on to a Hindi stem with Sanskrit roots. So while I may know what an Arab would call mustard, I am quite at a loss if the cook speaks of it by its Persian or Sanskrit name. Iba seems to know all the possibilities,—Iba who never went to school a day in his life, and to whom this speech is no more natural than it is to me!

Yesterday we went to take tea in the Raja's garden. The Raja is a nice old thing. We feel well acquainted with him, because this is our second visit to Shigar, and we've made rather a long stay each time. The first time we camped in one end of the long green polo field. (It was a month of mourning, so there couldn't be any polo.) The Raja came to call, preceded by a long line of servants bearing gifts. There was one great plate of fine white flour, another of rice, another of grapes, another of strips of cinnamon bark, another of raisins, another with a pat of butter between grape leaves. And still others of fruits and vegetables: one little yellow plum from a tree of his own, the only one of its kind in the valley, so juicy and delicately sweet that I immediately conceived of Olympian nectar having tasted like it. I forgot the last of that string of gift-bearers, leading a fat ram by a horn! When he heard that Chot was ill at Askole at the far end of the Braldoh, the Raja sent a runner up to our camp with offers of help. And I had hardly got off my horse on the highest of high terraces above the village when we came the second time, to camp in a place of the Ri Sahib's choosing, when the Raja's cook appeared with a tray and an English tea service and square cakes with roses on them in high relief. So you can imagine we felt friendly towards this nice person and were glad to go to visit him in his garden yesterday.

The great gate opened on a courtyard in which there was a huge old chinar tree. Behind it rose the palace, as old as the tree, several storeys high, built of wood, beautifully carved and weathered. A little markhor was wandering up and down the broad outer stair. There was hay sticking out of the windows of the lowest storey—probably the animals lived there. In the third storey I could see, in a loggia, women in purple gowns, leaning out.

The Raja received us in a little open summer-house in the very centre of his great walled garden. There is a square moat around the summer-house, crossed by a wee Chinese bridge, the work of the carpenter who has been making my litter. The garden is beautifully orderly,—three gardeners at work on it all the time, the Raja told us. Fruit-trees, pear, apricot, the plum, a kind of olive, line the walls, and at the rear a great grey cliff rises up and up, with a little structure on the top which was a fort in the last Raja's day.

Our host asked us questions about the world,—was it really round, as he'd heard tell? We demonstrated with a melon— a file of servants had come down the markhor's stair and along the path with great platters of fruit on their heads—showing him that his country was on top and ours on the bottom. He told us there had been an earthquake in Japan, indicating that the people must have misbehaved to have incurred it. He offered us our choice of teas, English style in cups from Lahore, Arabian in tiny glasses, and cardamom-and-cinnamon-flavoured in Chinese cups with silver covers.

The cook and the silversmith and the tailor and the Zildar's little boy squatted under the summer-house roof too, Ibrahim, of course, being treated as a guest, though sitting at a little distance. They say Asiatic kings are always accessible to their subjects. Certainly, we have never had an interview with any "big man" without an interested group of watchers and listeners crowding close around.

The *New Testament* came into play again. I asked the silversmith if he had made the handsome tray from which I had taken the melon, using, with some misgiving, the word for John the Baptist's charger. It was accepted serenely. He had made it. I gathered that some of his ancestors had made the tremendous trumpets we saw at the polo game, but I'm not quite sure. In fact, nothing that I infer in my conversations is to be sworn to, at this present time, but the glossary of *St. Matthew* grows daily and I have promised the Raja that on my next visit to Shigar I shall be able to converse with him clearly and confidently.

As for ever learning to write to him or to any of the rest of them—I wonder? I've chosen for my signature the initials of "Khush Qismat Mem-Sahib." They read from right to left, and the M is really a "final" instead of an initial, but I like its conclusive shape and at least it's the final one of the three initials. The bird's beak with a dot above is Kh. (A dot below, or none, would quite change it.) The curly Q would become an F, if one of its dots were omitted.

P.S.—Tell Ruth Miner that the author of her favourite tale about Ducky-Lucky and Goosy-Woosy and Chicky-Licky knew Urdu. Our men say "pani-wani" and "roti-poti" and "chitthi-litthi" for "pani" and "roti" and "chitthi."

Gypsy Davy   CAMP 40
                                                  SHIGAR
                                                  October 23

Dear NORMAN,

Jim wrote us about the horrid skunk that came in the night and carried off seven of your baby chicks.

I haven't seen any skunks in these mountains, but there is something much worse. There is a horrid black man, with hairy black legs and long black hair, and a funny little acorn-cup cap, and dirty grey woollen clothes, something like an old monk's. This wicked old man catches the chickens when they are old enough to be running about without their mother, and claps them into a curious coop make of willow withes, and straps the coop on his back, and carries it up long ladders, scaling cliffs, and along narrow ledges on the faces of great precipices, and across long bridges of braided birch rope, one rope for his feet and two for his hands to hold on by,—spider web bridges you might call them. And out in the middle of one of these the man stops for a minute to get his courage up to go on, for he doesn't like the swinging of the long spider web, and the chickens thrust their necks out between the withes of their coop and look down, and it seems as far down to the water as it does up to the clouds, dreadfully far down, and they pull their heads in and they all huddle together and shiver with fright, and presently the man goes on again.

And after a long time, the man sets the basket down by a little tent, where another black man is cooking over a fire. And the cook comes and opens the coop and takes out one of the chickens and does halal to him and claps him into a pot on the fire. And when he is nicely cooked, he is placed before two enormous ogres, who eat him up in a very few mouthfuls. And one of the ogres is Gypsy Davy, and the other, would you believe it, is Lady Ba!

We are sorry for the little chickens. Sometimes we think we will never eat any more of them.

There isn't an animal in all these mountains that is safe for long, though. Sooner or later, some other animal will kill him and eat him. The yak and the dzo are under Maharaja's protection so they are safe from men. I think they can defend themselves and their young against everything else until they get very old and feeble, or grow weak with hunger in time of famine. Then the wolves get them.

But the little lambs and the kids that are born on the high pastures, 'way up at the edge of the snows that lie deep all summer long, days' and days' journey above the villages,—the lambs and kids are not so safe. Their mothers are very little things, not much bigger than a turkey hen. The huge lammergeiers that sail overhead are strong enough to carry off the mother herself, I think. I am sure they would think nothing of carrying a lamb to their eyries. And the ounce and the lynx and the bear and the wolf are always prowling about.

But all the dreadful things that there are in these mountains are not nearly so dreadful as the swarm of horrid char-à-bancs and motor cycles and motor cars and motor lorries forever sweeping over England.

We love your England behind garden walls, and in narrow lanes, and on its little mountains where that dreadful swarm is barred out for awhile. We hope some day a mighty ogre will come to England and eat all the motors up.

The Himalaya we love always and everywhere. We are even glad of all the wicked animals there are among them.

Our love to you and Jim and your mother. Remember us to your governess playmate.

Gypsy Davy

Lady Ba

CAMP 41
KAPEHAN

October 30

Dear RUTH,

We galloped over the dunes in the Indus Valley yesterday
and of course we thought of you. The dunes are splendid
just over the little pass from Shigar. It was a superb day.
Tomar felt like flying, and I felt like it too.

It's good to get on a horse again. For a whole month in
the Braldoh we had to go without horses. The trails are
difficult enough for bipeds. I'm so slow that Gypsy Davy
devised a kind of short stretcher for safe parts of the trail,
to carry me sitting with my legs dangling. On very unsafe
ones, they took the stretcher to pieces and put me into a sling
in the middle of a long Alpine rope, two men climbing ahead
with the ends. The sling went below my hips and over one
shoulder so that I could sit and lean back in the thing, the men
carrying most of my weight, while I used my legs somewhat
as the donkeys use theirs when the boys are hauling them up
steep places with block and tackle in the Sierras. On the
worst traverses I trod close on Gypsy Davy's heels, holding
fast the hand he held out behind him. And as for the
bridges——!

It wasn't high enough—seven thousand, rising gradually
to twelve—for altitude to bother much, though sometimes the
steepness did. I had ridden Tomar so steadily since Sonamarg,
instead of walking as the Bara and Chhota Sahibs do, that
I was soft and a good deal of a nuisance, tucking into bed the
minute we got in, and once having to camp prematurely in the
river-bed. I'm no mountain climber, as you know, but even
Fanny Bullock Workman found the Braldoh trying!

I'd have gone in a sack, though, to have that month to
remember. I have stumbled and climbed for what seemed
like miles along the bank of a grey swirling river between a
high mountain wall and a high ice wall, the advancing end
of the uneasy Biafo, dripping and grunting and spilling down
piles of gravel and occasional big boulders. I have crossed
a boiling river on a span of men's bodies between two of those
boulders as big as houses. I have run for my life under showers
of falling rocks. Pulled Gypsy Davy's shoe off once, and he
stopped and put it on again neatly! I have seen Paju Peak.
I shall know all the rest of my life that such regions are.

There! That race over the dunes was exhilarating, you see.

And so is the fact that after ten whole days in Shigar we are on the trail again. Headed up the Shyok, a month's journey at our rate of travel, before we reach the Khardung and Leh.

And so is the fact that at last Rasul is with us. Nice old Rasul! He rode two or three marches a day for a fortnight, getting to Shigar to join us. It was pretty to see all the men's pleasure at meeting him again. And his words when he came into his sahib's presence were a veritable Nunc Dimittis. "I have ask–ed God to let me see you again and your mem-sahib before I die. Now, is finish." Then, his humour twinkling up, he added with a glance at the Gypsy's neatly patched Shetlands: "You look same poor! But is only little grey your beard. Mine is white now. I am Aq-saqal—that mean 'white-beard.'"

He is to be our honoured guest the whole month of his leave. I've always thought it would be thrilling to have a court minstrel or bard at your command, and here we have one. Every evening he comes to our tent, sitting in the door-way, while we eat our dinner, to tell us a story. Pleasant voice, gestures of flexible hands. When he has gone, with his polite good-night—the first night he said: "Madam, I have said many times good-night to your husband. Now for first time, I say it to you"—I hasten to write down all that I can remember.

A most remarkable man, Rasul. He has been the servant of many sahibs, most of them, I judge, interesting men, real persons. He has been headman on important expeditions. Many of the sahibs he has worked for seem to have become his personal friends. I, only reading his story, have felt him as vivid and vital.

Up to now the mountains have been earth to us, beautiful, austere, impersonal. To Rasul they are places, backgrounds for stories of people. He is making the men in our caravan seem vivid too. We are learning of little intrigues that have been going on among them. We are given sage hints: "Always looking what man going first on trail. That very lazy one man. If going last, must seeing if go wrong loads. Lazy man going first, that not seeing any work. Lazy man like that very much. Sahib not can know which is good worker, which not is. When looking Sahib, always very good working. When not looking Sahib, there lying down and sleeping."

He is writing now an account of his share in De Filippi's big Central Asian expedition in 1914,—he was caravan bashi. Every rest-day (I don't march two days in succession if it can be avoided) he sits in the guest-tent which has been made over to his uses and works at his story. He made a half-dozen starts, "but not come very good in my head, madam." Now he is well off, and is lost to the world. He is a true poet, able to tell "a tale which holdeth children from their play and old men from the chimney-corner."

He told me today that he had been explaining our curious habits of travel to an inquiring headman. "I said to him: 'No, not shooting; not rocks-collecting, not flowers keeping; not heads measuring, not mountains measuring; not pictures taking. This my Sahib and my Mem-Sahib travelling where their felt are liked, camping always high place to look the country. I, Rasul Galwan, am Aqsaqal, but I am my Sahib's servant'." Then he added with his illumining smile: "Now he thinking is very big man, my Sahib, the Aqsaqal to his servant. Therefore I telling!"

To your dunes from ours, salam!

Yours,
RASUL'S MEM-SAHIB

Gypsy Davy

CAMP 41
KAPEHAN ON THE INDUS
October 30

Dear "WILKINS,"

It is a long time since we sat in your dining-room at those high teak tables, and you played "Wilkins" in earnest. You didn't have to go very far to the kitchen. And you didn't have to go out into the night to get there.

The walls were very thick and the shades drawn. We could not see the night. There was so much light in the room that we forgot it was night.

But out here in the high Himalaya things are different. Our walls are thin—green, close-woven flax. There's a green sheet on the ground, and a gay little Lhasa saddle-rug and gay saddle-bags and a black iron brazier filled with glowing coals, and a single candle shining through a sheet of mica, and our door wide open.

And just outside, close, the night. No question now about its being night.

There is ice forming on the rivulet that ripples in a little ditch on the terrace edge by the tent door. The cook-tent down below, the village and the orchards and the people and the cattle and the wide Indus and the high valley sides, are all hid in the night.

And overhead the dark field of the sky, fenced by sharp peaks, lit by a thousand fires.

GYPSY DAVY

Gypsy Davy   CAMP 41
KAPEHAN ON THE INDUS
October 31

Dear ALBERT,

I wish we had you with us. We are sitting in our door-way, —door-way of a dark-green Arab tent.

It is a cold morning. We are huddling round the brazier. A rivulet, ice-fringed, runs purring in a tiny ditch at the terrace edge, just one step from the door-way.

There's a village on a terrace down below us, but the houses are such little houses, so hidden among crimson and gold fruit-trees, that you'd never know it.

There's a purple hedge of thorn-bush just before you come to the crimson and gold orchards. We can see a lot of big old black dzo with very long horns in front of the hedge and a flat mud roof or two behind it. Sheep, too, all about on the ground, nibbling everything they can get at, without risking their silly necks. And goats everywhere, on roofs, on walls, up trees, thinking little of risking a neck for a juicy crimson leaf in the very top of an apricot tree.

You'd love the apricot trees. Their leaves all hang straight down, golden yellow, tinged with crimson. They look as if they were dripping blood from the trees' hearts. Perhaps they are.

Behind the orchards lies the blue-green Indus, flowing quietly between steep sandy gravelly banks.

And on the further bank, great tawny cliffs tower up into blue sky.

And through a gap, right opposite our door-way, giant snow mountains loom, glistening white snow and ice, and peaks as sharp as any you ever saw in picture-books.

GYPSY DAVY

Gypsy Davy   CAMP 42
                              ABOVE GOL ON THE INDUS
                                        4.30 a.m.

Dear JIM,

We had a nice letter from you. I haven't it by me now, and all the matter of it has quite slipped my mind, out here in the starlight.

Sirius has crossed the meridian. Procyon is approaching it. Castor and Pollux are not far off. The old moon is riding high in Leo. There is a faint brightening in the east above dark mountain tops.

A snowy arête lies glistening below the Dogs, and a fairy cliff towers toward Capella. It seems to rise infinitely high. I cannot see where the cliff ends and the dark sky begins. But every now and then a star is suddenly blotted out there, and I know the invisible top of that cliff is riding up on the rim of the world.

The high old moraine, on which we tarry the night, is white in moonlight. Huge boulders lying about have a ghostly look. Jackals slink among them. I saw the old caravan dog, at midnight, mounting guard on one of them.

The roar of the Indus mounts from far below, like the roar of a great city. But there is no city near. For hundreds of miles there is no city, whichever way you travel.

The ways are ways merely, some few of them fit for ponies, the rest for men only, some only for skilled climbers. Many are closed now for the winter.

You would think that passes between fifteen and twenty thousand, anyway, could be considered closed, but the dak runners on the Gilgit trail to Kashgar run pretty high all winter, I believe, and caravans from the North are still coming in to Leh over much higher passes than theirs. Iba has just had a letter from his wife saying that she has secured several maunds of Yarkandi flour for us from a caravan just in, over passes more than eighteen thousand.

Roger is risking his neck across avalanche tracks on the Zoji which is low enough in all conscience, the lowest in these parts, eleven thousand. But Chot is a long thing, and we are thinking one end of him will maybe be sticking out at one side or other of the avalanche for someone to get hold of, and pull him out by, along with our cash for the winter, the which he has with him.

I have been writing by firelight. The men build a big fire

before day-break against a great boulder, for me to strip before, and, as they doubtless think, worship at. It's fun to strip, and stretch your much-swaddled muscles in the crisp night air before a blazing fire.

We are real gypsies. We have long suspected it. Had you been with us in London and gone with us into Benjamin Edgington's tent loft in Queen Elizabeth Street, and watched us looking very much bored while Mr. Williams set up first this handsome tent, and then that,—"like the Duke's," "like the King's,"—until he presently pulled out an old museum piece of an Arab tent—had you seen us pounce upon that, knowing it for our tent, you would have known, then. (It was Galton's favourite!)

If you get it in silhouette from the side, it looks something like a big dromedary lying down, with his neck stretched out on the sand. It's a darlin' dark green with a faint suggestion of old gold about it, and there's a red knob on the hump and a red knob, lower down, on either end. It's not so unlike the hull of a yacht upside down; hull of a yacht with a deep keel. It will cleave a high wind, if you set it right, as neatly as the keel cleaves water.

By the way, we hear of your going straight to Oxford. We are for it. We will come to see you there.

Dear JIM,

Lady Ba says it was all nonsense writing a playwright about stars and jackals and all sorts of irrelevant things. It's plays and players and playhouses one should be writing of.

You would never think, to look at these villages, that playhouses might be found in them. To the smoke-blurred Cleveland eye, I doubt if the villages themselves would be instantly visible: little clusters of low, flat-roofed, mud-and-pebble houses, one colour with the soil about them, buried in orchards all crimson and gold. And the people are hard even for me to see, sometimes, so like the soil are those heavy Gothic folds of their homespun. Nevertheless, there are theatres, actors, and audiences, with close scrutiny, discoverable.

The stage is a more or less circular bit of bare ground, some thirty feet across, hemmed in by those low, flat-roofed houses, and perhaps the corner of a carved masjid, a bit of garden wall, a big clay archery target decorated in colour, a dung-tower or two. Towers, walls, roofs, target-top, stone slabs about the edges of the stage, all occupied; the roofs and walls by women and children, a touch of colour there; the slabs by

badshah log like ourselves and the Zildar; and packed in
between the walls and the edges of the stage, the grey rabble
of men and boys, standing.   Squatting under a huge chinar,
the band: two home-made bass drums beaten with one stick
and one hand; six little copper kettles, beaten in pairs with
two sticks, one tuned in E, the other in B, single taps played
on the lower one, and the tremolo done on the higher;—(fire
of reeds built close to the kettles so as to warm one in each
pair and alter the pitch, tightening the net of leather thongs
which envelops the kettle and holds the drumhead taut); two
oboe-like wood winds; two huge ancient trumpets, over ten
feet long—tremendous effort to produce reluctant sounds
which once produced, endure adequately.

Actors all men, of course.   Thrilling sword dances by
ragged fellow and dandy side by side.   Weird dances with
strange gesture and terrifying grimace.   Intricate steps by
black men still further blackened with charcoal, barefoot,
heels cracked like old potatoes, toe-nails touched with rouge.
Most satisfying dance by two tall Ladakhis, come from the
high mountains, trading, gay with colour, from the crimson
in their dark cheeks to the scarlet yak-hair in the pabu on
their feet.   Iba saw them watching from a tower, and impressed
them.

A side-splitting monkey, well-acted, striving to find something good to eat in the dust, tasting critically, ejecting, finally
confidently leaping upon his owner's back, pulling off his cap,
seeking, finding,—licking his chops.   A rough jungly trader
from the hills, an excellent piece of acting.   A little palanquin
set down in the centre of the stage: a shrill child's voice singing
from under the curtains,—suddenly a dreadful bray apparently
from the same source.   Audience roars with laughter.   And so
on and on.

All actors doing obeisance to the Badshah and the Begam.
The Badshah has had enough.   He rises.   The big-nosed
Aqsaqal distributes largesse.   A way is cleared.   The Badshah
and the Begam are escorted to their tent.

Yours,

GYPSY DAVY

Gypsy Davy   CAMP 43
                        ABOVE KIRIS ON THE SHYOK
                                          November 4

Dear ALICE,

Come see the camp with me. The rosy morning flush has faded from the cirrus, racing eastward overhead. The sun has lit the highest snowy peaks. The valley's all in shadow: the tawny cliffs; the purple screes; the broad yellow terrace far below, some old lake bottom; the grey shifting sands of wide flats further down; the blue-grey Shyok swinging in quiet curves, with here and there a rapid; the square mile of old lake-bottom brought under cultivation in some twelve hundred tiny terraces; the half-dozen villages scattered over the terraced land, clusters of doll-houses half hidden among trees, apricot, walnut, mulberry, chinar, willow, tall poplar, foliage dim now.

Hold! I am gone astray. It was the camp I set out to show you. Now we must climb all the way back from the villages.

The Lambardar of one met us yesterday as we rode in, and showed a shady garden that his men were busily sweeping with brushwood brooms. We thanked him and turned a blind eye to his garden, and presently, to his ravings, a deaf ear. It was not shade and garden walls, but sunshine and wide spaces that we wanted. He said the valley sides were much too steep for us. At our insistence he led us up one blind trail after another to isolated terraces, cliff below and cliff above, quite inaccessible to ponies, but with fair prospects, and with clear water rippling by in sinuous ditches. At last the Bara Sahib's patience reached the tether's end. He gently left the Lambardar, found his own trail, leading up and up, far above the highest terrace, to a clear spring issuing among boulders, on a most forbidding slope, and left the caravan to follow as it might.

Now, the next morning, the Mem-Sahib sits like a mermaid in her green bed, which quite fills the little forester's tent, wide open upon such a prospect as the gods enjoy. The Bara Sahib sits like a merman in his green bed, on a narrow terrace a foot or two below, his upper half in a big postin, a brazier full of glowing coals between the two of them, a warm breakfast within them.

A long way down, by the rivulet from the spring, the cook's tent, hidden. A long way further down where the rivulet empties into a tiny pond, fringed with poplar and apricot trees, the men's tents, and the ponies feeding, bells tinkling, piles of hay and grain and firewood being carried up a weary way on men's backs.—One of the men's tents, a beautiful green one like ours, Rasul's masjid, a scarlet namda on the ground at one end, and should you look in, after dark, a candle burning there and the Qoran open before it, and Rasul alone, reading aloud.—And all about the camp, for a long way below on either side the rivulet and far above, a desolate steep waste of tawny boulder and rough scree and finest silt. And above that, tawny cliff towering into cirrus-streaked blue sky. And yawning before us the great valley, restfully simple in its big outlines, nervously complex in its man-encumbered bottom.

GYPSY DAVY

Gypsy Davy   CAMP 43
                               ABOVE KIRIS
                               November 4

Dear JIMMY,

I have your letter about the horrid skunk. I wrote Norman about the chickens' enemies in these mountains. But I think the chickens really have a pretty good time until the black man gets them. They run about everywhere, unmolested. They come right into the houses and into Iba's tent, and nobody minds.

All the animals seem pretty free of the houses. It is not so easy as you might think to tell which are their quarters and which their masters'. They are side by side and they look very much alike. I should think an old dzo or an old billy-goat whose senses were no longer very keen might easily stumble into his master's quarters by mistake. The men and the women and the children and the animals are all mixed up together, as they were at our picnic in the buttercup meadow when the cows and the goats and the hens and the donkey all came.

You and Norman would love the funny twisty little lanes between the crowded houses: flat mud roofs at many levels, crowding together, each with little piles of melons and grain and drying apricots upon it, and hay and winter wood and un-threshed grain piled high. The ladder-ends sticking up out of hatches in the roof would tempt you down into dark caves of rooms, with funny little cubby-holes to put things in about

the walls, and floors that don't need sweeping, because they are
made of dirt and couldn't very well get any dirtier.   And you
would like the lovely little mosques where people come to pray.
In the beautiful carved porch of one we saw a weaver at his
loom.   You'd like the gay flower gardens, too, and the vegetable
gardens and the orchards.

You would, love to see the goats balancing themselves on
their hind legs on high garden walls to reach leaves on the
trees, or climbing trees like squirrels to get still higher and
probably sweeter leaves at the top.   And you would love to
see the sheep and the dzo patiently waiting under the trees
while the shepherds and the dzoherds knock leaves down for
them with long willow poles.

Such lovely leaves! Crimson of apricot, pale yellow of chinar
and sarsing, and walnut of the golden browns your Aunt
Roslyn wears.

You would love the terraced fields and the tumbling water
in the ditches and the little boulder mills, grinding away beside
the ditches.   But the cold grey river thundering down its barren
gravel bed would make you shiver.   And the tall cliffs and
long snowy slopes, and great slabs of rock, hanging ready to
break loose and come crashing down upon the fields, would
trouble you, and the great glaciers and the mountain peaks
against the sky would frighten you, I think.

GYPSY DAVY

Gypsy Davy   CAMP 44
KURU
November 6

Dear ELMER,

Have you heard anything about our donkeys? Have you
been up to that first camp on the ranch, where Lady Ba wrapped
you in a red blanket and you said you felt like a king? I suppose
kings do have people to wrap them up, even when they are
quite old.

In these mountains I really am a king almost, and Lady
Ba's a queen.   You would suspect it if you should see us on
the trail.   A tall black man in a long purple gown and white
pagri precedes us, ordering everybody off the trail: ponies,
donkeys, yak, dzo, sheep, goats, coolies, all, except the goats,
loaded with wool or salt or sagebrush or dried apricots or what
not.   Imagine ordering all the freighters off the trail, sometimes

driving them into dreadful places, and making them wait there until the Badshah's caravan passes by! And such freighters! Dark tall men with heavy sheepskin coats that reach to their feet (wool inside and skin outside), and jaunty sheepskin caps, and long turquoise ear-rings, and long black pigtails. And such pack animals! Donkeys so small your feet would touch the ground on both sides if you sat astride one. Sheep hardly smaller, with long spiral horns, straight out on either side their heads. Yak, looking to us as big as bison, jet black, with long fringes on their sides and big bushy tails. And such a trail! Up valleys that you would say no man in his senses would ever try to build a trail in, let alone a village.

In such a valley on such a trail among such freighters, pick out our caravan. That black and purple herald ahead. Behind him the Begam, the Queen, apparelled in red and blue, riding her white pony, though you'd scarcely see his colour for the trappings that he wears. And after her, the King's gay little iron-grey, cavorting dangerously with His Majesty. And after him, Her Majesty's litter, borne by four dreary Baltis, with long bobbed hair, and dingy woollen smocks, and grey shawls hung in heavy folds about them, walking in single file and four others walking ahead, ready to relieve the first. And behind the litter, the Aqsaqal of Ladakh, our Prime Minister, a very black, very fierce-looking little man, grey-bearded, white-turbaned, clothed in a long grey robe of homespun goat's hair, riding a richly-caparisoned bay. And behind him, eight black retainers in camel's hair gowns mounted on ponies all gay in the sunshine, with yellow and scarlet and flashing silver. And behind them as many more retainers on foot, scattered among the load-ponies, ponies carrying black iron boxes, yellow wooden boxes, and dark-green bags. And after these, I don't know how many coolies, all swathed in heavy folds of dingy grey, bent under every kind of load, and hung about with pots and kettles and baskets of eggs, and fruit and vegetables, and curious crates of chickens. And behind them all, Ibrahim, the Karawan Bashi, tall and black, in scarlet fez and crimson robe, perched on a long-legged dun in the odd fashion of the country, an orange namaz-rug rolled up behind his curious saddle, and trappings as rare as the best.

If all this did not convince you that we are royalty, perhaps the reverence the heads of the little mud-and-cobblestone villages show, would, coming out a long way to meet us, bowing low, presenting gifts of fruit and nuts on silvered trays. And if you were still doubtful, surely the rajas would convince

E

you coming to pay their respects in camp, preceded by long lines of servants, bearing gifts of cake and fruit and vegetables and flour and rice and butter and hens and sheep.

I quite forgot to tell you how every mounted man we meet dismounts the minute he catches sight of us, and doesn't remount until he thinks we are out of sight. Our servants ride when we ride, but dismount immediately when we do. I think Roger and I make our sais very unhappy because we walk so much.

Our greetings to Francis.

GYPSY DAVY

Gypsy Davy   CAMP 47
                              7,000 FEET ABOVE KHAPALU
Dear ROLAND,

We are always thinking of you now we're on your ground. And you all the time in such a sweat to get on! We could not hurry by this.

Rasul has come to meet us and would show the Mem-Sahib what a caravan bashi can be. But in his present absent-minded state he hasn't much to show. He chafed a bit at this pilgrim pace of ours until I set him to work on De Filippi's story. Now he forgets everything but his new drama, right in the presence of a Raja come to pay his respects, even.

I don't think you knew Ibrahim, for so many years Rasul's right arm (as predicted by his wise old mother). The Mem-Sahib has quite lost her heart to Iba. I commend him to you as a most excellent caravan bashi.

Rasul and Iba are below in Khapalu band-o-basting for the Shyok. We may be the better part of a month on this trail and have to take the Chang La instead of the Khardung at the finish, but nothing can hurry us. The cook and Khalik (nice boy of forty, Khalik—we like him immensely) and ourselves are here in camp, the two tents being well out of sight and sound of each other, by Mem-Sahib's orders.

The Mem-Sahib is napping against a clear night of stars— to be fresh for that, I mean. I am sitting by a three-foot brazier in the open door-way. Supper is a-cooking: roast chakor and grape pilav.

We hate the villages. We love their picturesqueness and enjoy sketching in them,—but camp in one of them? Not we.

We hurried through Khapalu ahead of the caravan, which had quite a time of it at the zak ferry, swimming the horses. We climbed and climbed, hoping for a glimpse of Masherbrum. Each one of those aiguilles to the east of it, our guide pronounced Masherbrum as we lifted it. He was a friend of Rasul's, over-anxious to unload us and get back to the village. We kept on as long as we dared, and then ducked a branch trail over to the edge of the moraine and halted. Ibrahim didn't get in until dark, as it was. Of course we didn't lift Masherbrum, but the arête was a thriller, and a grey pyramid 'way back north, going black before even the lower of the aiguilles, what do you think that was? It seemed a little thing at first, but it took on immense proportions as we watched it, despite an ignominious shadowing it had to submit to, both at sunrise and sunset. I thought it must be K², but the *I.S.* will not have it so.

We rested the Mem-Sahib the next day, according to our custom. I got up about four a.m., as usual, worshipped before a blazing fire naked, and climbed a nub of the moraine about a mile to the east. There I lifted Masherbrum in a clear sky, a very beautiful mountain. I hope you did that high trail at sunrise or sunset.

Rasul sent up word that he would not be ready for a day or two. The Mem-Sahib climbed the nub with me in the afternoon to watch the shadows creep across. She had been thrilled at Doghani, a good ten hours downstream from here, watching Mango Gusor take the sun extraordinarily late, and, all of a sudden, show the unmistakable shadow of Masherbrum come slowly slipping down the face, first hint of its proximity. As we saw Masherbrum from the nub, it was smoking from the southern spur-crest, and the summit was hidden. We didn't get a good look at it.

The next morning I set off at four to find a proper camp,— two or three miles on, I promised Rasul in my note. I was continually stopping to look back. I even tried a sketch in a deep gully which framed the mountain well, but it was rather dark down there. Each step seemed to lift the mountain higher and fit it more perfectly into its Hushe Lumba frame. But something was keeping the sun off it. It seemed as slow in taking the sun as Mango Gusor had been. The long arête on that side of the Shyok bristles with sharp rock needles pricking through snow and ice, but the highest of them could not shadow Masherbrum. The crest of a big nameless snow dome, marked twenty-five thousand on the map, much lower than Masherbrum, shows between two of them. This might. And another big peak shows through a gap east of the last aiguille. This might. The sun struck both these peaks, and lit up the whole eastern face of one of them before it struck Masherbrum.

I climbed to about sixteen thousand, marking the trail with little stones in piles of three for the caravan to follow, and found a perfect camp on a little loess flat in the crest of an old moraine. It was no three miles' journey for the caravan, but a long hard day's march.

The tent is pitched there now, a good seven thousand feet above Khapalu. I can command the whole of Masherbrum from the tent door. It must be a clear sixteen thousand feet from the top of a severed spur-end almost buried in the gravels in the bottom of the Shyok, up to the summit. The mountain dominates everything in sight as if a dozen of the forty miles between us and it were vertical miles.

The shadows of the mountains behind us are already half-way up the slope of the aiguilles. There! Masherbrum has lost the sun along with those two big peaks, all three at the drop of the ball, though they took it so irregularly. The easternmost of those big peaks is entirely beautiful now. We call it "Tyrian Purple," choosing the words from our lean vocabulary, not for any fitness there may be in them, but for an association in our minds between them and a most rare lovely colour. This same splendid thing at sunset was nothing much at sunrise. Masherbrum takes the palm for that. Masherbrum, huge massive thing, seems to be rising now. Now it's fading. Now it's gone, merged in a long ghostly skyline. We feel a presence there but have no certain knowledge of it.

Masherbrum is a most stately mountain from any point of view. I saw it from an old moraine in the Braldoh at the snout of the Baltoro at about twelve thousand, and again from a shoulder on our Dontok (the peak which De Filippi doubtless rightly calls Paiju) at about eighteen thousand, across the snout of the Baltoro, an immense white tower rising through mists which alternately hid and discovered it; two tall gendarmes, like battlements, near the western edge. The tower seemed to rise miles above anything else. Gasherbrum at the head of the Baltoro and K² and Muz-tagh Din in the northern arête seemed insignificant.

Dontok, by the way, from its shoulder at seventeen thousand where I saw it and from the old moraine at its base where the

Mem-Sahib saw it with me in late September, is far and away the most lovely mountain either of us has ever seen. I stood on the narrow shoulder between the snout of the Baltoro on the south and a truly awful gorge on the north-east, and watched the mists play among rosy pinnacles and white seracs. Stones fell continually, dislodged by invisible ibex, climbing recklessly to escape me.   And now and then a lammergeier soared across the gorge.

Yours,

P.S.—Rasul and Iba have come up to drag us off our high perch at last.   Rasul took a long look at Masherbrum and said: "You see that mountain other side from Baltoro.   Now see this side.   Same friend.   Look back, look front, look different,—is same friend."

Gypsy Davy   Camp 47
                                            Above Khapalu
                                            November 9

Dear Stuart,

We have been thinking that maybe time enough has elapsed to make a reply from us to your letter acceptable.   I forget whether the approved interval in Hamilton is six months or eight. We have been stalking K^2 for the last three months.   It is big game, second highest, they think.   But for all its immense height, not often seen.   There are not so many who know its name even, though it has names enough: Godwin Austen, Chigoro, Lamba Pahar.   De Filippi mentions Chiring, Chogo, Depsang.   Much smaller mountains of striking shape, more easily seen, within twenty miles of it, are better known.

I had my first glimpse from about seventeen thousand: a mountain on the western edge of the Deosai.   I was up all day till the stars came out, alone.   The northern skyline bristled with great snow peaks, pricking through heavy, fair-weather clouds, from the grand ones above Hunza, to fine ones east of K^2.   But no sign of K^2.   I kept sweeping the horizon, first without and then with the sixteen-power glass, in vain.

About noon I got a glimpse of a very small bit of white snow with sharp outlines, in a break. About two minutes, I think, and the break closed.

But what a place for snow to be! I had thought the other giants big, but this seemed to be miles above the highest of them. I misdoubted my eyes until I had another glimpse of a larger bit of the summit for a moment, and then a still larger bit, and presently a bit of the base, to prove that it had a base on earth. All the while I was sketching industriously, trying to catch each glimpse.

At last, the whole peak stood out, clear of cloud, a huge steep-sided pyramid of dark rock and snow and ice, a long snow pennant flung eastward from the summit. The glass showed very distinctly two sharp nipples above a flat shoulder.

It was a long shot, to be sure: a hundred miles. But I never thought of that. Couldn't believe the distance when Chot proved it to me. It stands just north of the upper part of the Baltoro, you know. Its snowfields feed a long steep tributary to that big glacier.

When the array of peaks over there rode down on the earth's rim into the shadow, K^2 held the sun after the others near it. But the peaks to westward, though much lower, held it longer than K^2, for the sun can't shine far around a curve, and there is much curve in seventy miles. The westernmost peaks are surely that far directly west.

K^2 rode down deeper and deeper into the shadow, and when the stars came out, for all its hugeness, vanished in the night. The earth's rim, over there, where I could mark it on the sky, looked level.

My next shot was from about sixty miles, a high point in an arête stretching eastward from the Burji La. Roger and I were up at over seventeen thousand, under bright stars, drinking hot goat's milk chocolate and eating scrambled eggs and toast by a fire, in the lee of a bit of ledge.

From time to time, we peered over the edge into the wind and scanned the dark skyline, apparently unbroken. The zodiacal light shot up almost to the zenith, foretelling day, while the rest of the sky was still as dark as midnight. We felt the rush of the earth, a mad ride in such a place. But for all our speed, the day's approach was a stately thing. Earth's speed is gauged to the magnitude of herself and the Sun and the space between. Slowly the peaks took form and gained height. They were all big when they rode down into the glare of the daystar but K^2 was huge. Of a sudden, the sunlight streamed through a gap, and fell right across the face of K². You know what that's like.

This was not the end of our stalking, but it is the end of this letter. I pray I may not be digressing from Hamiltonian customs in this so prompt reply, not to a letter exactly, but to the friendly thought of the writer.

Think of us travelling slowly up a great valley, the Shyok, with huge peaks to the south of us, and the great Kara-koram range, close at hand to the north, and Winter steadily tightening his grip. It will be a full month before we emerge from the shadows of this valley, over a snow-covered pass of some seventeen thousand, into the bright winter sunshine of the Indus.

Yours,

P.S.—There is a very striking pyramid not far west of K² north of the Baltoro which I have not identified. It is considerably lower than K², but is so conspicuously higher than anything else in its vicinity that you might easily mistake it for K², if K² were covered. There seems to be nothing like it in the panorama from the Burji La, or in any other of the panoramas in De Filippi's book of the Duke of the Abruzzi's expedition, or on any map. Is it possible that the slim Muz-tagh Tower could look like this from any point of view?

Gypsy Davy   CAMP 47
                                ABOVE KHAPALU

                                November 11

Dear JACK,

I asked Stu to show you his letter on the early days of our stalking of K². Here's more of it, which you can pass on to him.

We travelled a long way, and were a long time about it, from the Burji La, before we had another glimpse: travelled up the Shigar, up the Braldoh, beyond the Biafo. Somewhere between the Biafo and the Baltoro, one day, from a point high above the trail, we lifted a huge massive thing filling the narrow space between the steep walls of the valley. The Mem-Sahib thought it was K², but didn't dare say so. And I did not suspect it then.

But later, at daybreak, from some seventeen thousand on the steep slopes of Dontok (Paju Peak), at the point where its cliffs and pinnacles begin to tower sheer into the sky for another mile or so, from this point I had a clear view of that great massive thing, standing, according to my map, where K² ought to stand, on the north side of the Baltoro. I saw the upper part of Muz-tagh Din, much nearer, and Gasherbrum at the head of the glacier, further off, and Masherbrum, nearest of all, across. Masherbrum looked much higher than any of them, but there was nothing that looked high enough for K², or in any way resembled the views I had had of it from very different angles. That big thing between Muz-tagh Din and Gasherbrum must have been Broad Peak, and a rather chunky mountain, standing just clear, to the left, appearing of about the same height, must have been K². The Duke's panorama C shows K² under just such humiliating circumstances. A sketch of mine suggests this, though my K² has a surprising precipice on the left, from some distance below the summit down to the skyline, which the panorama does not show. Perspective plays curious tricks with big mountains. Makalu dwarfs Everest sadly from the Singalila ridge, being only twelve miles nearer, and a good ninety from the ridge.

The wind was too bitter on Dontok, the weather too un-promising, and the climb down too arduous to wait for sunset to prove K²'s height. Sunrise would have shown nothing, as the sun rose in late September right behind these mountains. This test is none too reliable, we find, as there is a most surprising shadowing of higher peaks by lower peaks about the world.

Today we are camped at sixteen thousand on an old loess smoothed moraine, on the south side of the Shyok, opposite the mouth of the Hushe Lumba, which heads on Masherbrum —south side of Masherbrum this time, and forty miles away, looking not a step over ten.

In the gap between Masherbrum's eastern slope and a terrific grey arête stretching eastward, there stands a modest little grey pyramid, or wedge rather, a broad-based wedge. We have watched it at sunrise and at sunset at various altitudes for several days. It goes black at night before the aiguilles in that arête, not over twenty thousand, and takes the morning sun later than they, and on the end of the wedge towards us, not on the side of it toward the rising sun. Once a shadow darkened the top after it took the light, and swept down the face. We thought for some dizzy moments that it might be K², but the *Indian Survey* places K² too far to the east. I wonder if it can be the pyramid to the west of K², so high and conspicuous from my station above Charchur La on the Deosai, and from the station above Burji La. It is a long way off from here, across the Baltoro. It is shadowed at sunset by Masherbrum, I suppose. And Gasherbrum or K², or some other peak that way, shadows it at sunrise. It looks big when it has the full light of the sun.

We waited at the Baltoro snout as late as we dared. There was a wicked trail behind us. We have waited here as late as we dare, for there is a wicked trail ahead, and a pass of some seventeen thousand.

Our best wishes to your ma-bap.

GYPSY DAVY

Gypsy Davy POTHOLE CAMP (49)
SHYOK
November 13

Dear HILMA,

It is 'most a year since we dragged Wanda out from under a great pile of washing in the laundry, spitting and scratching like a cat, and dumped her into the lake. What a wonderful laundry that house has, with set tubs and washing machine and ironing machine and roller drying racks! I suppose you have great bins of soap stowed away.

We have been travelling in deep mountain valleys for months, where there is no soap, except what we have with us in our little caravan. The people, at least the grown-ups, wash their hands and faces in cold water, because their religion demands that of them, but I don't believe that they ever bathe, and we have never seen a child with clean face or hands.

Their clothes they never wash. Once, for a moment yesterday we thought we were mistaken about this. We are camped among some great rocks in a river-bed, very like the rocks on the shore at Newcastle, except that they are all worn smooth, and have no barnacles. Here and there are hollows that hold water, splendid natural wash-tubs. Soon after we arrived, Lady Ba saw a man's head, a very black thing with a little grey acorn cup on it, bob up from behind a rock and then bob down again. It kept doing this till Lady Ba got worried. She thought the owner must be crazy. Iba and I went over to drive him off. He wasn't crazy at all. He was tramping cloth in one of those wash-tubs. They wash clothes that way down in India, but this man wasn't washing clothes. He was shrinking a piece of dirty newly-woven woollen cloth in O such filthy water,—the only washing that sheep's wool is ever going to get. They didn't wash it on the sheep, and they didn't wash it after it fell off him. (It looks to us as if they rarely sheared their sheep, but rather waited until the wool fell off, so as to be sure to get all there was of it.) The sheep are either white or black, but newly-woven cloth is never white nor black, but always dingy grey or dingy black. When a garment is once made up, the owner wears it either until he dies, or until it falls from him, shred by shred, as the wool fell from the sheep in the first place. Such bundles of rags and tatters as some of the old women and some of the children are! Masses of woollen scales, layer upon layer of them.

I thought it would be a good idea to send in a big caravan laden with soap to be distributed gratis, but Lady Ba says this would never do, The people are gloomy enough as it is, and if any of them should set out to try to keep clean in their surroundings, they would die of despair.

You had better believe we wash! To be sure, we don't live in a house with dirt floors and soft mud walls. We don't play about on dung heaps as these people do. We live in a nice clean tent, swept out every day, more than once. We have a hot bath every day before a big brazier of glowing coals. We have several good washermen among our servants, who don't shrink our woollens, and who do get things as white as Wanda ever got them. Of course, we have no ironing machine, nor an iron of any kind. We have a very nice little clothes-line, though, stretched between two of the tent-poles and a third pole set off to one side the tent. We found that the wind blew the washing off—once a magpie snatched a long brown stocking of Lady Ba's and flew off over a precipice with it! So we had to invent clothes-pins. The first the carpenter made were not very effective. We had to change the model.

Yours,
Gypsy Davy

Gypsy Davy   CAMP 49
                                POT-HOLE CAMP
                                November 13

Dear ROGER THE YOUNGER,

We are camped on sand in a broad shallow pot-hole beside
the grey-blue Shyok, flowing quickly by our open door-way.
From downstream comes the roar of rapids, and from upstream
the same. Cliffs, streaked with many dikes of white and
black and brown, rise from their own ruins on the opposite
bank, and tower so high above us that we have to crane our
necks to see the sky. The roar of the river re-echoes from them.

At sunset last night we heard, above the roar of the river,
the thunder of an avalanche, starting high up some couloir,
across the valley far above us, out of sight. We thought at
first it was an earthquake. Perhaps a little quake did start
it. Great rocks came bounding down the scree ahead of it,
down to the water's edge. And then a torrent of little rocks
came tumbling, not so far down, and smaller and smaller rocks
came following, less and less boisterously, and a great cloud
of dust hung in the air a long time. And the ruin of the
cliff over there had progressed a bit.

There is a trail on that side as on this, and every hour or two
we had seen men passing there with heavy burdens on their
backs, or driving tiny laden donkeys or big yak or dzo. The
light was faint when the avalanche came down and men in dingy
grey look so like the rocks that they are not easily distinguishable,
even this close, in the twilight. We heard no outcry. We hope
no one was hurt. Our own men, carrying our packs on this
side of the river have had close calls, for much of our trail lies
over such ruins.

This is a young valley. Its walls have only begun to fall in
ruins. They will go on crumbling for thousands of years.
And while the ruin is going on, there will be danger to travellers.
A danger growing less and less, until each ruined cliff has
crumbled down to a smooth slope, gentle enough for grass
and birches and junipers to grow on. I think the junipers
will venture on it long before the grass does. But even when
the slope is all grassed over, the rocks beneath the grass will
keep on moving down, not in avalanche, nor in slides that
you can see, but so slowly that the grass and trees will keep
on growing, just the same, and seem, from year to year, to be
in the same spot. You wouldn't believe that anything on the
long slope had moved, unless you should dig down, when you

would find new boulders near the top, quite fresh and hard, and near the bottom, old ones rotten and crumbling, rotted in that tedious passage down the slope.

Of course, the mountains are young, too, like the valley; quite recently carved out of Tibet. I suppose this "roof of the world" was much bigger when it first went slowly and jerkily up, millions of years ago, perhaps; a more or less broken block, of course, a big fold on the south and a smaller one on the north and a fold or two in between—not a perfectly smooth block, but still on the whole an immense block.

If you could have landed in the middle of it then, you would probably have found it bitterly cold, fierce winds blowing continually, no people and no animals and no trees and no flowers. And when you got to the edge of it you would have found there was no getting down. The carving out of mountains would have begun on all the edges.

If you were to start now, down in the lowlands, say in Peshawar valley, and work your way up towards Tibet, you would find rather low oldish mountains, easy to get about in anywhere down there. They would grow higher and more and more precipitous eastward, until long before you got to where we are, you would find travelling difficult, often impossible, either on the mountain tops or in the valley bottoms. Travelling would get easier again as you neared the still uncarved plateau. The valleys would grow shallower and shallower until they merged into it. Of course where the rock was soft you'd find carving going on much faster than where it was tough. And where ice had been used, all set with hard sharp cutting tools, you'd find it easier to get about in the valleys than where it had not been used. In short, as fast as the outlying mountains wear down blunt, new sharp ones are carved out of the plateau to replace them, like shark's teeth.

Under this November moon, old Winter is slowly creeping down from the ice and the snow and the peaks, starting the avalanche with his heavy footfall, freezing the streams in the bottoms of deep valleys with his shadow, withering the leaves on the fruit-trees there, ruffling the hair on all the animals until they look much bigger than they did before—all except the birds. The magpies and the ravens look as sleek as ever, and as warm and unconcerned, but I must say they rise rather late. They don't come visiting till near sun-up.

There are three magpies now, hopping about near Hamra, waiting for a chance at a crisp louse or maybe one of those curious flies that dwell in his long hair. I think his hair is full three inches long now, and it all stands straight out. He has given up trying to catch the magpies, but he won't let one of them light on him. He is very foolish. All the other animals immensely enjoy being picked over.

My compliments to your cat, Pattikins. Would you believe it, I haven't seen a cat for months! They must be very scarce here. I don't know whether these people don't appreciate cats, or the cats these people, or whether the altitude doesn't agree with them, or whether all the cats are on the ships that touch at Indian ports. (We are told that every ship is required by law to carry thirteen cats!) Or it may be vanity, for if a cat had to grow winter hair, three inches long, standing straight out all over her—!

Yours
Gypsy Davy

Gypsy Davy   Camp 49
                                      Shyok
                                      November 14

Dear Carlos,

You remember how we used your string of burros in the Sierras as laboratory, to try out our ideas on linkings and come-alongs and lashings and what not, before we applied them to any of the other strings. The harness was forever changing, I like to think, evolving, and is yet. Reedy has an entirely new saddle in hand at this writing.

Out here our gear is in a similar state of flux. The litter in which the Lady Ba now so comfortably reclines, has evolved from a hammock. It's a peculiar sort of light stretcher, with a back and removable canopy, carried by four men walking single file, so harnessed in that they can turn sharp corners easily in narrow trails, and carry Milady up steep difficult places where there is no trail. It has a rather short canvas, part of the hammock, rather long shafts, two pairs of short swivel poles, and hinged legs nicely longer than village flea-hops. Nicely calculated, too, the distance between the ends of the green canvas and the heavy folds of Gothic grey ahead and behind, into which the ways are always open up black bare hairy legs, and on up to grey acorn cups on black bobbed hair, whence a successful leap might conceivably be made with a favouring breeze.

The litter's evolution was on this wise. It left Edgington's loft as a proper African hammock with a fine awning, handsomely lined and valanced, designed to be slung from a long pole with a crowd of Zulus at either end.

We unpacked it first at Dras, for they told us that no pony could carry load or rider across the Marpo La. We soon saw that no long pole would work on such a mountain trail, so we laced the ends of the hammock together, making a sort of roller towel of it, and hung it on two poles about twelve feet long, the fore end of one reaching out a stride ahead of the fore end of the other, and the hind end of the other a stride back of the hind end of the first, so that two men could go ahead, single file, each carrying a pole-end on his shoulder, and two behind. The Lady Ba had an uncomfortable seat, dangerously high, with her feet dangling and interfering with the man immediately ahead of her, and the poles had a tendency to pinch her.

We found the trail perfectly good for loaded ponies, and didn't have to use the litter till we got to the Braldoh a month later. You can't get a horse, loaded or unloaded, up that trail. There we found our contrivance much too clumsy and had to set to work on it in earnest. Any conventional palanquin I had ever seen was out of the question. Even the dandy, the neat but heavy little coffin mem-sahibs use in hill stations down in Hindustan, would have required too much room to manoeuvre in.

We shortened our poles, set the ends even, and tried making two men carry the thing like a stretcher, low, with broad slings on the shaft-ends to go over their shoulders, having relief shifts, changing at frequent intervals. Lady Ba weighs a hundred and sixty pounds, and that litter weighed about fifteen, but the Baltis in the shafts grunted and groaned and staggered so, that most of the time you couldn't see the litter for the crowd there was clustered about it, trying to help. This help was dangerous, for the helpers clung to the shafts when they fell, which they did frequently, and besides that, they mussed up the narrow trail.

One day Chot and I, by way of example, took the thing out of the Baltis' hands, and went careering over rough country with it, singing (anyway Chot sang!) as if Milady were a feather. We were discreet enough to choose the last few hundred yards into camp. When we set it down, two of our Ladakhis took it up and gave a much more dramatic exhibition with more convincing singing.

There were carpenters and blacksmiths working at the thing in every village all the way up and all the way down the Braldoh. There were changes enough made, but it remained a clumsy piston engine, as you might say. None of us thought of the turbine.

When we got back to Tisar in the Shigar, things began to happen all of a sudden. A certain degree of comfort had been attained by this. The shafts were now kept apart by bars, and half the hammock (the rest being rolled up) was stretched over a lacing of yak-hair rope, long enough for the Lady Ba to lie on, curled up. But the thing had still to be carried by two men. We tried lengthening the shafts to ten feet, and hanging them by rope slings from the centres of six-foot poles, one pole at either end, so that the shafts rode at about the height of a man's hips. Each pole rested on two men's shoulders. The leading men walked, one in the shafts and one just ahead of him, and the following men, one in the shafts and one just behind him, all four tandem. They could swing the poles at right angles if the men in the shafts moved up towards the centres of their poles and took most of the weight for the moment of a sharp turn. That is, they could if the pole happened to be resting on a propitious shoulder. It worked after a fashion, in bad places, but the men didn't take kindly to it, and there was always danger of upsetting a man in the shafts, should his pole happen to be resting on the wrong shoulder at the moment of a turn. Chot had to borrow an occasional oath from the cook-tent for me at this stage.

At Shigar we gave up the single poles and substituted two pairs of six-foot poles, attached to the shaft-ends by short iron swivels. There was a broad yak-hair shoulder-sling at each end of each pair, long enough to drop the poles to a convenient height for the bearers' hands, arms hanging straight. Four men, walking tandem, could carry the litter low, for the shafts hung even lower than the poles. They could make sharp turns by sliding the forward poles forward in the swivel rings, and the after poles back, as far as they would go, throwing the weight on two men for the moment of a turn, when these sliding poles could be swung at right angles. The hinged legs were put on here, too, to keep the litter out of harm's way, when the Lady Ba might wish to stop in a village and look about her.

Changing shifts was rather a nuisance, the relief was so hung about with plump kidskins of sattu, and their toiling comrades' shawls. I had to instal a scrip coolie, stooping sullenly under

a heavy load of plump kidskins and shawls, behind four comrades travelling light.

The Zildar's son, about your age, carved the names of the
smith and the carpenter on one of the shafts. And what a
smith! And what a carpenter! Both men were swaddled in
grey homespun except for their bare right arms, and wore
grey acorn cups on long bobbed hair. The carpenter had
better tools than the men in the Braldoh, those little homemade
adzes and homemade saws. He had a good adze and a good
saw and, besides these, a drill of the kind you whirl between
your palms, and a chisel. He sat on the ground and used
his toes for a vice, and did most of the work with his adze.

The smith was a big handsome fellow. He sat on the
ground by a bed of hot coals in a shallow hole which he had
just dug. He burned some kind of charcoal. They think
goat and sheep dung good smithing fuel further up. His
anvil was a big pebble. A ragged urchin worked a couple
of goatskin bellows for him, the whole goat with hair on, as
little cut into as possible in the process of getting him out.
The goats' necks were tied round the branching ends of a
Y-shaped iron nozzle, set in wet clay and pointing at the coal-
bed. A big pebble rested on this and held the nozzle
steady and protected the bellows from the heat. The smith
had a cutting tool, two pairs of tongs, a small hammer and
a large one, the large serving for a small anvil, and that's all
I remember. He couldn't spare much time for the litter as
he had to make all our horseshoes and horseshoe nails.

We had some saw-buck saddles made there, by the way,
as we were getting sore withers with ill-fitted knees. It was
hard to get good knees of the proper angle, and the saw-buck
I could fit exactly before they mortised it. I fitted two and
made a grand fuss about doing it, with all the men attending
closely, and left Ahmat, the best packer among them, to fit
the others. If you please, they fitted every one badly and
I had to do them all over!

We still have our troubles with the litter because we have
to change men every day or two. Rasul has a Ladakhi crew
on the way to meet us, coming over the Chorbat La.—By
Jove, they're coming now! I see eight strapping fellows swinging
down the trail toward Rasul's tent. They haven't any packs
on their backs or any pack-animals.

Yours,

GYPSY DAVY

Gypsy Davy   Camp 50
                                   Siari
                            Shyok Valley
                                November 15

Dear Leif,

Today was your day.   You would have loved the march, and so would Edward.   Roger is gone for a month after money. (It takes about a month to drop down to the bank, after tiffin, so to speak.)   Lady Ba and I had to have this wonderful morning all to ourselves.

The gypsy Queen and the gypsy King were up while the stars still shone bright in the narrow belt of sky overhead. They were off long before the canyon wall dipped low enough to let the sun in.

Silently stealing off in the twilight? Not a bit of it. It was no feeble, long-faced crew that bore the Queen's litter this time. It was tall, stalwart, gay Ladakhis, come over the Chorbat La, by order of the Aqsaqal, to meet us, wearing the jauntiest of sheepskin caps, silver and turquoise ear-rings swinging in their ears, black pigtails hanging down below their waists, long woollen coats almost touching the ground, scarlet sashes, gay pabu of yak-hair on their feet.

They walked with a swinging, springy gait, that made the Queen bob up and down like a cork on rippling water. And the four men in the shafts, and three men of the shift, all sang and the fourth piped Ladakhi working-songs, that made the litter light as air—carried it up steep hills as easily as down.

> "Your merry heart goes all the day,
> Your sad tires in a mile-a."

They charged bad places with savage rhythmic yells.   They danced in easy places, before and behind the Queen.   When we met trains of tiny donkeys, just showing black noses and long ears and tiny feet under huge loads of wool, and trains of big black long-horned dzo under heavy loads of salt, the tall leader would drop on all fours and charge, yelling, in amongst them.   The travellers they met they either frightened out of their wits with fierce gestures and grimaces, or embarrassed with low salams, touching their feet in jesting reverence. Red-cheeked little women, bent under great loads of burtsa bush, little of them but their red cheeks showing, laughed at these antics, or dropped their loads and ran and tried to hide behind big boulders.   Men hid too.   Did the trail lie close

F

under some great echoing cliff, the littermen made it echo all it would.

Whenever we approached a village, the Balti Lambardar met us with a little group of henchmen, bearing gifts, and behind them came the village band, a pair of kettles, a bass drum, and wood winds. The band struck up as merry a tune as a Balti can play, and will you believe it, even the men in the shafts danced! Men, women and children came running, jumping down terrace walls from above, or climbing them from below. And in the village, women, all hung about with silver and brass, flocked to the edges of the housetops along crooked alley-ways so narrow that the King, riding between high cobble walls, had to mind his knees. And the Balti band and our Ladakhis made the narrow passage roar with their music. And in every open spot a troop of urchins, naked but for a rag of dirty homespun or two square feet of goatskin with the hair on, danced and yelled before us.

When the band dropped off at the further edge of the village, the villagers all collected on the housetops on that side to watch us out of sight, and we heard the band playing until some tall crag hid and muffled it. But the Ladakhis kept right on. Amazing lungs! No grade could wind those singers.

At times the Queen descended from her litter, and the singing stopped for a brief space, while the company hurried across an avalanche track, eyes and ears alert, looking furtively up dangerous slopes and cliffs, hurrying a little more at sight of some fresh bruise or bit of new-broken rock in the trail.

On safer stretches, when overhanging ledge protected a narrow shelf of trail, supported on rude props, the music broke out again,—bare cliff towering to right, bare cliff to left, descending straight to deep, blue-green water, far below.

One village band of five dark ragged fellows, preceded us for miles. The trail led up brown cliffs, zigzagging. At each zigzag, the men would halt: dark figures against dark cliff, a marigold in the leader's cap, black acorn cap on black bobbed hair, dark face, dark oboe bound with silver, held high like a trumpet; clear call of oboes, roll of drums,—then on again.

Hours and hours of this. Belonging in tnese mountains as truly as the eagle's scream does, or the hoarse croak of the great black raven, or the roar of the river, or the whistle of the wind, or the thunder of the avalanche.

Tell Edward that we brought a flageolet like his, and one of our Ladakhis, although he stood aghast at first at all the fixings on it, can now so far outplay us that it is his.

Gypsy Davy

Next Day. P.S.—Tell your mother that I have made one of the littermen hawaldar and charged him to teach the men to break step at any cost, because the Lady Ba doesn't like to cut the figure of a cork on rippling water.

Gypsy Davy   Camp 51
                         Prahnu on the Shyok
                                November 16

Dear Pat,

A gypsy foot is a restless thing, will carry you far afield.

Ours have been supplemented of late by ponies' feet and yak's, and I have counted as many as eight men's feet under the Lady Ba in the shafts of her litter, and as many more ready to relieve the first lot, stepping lightly on this side and on that, to a simple ditty on a pipe, accompanied by lusty voices,— here in the bottom of this Himalayan canyon at nine thousand feet beside a jade-green river, studded with blocks of grey November ice. On either hand tall buttresses of naked rock beneath great roofs and domes of snow and ice, twelve thousand feet above us, and spires and pyramids on up to nineteen— at any rate one is. And all the time, looming ahead of us, a distressingly long way ahead, a glacier-saddled pass some eighteen thousand feet above the sea. Vague rumours coming to us: "The pass is open still." "The pass is shut." "Men swept down by avalanche."

Yours,

Gypsy Davy   Camp 52
                                              Turtok in the Shyok
                                                     November 18

Dear Alice-of-Idyllwild
   Chief of the Wild Men's Club,

We are camping the night in very wild mountains, few of
them hereabout under twenty thousand feet; in a very wild
valley, nothing in sight but brown cliffs and grey gravel, and
jade-green river, roaring far below us; on the edge of a high
terrace, just below the village of Turtok. I mean, on the
literal edge. If I step three feet outside my tent door, I fall
over a tremendously high bluff, and break my neck, and my
corpse goes floating down the jade-green river.

The people in this village look and act much wilder than
the Idyllwild wild men. They call their Chief a Lambardar.
He met us peacefully enough a mile outside, a half-dozen
henchmen at his back, bowed very low and extended a handful
of silver. I said, "Your gift has arrived to us. Thank you.
Kindly take it back." Which he did, much relieved, I thought,
to find it was not Maharaja's minister travelling at the villagers'
charges, but a mere sahib travelling at his own.

The villagers act as if they had rarely seen a sahib. I wonder
if they've ever seen a mem-sahib. They came trooping up
and down the flights of little terraces, crowding along the line
of march, squatting on dung heaps and terrace walls, and
every point of vantage, staring and chattering like monkeys.
Our men have driven most of them off now, but little groups
come sneaking back to get a look at us. They run if I so much
as look their way.

I doubt if they stew their Chief when they have done with
him. If they do, they must wait until he cools off, for they
eat with their hands. We haven't seen a spoon for months,
except a big iron one that belongs to the blacksmith. He uses
it for heaping his coals of thorn bush. I don't believe, by the
way, that you would have had any idea that that wild fellow
was a blacksmith, or that little hole in the ground, a forge, or
the boulder beside it, an anvil. It was a wild ragged urchin
who blew the goatskin bellows for him.

I like the village best when all the people have gone to bed,
and the moonlight is flooding the valley, and the towering
cliffs are silvery, and the naked trees have a ghostly look,—
the tall straight poplars, the writhing walnuts, and the big
chinars, all very white in the moonlight.

There is firelight coming from a little pile of boulders by a boisterous streamlet, and the sound of millstones, grinding. A farmer, squatting there with half his family, by a fire on the floor of his boulder cave, grinding away,—all night, I wonder?

Remember me to your father and mother and John and Junior, if any of them have escaped the stew-pots of the Idyllwild Wild Men.

Yours,
GYPSY DAVY

Gypsy Davy   CAMP 55
THOISE
On gravel terrace near the Shyok
November 23

Dear ROLAND,

Rasul tells me that you and he and Dorje turned off at Piun to cross the Chorbat La. We kept right on up the left bank, the Piun hautboys a-playing before us, O!

The mapped trail on the French map crosses at Piun (Paxfain, *Indian Survey*). We saw a good bip moored along-side the trail there, where a narrow ledge carries it close to the river. The large scale *I.S.*, corrected to 1916, shows no trail on either side between Paxfain and Biagdangdo. A small scale *I.S.*, corrected to 1923, shows a detour for this stretch, crossing a glacier pass at eighteen thousand and meeting the Shyok at Chalunka. The Dehra Dun route-book shows trails near the river on both sides.

We found our trail in good condition, recently worked by Rasul's orders, for our benefit. It was exposed to falling rocks here and there rather dangerously, as the rocks start at great heights and fall under cover for a long way, so that they are moving at high speed when a traveller gets warning. The trail was not under fire when we passed, but the Mem-Sahib's littermen didn't sing on those stretches.

It had a cliff or two to traverse near the water's edge of course. The parri (?) were substantial enough as those things go. The British say: "carried on props," don't they? It isn't altogether clear to me how those narrow railingless scaffolds are tied to the walls they wind about. The props always seem to be fairly securely footed, but they rarely stand at such an angle as will make them effective in holding the scaffold securely against the wall. Perhaps the horizontal sticks are pinned down into a crevice in the narrow ledge they rest on. How do they ever persuade those uneven flat rocks they floor the things with to nestle down among the crooked sticks and branches of the frame, to a point where they will lie solidly enough to let a yak tread on one corner without calamity? They don't lie quite still under that strain. Perhaps the yak doesn't throw his full weight on a corner until he has tested the come-and-go.

There was almost no traffic. I don't remember any villages. We missed the caravans, and the thrilling passings in impossible places, and those funny big piles of burtsa coming down the screes apparently on their own legs. I suppose there was always a little red-cheeked woman discoverable at the core.

At Siari the Mem-Sahib took her alternate day of rest on a commanding little terrace at the very edge of things. Rasul has long since ceased to challenge these rest-days. He continues absorbed in writing up the De Filippi safar, and welcomes a long quiet day in his green masjid. That Edgington three-pole fly makes a perfect masjid.

We crossed a winter bridge at Siari. I don't think you saw any of these things. Narrow boulder causeways built out from either bank to caissons of willow withes, causeways always rough, but usually substantial. Then the span between caissons still narrower, fairly rigid or somewhat elastic according to the relation between the length of poplars available and the necessary width of the span. In this case the small ends of the poles were pretty small. There were longer poles on the sides, whose diameter toward the small end, where they rested on the caissons, was slightly reassuring. The small ends of these side poles projected out over the causeways some five or six feet and served as levers, with a man at each, for quieting the nervous thing. We swam the ponies, but the loaded coolies took the bridge, five at a time. It sagged to a point where I thought the pole-ends must snap off the caissons.

We had to climb and descend on the right bank more than once some fifteen hundred feet or so, on gravel, between severed spur-ends and the valley wall.

We got a good bird's-eye view of Prahnu down below us: a broad flat, pretty high, in behind the conventional spur-end, the village on a rocky fan, skirting the inner edge of the flat, little terraces stepping up behind it, climbing steeper and steeper slopes. Across the flat, on the barren side of a moraine piled up against the severed spur-end over there, standing apart so that no ditch could reach it—in this out of the way place, a lot of circular low-walled flat spots like Braldoh threshing-floors except that they lack stakes, a number of low buildings that might be storehouses, interspersed. I wonder, do they carry their grain all the way over there to thresh, and bring it all the way back to grind?

Iba says there is a Bara Maulvi at Prahnu. There are masjids enough there under big chinars, and a wide qabrstan in a most desolate boulder-strewn part of the flat, surprisingly well kept, as if the bereaved were well-to-do. By the way, Iba says the Braldoh Maulvi, who appears to be the really big one in this whole region, is inclined to be hard on wealthy men. He stays with Iba when he comes to Leh.

A little beyond Prahnu the trail is carried back to the left bank on a fairly substantial poplar cantilever, with railings, if you please. The riven planks tip very slightly under your tread, and the sag and sway of the span is moderate. But even so the dog Hamra funked it, as he has every bridge thus far. I don't suppose the people consider that a bridge needs repair until it goes down with all on board. Very likely Hamra could give us information on this point.

Curiosity about us, especially about the Mem-Sahib whom Rasul delights to honour, seems to increase with each day's march up valley. Much of the trail beyond the bridge lies on young fans at the foot of high bluffs in old ones, villages perched well up the old fans, out of sight. The villagers came crowding down to bluff edges to watch us. We saw a long dark file ahead zigzagging down one bluff face. When we came abreast, there was a whole village lined up on one side the trail, first the women and then the men, all in their Friday best. And they all bowed low as we passed.

Turtok is a shaggy little village, literally bristling with curiosity, but very hospitable for all that. We kept the smith busy all day long making a proper brazier. The weather's snappy. Apricot coals need draught. (Rasul's Turtok, which is also mine, is close to the Shyok, a few miles down stream from Chalunka on the opposite bank.)

There were ponies grazing at Prahnu, but practically no traffic between there and Turtok. There was a surprising amount of pony dung on the trail beyond Turtok, however.

The winter bridge there is more substantial than the one at Siari. The ponies took it light.

We passed through a land of colour would dazzle your eyes where the Shyok broadens out opposite Tebe Nala. The nala's mouth itself is pretty wide. The sun shines fairly in, and burnishes all the high wainscots of the place. A rare place to camp, on a high river terrace opposite the nala. No such colour have we found yet elsewhere in these mountains. The colour gives place abruptly to black scree up valley, but the boulders are streaked with serpentine and one scree was thick with yellow dust, suggesting recent avalanche.

We camped near the river for once, under Biagdangdo—village out of sight on a high terrace.

The Ladakh line, Rasul says, runs down the Tebe (a high pass to the Indus, by the way, reported at the head of that valley, and a village this side of it) and crosses the Shyok below Biagdangdo. But you'd never have suspected you'd crossed the magic line if it hadn't been for a crimson-gowned chaprasi from the Leh Tehsildar come on business of state, incidentally bearing the Tehsildar's compliments to us, and news of home for the men, four months out. "We every one Ladakhi wanted the long news of Ladakh." (Sheet 52F Provisional Issue *Indian Survey*, one inch to four miles, corrected to 1922, states: "No information available on boundary between Skardu and Ladakh tehsils.")

They told us that the trail on the Biagdangdo side makes a wide high detour crossing sixteen (!) passes before it gets back to the river by Waris Nala. The *Indian Survey* shows this trail bereft of most of its passes. It crosses a number of spurs, I suppose.

There was a new bip moored near camp, got ready for us, Rasul said. A fragile-looking bundle of crooked poplar poles with very crooked tops reaching out behind, like angry tails lashing the water. We swam the ponies about noon while the sun was peering over the valley-rim. The water was icy cold. They were a long while racing up and down to get warm after the sun withdrew. We crossed dry on the bip early next morning, sitting high on boxes in the middle of a handsome rug that lent an air of solidity to the frail thing, but covered wide interstices, and made stepping off precarious.

There is a long stretch on the left bank above this crossing, uninhabited, uninhabitable, bone-dry. No trail marked on the British or the French map, but one shown in the route-book. We found a good safe trail there. We crossed a broad flat opposite Waris Nala like a lake-bed, properly bastioned toward the river by severed spur-ends, but on the wrong side for the winter sun's peep in, and without water.

It was late afternoon when we struck the first water at a place the men called Pachathang, a frozen trickle in a little nala. There were rock shelters on the trail in the nala, and one house reported a mile or two up, with two men and a woman living in it. This camp is not marked on any map I have seen. The *Indian Survey*, large and small scale, puts Pachathang some three miles up a much bigger nala, a nala a few hours further up the Shyok, with a bridged stream in it, and a strong trail. We forded this at dusk. It was only partly frozen over. The bridge was solid enough, but needed caulking, as one might say.

It was pitch dark when the Mem-Sahib's littermen, singing, bore her up a steep trail to the brow of a high terrace. There was a pan of coals in the open door-way of the tent (we never shut it) that glowed with a most unusual brightness and emitted heat in plenty. There were big fires down below us, such as we had not seen before in the men's camps. The coolies lay swaddled in grey shawls in a ring round the biggest, and all night long one or another fed it.

Morning showed a broad valley ahead, with gently sloping fans on either side, no more "darksome narrow straits." On both banks wide groves of a peculiar wild tree, a crooked low-branching trunk about twenty feet high, with shaggy red bark, and leaves of three very different shapes. Tograk in Turki. Hotang, I think, in Ladakhi. The coals of this wood are far and away the best we have found. They fall slowly away to fine white ash without any draught. Even so, Rasul says: "This wood is only queen of woods. In Ladakh will come king of woods, tset."

A very few hours beyond that camp, the first gompa, a little one, waving black yak-tails at us from its parapets. There were two black cats making the circuit of the walls. The gompa was little, but had full store of red jinn and blue jinn. The first chortens. The first mani wall. And high up the valley side, across the river, crowning a spur there, grey battered walls of a big lama castle.

No more dull houses of dobe, or sombre cobbles, but cheery whitewash and daubs of red. (Is that red paint really efficacious in keeping out lhas? How do they make it?) And that lovely turquoise head-dress, and all the rest of it!

Ladakh for us!

BA

P.S.—Tantric divinities? Worshipful or propitiable or bribable? Maybe, but for Rasul and Iba and us, blue and red jinn.

Can all those hideous figures and more hideous masks be

tantric? Is no one of them Kurulugu? Were the old gods of the country all too modest to find places in the lamaist pantheon? Are the lhas up the nalas that all those little piles of stones stand out against all tantric too? Rasul showed us in pantomime how a man's nature might suddenly be changed if a lha should get by a stone pile and into his house. "Now I am Rasul," most sedate and mannerly. "Now I am the lha," grimacing, glaring, savage.

Later.—Waddell, in that old book of his, I notice, credits the pantheon or the pandemonium, or whatever you call it, with a lot of Tibetan celebrities, though he doesn't say who they are.

Lady Ba　　　　　　　　　　CAMP 58
　　　　　　　　OPPOSITE THE MOUTH OF THE NUBRA
　　　　　　　　　　　　　　　　November 28

Dear PRUE,

Your letter of September first reached us with a certain casualness. We had instructed the Leh postmaster to hold our mail for us, but he is a kindly soul, and hearing that we were travelling slowly up the Shyok, sent our letters along by some one who might meet us.

It's a nice letter, full of plans for autumn and winter, children's school and clothes, wood for the fireplace—a domestic letter calculated to make a gypsy sister breathe a sigh of envy. But this time I can answer.

We know where we are to spend the winter! That is, within limits. My rom has no desire to attempt snow-closed passes, thus encumbered. Which means confinement, within a radius of two weeks' journey.

Rasul wants us to spend the winter in Leh. The Raja has sent us an invitation to camp inside or on the roof of the palace—a huge old building, they tell me, with a hundred vacant rooms, perched high on a crag. The Moravian missionaries in the village have most kindly offered one of their cottages free for the moment. The Tehsildar sends word that the dak bangla is at our service. I suggested the serai where caravans put up, man and beast. Chot says he spent a day or two in one, in a room all hung with rugs, opening on a balcony overlooking a courtyard with trees in it, where great bundles of silk and charas were piled and where the traders came to say their morning prayer, kneeling toward Mecca (westward).

My sahib greets all suggestions with polite appreciation, but I see in his eye a look of remoteness. We'll not be camping in an echoing palace chamber, nor yet in a cosy cottage.

Iba's wife (an executive woman, apparently), wrote him that a lot of fine-ground flour had been brought from Yarkand over the Sassir down to the Shyok on camels, and been transhipped into Leh, from there on yak. He wrote her to buy up a lot of it for us. He laid in, in Shigar and Khapalu, two maunds of the best dried apricots, the kind with the stones left in. The stones are valuable themselves. I've seen a circle of women kneeling under a chinar tree in the centre of a village, rubbing the oil from apricot kernels on hollowed slabs of granite. Like Milton's Eve, making a creamy curd from nut-meats to give Adam a bit of variety in his Eden diet. They're good to eat, too, these "apricot-rocks," as Rasul calls them. And then there are almonds and walnuts. When we get into a camp someone always arrives offering to massage the Sahib's legs, which bores the Sahib, and, just as regularly, someone brings the Mem-Sahib a plate of walnuts—which pleases the Mem-Sahib. Iba has two sacks of them on the back of a big black dzo, coming along with us.

The Ladakhis come habitually to Baltistan for butter for their tea, so we are taking along a lot of it in skins, with the hair on, for our men this winter. We'll have to keep a staff, of course, pony-men and cook and room-boy. They say there's Balti honey to be had too, with the bees in it. And, because only the missionaries and the B. J. C. in Leh raise potatoes, we've stocked up with some of the funny little yellow ones, descendants of those sent by Hügel to the King Ahmed Shah of Skardu a hundred years ago, I imagine, and not prospering greatly.

These expenses were so heavy that we were thankful to meet Chot, bulging with money, yesterday. We had brought only a couple of horse-loads of silver when we came into the mountains, thinking we could get more in Leh. When we heard how difficult that would be (Leh is quite dead in winter, they say, and even in summer there is never anything approaching a bank, of course), Chot went off for a month or so on a private adventure to see what he could turn up.

If this doesn't match your forethought, add this bit: I can see the men at Iba's tent, arrayed in white, forming into line to come up to our tent and thank us for their new sheepskin coats—skin and wool, worn just the reverse of the sheep's way. It will be good and cold going over the Khardung, and Rasul waylaid a caravan coming down the Nubra, and fitted them all out yesterday. They've left off their pagris, too, and put on the horned fur caps of Ladakh. And their feet are gay in red charoq. It costs about a dollar for a sheepskin coat, but as a man's pay isn't more than fifteen cents a day (with about as much for his food), it's a present worth a "thank-you!" Nice fellows! We like providing for them.

I feel vicariously like the virtuous woman of the Psalm. We have seen her all autumn, in black or faded purple, on pumpkin-decorated roofs, plucking wool apart, passing it from one round box of birch-bark to another, and spinning, spinning, endlessly spinning, no wheel, but spindles twirled in cups of that hardened apricot pulp, and spindles tossed over the roof edge to be caught back and tossed again, till the yarn is ready for the weaver, setting up his loom in the open street before the house—we saw one at work in the carved porch of an abandoned masjid.

Rasul and Iba have beautiful robes, Rasul's dark grey, Iba's deep red, of wool of their own wives' spinning, the weaving and fashioning done by men. I'll try to get some strips of the narrow cloth for coats for your children, not for this winter, but for another one.

Yours,

Gypsy Davy

CAMP 58
OPPOSITE NUBRA VALLEY
November 28

Dear PAUL, potter,

There is an extraordinary dearth of pottery in these mountain valleys. I don't think it's lack of clay, though it may be. I have heard of but one place where pots are made, in four months' travel. We have passed but half a dozen man-loads on the trail so far, loads rather larger than the men, pots all red. They are said to pat the clay on to the mould of half a pot, and at some stage in the drying, stick two halves together.

We saw some rather neat work in serpentine, little cups and inkpots, rather good lines, hacked out with a hammer for the most part, and turned down a bit on a rude lathe which makes a couple of revolutions one way and then a couple the other

way. Workmen sitting on the dirt floor in a room with no
other opening than a hatch in the ceiling, typical winter quarters
in those parts. Rather interesting carved pillar holding up
the ceiling, but rudely made ladder. The sheep and dzo
make so free of a man's house that the fastidious must have
to resort to the hatch and ladder for protection. Even this
won't keep out the goats. As a matter of fact, these particular
fellows were probably smuggling—the Maharaja holding rights
over all rocks and minerals of any value—so they'd not mind
the darkness and the inconspicuous entrance.

We poked our noses into a cave on the Shyok trail, which
had been dug in a soapstone vein. The walls were warty with
incipient pots. They apparently cut the pot out in the vein
as far as they can, before cutting it off. How they detach it,
I can't guess. Rasul says these pots are prized for making
soup. I suppose in time the pot gets a flavour like an old
meerschaum which it lends the brew.

There's quite a lot of rather pleasing wood-carving in the
villages. The Mussulman seems as set against repeating a
pattern in his masjid as the old Gothic builders were in their
cathedrals, but these up-country Mussulmans are much oftener
reduced to ugly patterns.

I suppose these artists are all Baltis. The best of the Baltis
are fine stalwart handsome fellows, but there are over many
among them not like that. There are altogether too many
Baltis, anyhow, for the occasional boulder patches which lie
enough off the perpendicular to admit of being terraced, and
to which it is possible to bring irrigation water out of narrow
slits of canyons in the valley walls,—water from snow and
ice, lying at twenty thousand and more.

There is almost no colour in their dress. The coolies wear
dingy grey, homespun of course: little acorn-cup caps; wide-
sleeved tunics hanging in heavy folds such as Giotto would
draw, caught at the neck with one button (sometimes a British
trouser-button); trousers reaching nearly to their ankles, a
full yard around each leg; in this cold weather shawls much
longer than Scotch plaids wound and draped about them in
a dozen different ways, sometimes enveloping them to the eyes.
Feet usually bare—live sole leather very poor, often badly
cracked about the heel. The limpest lot of fellows you can
imagine, mere dish-clouts of men apparently, yet carrying all
the loads of the country on their backs.

We have rarely caught a Balti laughing or seen him eat
anything but dry bread and water. But they all love

to wear flowers in their hair, and can shake a leg on
occasion to an extraordinary band, and there are those in the
country who can ride a polo pony. (Polo has been played
here since the time of the Moguls.) They don't drink for
religious reasons. And for most of them it's a long while
between smokes, and it's rarely tobacco they get when they
do smoke. They must have some drug or other to pull through
on, but it's not in evidence.

We crossed the line the other day into a land of singing and
dancing and colour—Ladakh. Silver and gold bracelets on
men's wrists, big silver rings studded with turquoise swinging
in their ears, jaunty poke-bonnets brocaded in green and gold,
crimson girdles, crimson robes, even. And that dye, that
crimson dye! As precious as Tyrian purple. Boiled for an
incredible time, long enough you would think, to ruin the
stoutest wool, in fine old seasoned yak urine, with the root of
the broom, a powdered red stone, soda, and I don't know what
besides. No two shades alike.

These men, mark you, eat meat and drink beer in plenty.

Yours,

Ba

Lady Ba   At the Snout of the Baltoro Glacier

Dear Jack,

[I'm really in a camp just under the Khardung Pass, but
this letter was conceived at the place of the heading. Not
more than conceived, because the Lady Ba was physically exhausted. The body of her lay in a cocoon of soft brown blankets
beside a brazier, and the mind of her turned, between naps,
to you who should have been at the Baltoro snout in her place.
It's not in blankets you'd have been at that juncture.]

We set out weeks ago to get as near as we could to K². We
left our ponies at Tisar at about the point where the grey waters
from the Chogo, the Biafo, the Baltoro and a host of minor
glaciers come together to make the Shigar River. We left
our heaviest impedimenta there and several of our servants.
Then, after days of following a trail up vertical walls,
across cliff faces, on ledges where there was barely room
for one foot at a time, and across slopes where loose stones
might come down upon us from above or be dislodged by us
on coolies taking short cuts with our luggage far below,

across dizzy bridges, rising from a comfortable seven thousand
to a less comfortable ten, we reached the last village on the
map, Askole. Beyond lie the greatest glaciers, the Kara-koram
range and an UNEXPLORED region.

At that last village of all, Roger, our bahadur Chhota Sahib
fell ill of a fever. We pitched his little forester's tent a few
feet from our big one on the sunny edge of a terrace far above
the river and watched over him till the fever was gone. Then
we pushed on, leaving him in a self-enforced quarantine, one
of our servants within call, and arrangements made for couriers
to run between his camp and ours daily, while we raced against
bad weather already overdue—if "mem-sahib marching" can
ever be called "racing."

Yesterday, four of my marches beyond Chot's camp, I, dragged
and hauled by ropes up to a shelf far above the valley bottom
(there, twelve thousand), caught a glimpse of some of the great
peaks, one of them, I long to believe, K² itself. But today,
there is no more spirit left in me, and here I lie, gazing at
the vertical ice wall before me, while my lord, sole survivor of
our little band of "explorers," was at dawn high up on the
shoulder of Dontok, accompanied by a nimble little old man
whom Iba calls "Appo Mahmat."

Iba has just been in to see me. He says that Grand-dad
Mahmat says he remembers a patch of grass and jungle on the
left side of this valley, covered now by the thick dirty ice of
the glacier. He also says that last night by the camp-fire
Grand-dad Mahmat told the men that years ago when he was
a youngster, there came down into Askole from up this way
a queer little party of men, ragged, hungry and exhausted. The
villagers were amazed and alarmed. Askole has always had
a fort up valley, for defence against Hunza raiders. But
these were not Hunza men. One of them, dark and ragged,
his feet bleeding from long marching on ice, was a sahib!
The Askole people had had trouble enough with the Hunza
raiders using the old Muz-tagh Pass when it was open, but
it had been closed for years by impassable ice. And here
was one of those indomitable white men come over it! They
treated the Sahib well enough. But they showed such angry
faces to the man who had guided him, a former dweller in Askole,
that he didn't dare stay as he had intended.

Ibrahim told me this story, and my sleepy mind came wide
awake to listen. "It was Younghusband Sahib," I told him,
"when he was very young. He came all the way from China
to India by land. He came over that terrible pass. Nobody

who was used to climbing would have thought it could be crossed, unequipped as he was, without ropes or ice-axes,—or even proper boots, and no men with him used to such work. He showed us the boots he wore to the pass-top,—nothing but uppers left. He had to wear pabu all the long way down over the ice, soft slippery pabu. His men were Ladakhis. It was Shukur Ali who came over with him. Mohammed Isa was with him up to the pass, but turned back there."

Iba was thrilled. Of course he knew about Younghusband Sahib. All the mountain people know about him. Iba says that if all the English were like Younghusband Sahib, there would be no hard feelings between dark men and white men. Shukur Ali was a great servant of sahibs when Iba was a little boy in Leh. And Mohammed Isa—why, he married Bulla's mother, and Bulla was our cook, making sour-dough bread in the shelter of a boulder that minute. "Mohammed Isa went to Lhasa with Younghusband Sahib. He's dead now. And Shukur Ali is dead, too," he said sadly.

"But Younghusband Sahib is strong and well," I told him. "He walks miles and miles every day. He is a very big man. They call him 'Sir Francis' in England. Only last spring we went to see him, not on ponyback, but in a high cart with big wheels like a Yarkandi araba. A horse taller than the Yarkandi horses drew us over wide smooth roads with no rocks or sand in them. He lives in a lovely country. They call it Kent. It's all trees and flowers and beautiful green fields. Bluebells are like a carpet under great trees by the roadside. By and by we climbed a hill and there at the top of it was Younghusband Sahib with a wide view before him. He talked with us about Ladakh and the Ladakhis. He loves the Ladakhis, men and ponies. I shall write him a letter and give him your salams and Appo Mahmat's."

Iba put his hands to his forehead in gratitude, and then had to be off to send food up the mountain to the Bara Sahib, sure to stay aloft till sunset.

Poor Chot! nursing himself at Askole! How he will hate to turn back at the very edge of UNEXPLORED country! I have a feeling he'll be coming down off the glacier's snout here some-day, with who knows what adventures past, glad to see the wild rose bushes and tamarisks of this valley. Perhaps you'll be with him. When you get to Askole, ask for Appo Mahmat and give him my greetings.

[Well, here I am, back in the Khardung camp with a great range of snow mountains between me and all that. I have been telling Rasul the story. Rasul says that on his first long journey, as sais for Captain Younghusband, they camped one night here, near where we are camping. It was a cold night and Rasul slept under the fly of the Captain's tent, to keep warm. "Not know if Sahib know is boy under tent, or not know."]

Yours,

Gypsy Davy   CAMP 59
                                          KHARDUNG
                                        November 29

Dear ROLAND,

I think Ladakh must miss its king and queen. Or is it that so merry a land is always treating strangers thus? This land where all the women at their daily work dress like the queen on state occasions, and all the men like kings, and all men, whether at play or work, sing, dance, pipe and drink deep the livelong day and far into the night. Our progress since we crossed the border has been one long ovation.

The merry little villages have all been small, until the other day we came to Hundar, sprawling over a whole fan below the crag from which its gompa frowns.

The Zildar met us a long way out with a big retinue, himself robed in ancient state, wearing the long sword and that huge tall crimson hat that looks so like a brobdingnagian oyster, small end down. He bowed low and held out a handful of silver, and the little group of crimson-robed Lambardars immediately about him all bowed low. Then we rode down a long line of gorgeous women: black eyes, rich crimson in dark cheeks, all hung about heavy with silver and coral and turquoise, from those wide turquoise-studded cobras on their own black hair between wide elephant ears of yak's, down to bossed silver girdles on crimson gowns, passing what wealth of silver and pearl and coral on the way! What an incredible harness! Has each part significance? They all bowed low to us, clicking those white cuffs cut from that big sea-shell. And at the far end of the line stood one of the gorgeous creatures holding a handsome brass jug of beer all set about on the rim with little dabs of butter, and one holding a bowl of sattu

G

likewise set about, and one a big iron ladle burning incense.
Wert ever entreated in this wise? Is the beer and sattu wholly
symbolic? Or may a hungry man eat and drink with the
sweet scent of juniper twigs in his nostrils?

Then the band struck up—oboes and kettles. No splendour
about the musicians, just plain grey homespun, none too whole.
There was dancing and singing on every hand. Up a long
trail they led us to get round the ice that crept out over the
main way. The boys were sliding on crimson gowns instead
of sleds. They'd all been spanked the day before by Rasul's
orders for digging pitfalls on the public way. I wonder who
the culprit was they laid those traps for.

We climbed higher and higher, for the whole valley knows
by this,—we are the Ri Sahib. We caught a strain of distant
music from the crags above, looked up and saw the gompa
parapet all crimson with lamas. Our men showered pellets
of pony-dung at the village musicians until their hubbub
ceased, and the lamas' music came to us, clear and sweet.

We climbed on up by grey mani walls among white chortens
beside a narrow gorge, until we came abreast the gompa,
then crossed a bridge and made camp under the gompa walls.
The lamas came down, trumpets in hand, and all the gay throng
gathered round the stage to see our play-acting. One beggar
woman of a "looped and windowed raggedness" grotesque,
hung about, watching the Mem-Sahib's every movement.

Next day there was some real play-acting down in the village
in the garden of the great house,—Nono Sonam Wangdus,
if you please, now fallen upon evil days. Nono Sonam Wangdus
is now "same donkey. Not same dog. Dog can sleep on
master's bed. Donkey nobody wanting."

The acting was preceded by singing and that slow dancing,
now by men, now by women—the Lady Ba's first sight of those
amazing capes of green and scarlet with the long white goat-
hair fringes. My chang, ladled from big jars in the centre of
the dusty stage, went round continually, the stage merely a
clear space in the midst of the crowd.

At last the acting. Head lama, Rasul said, a long lean
fellow, and several of his men, all in beggarly attire, squatting
on straw, all drinking hard and getting drunker and drunker.
The underlings wipe the Skusho's running nose from time to
time with straw, and now and then his mouth. Crowd hilarious
with delight. Hindu Naib on safar sitting next me, disgusted
beyond words. Presently the actors rise unsteadily and the
Skusho staggers about, mock-blessing the gay kings and queens

in the front row, chucking a queen under the chin now and then, frightening a baby, his followers mimicking.   Rather startling this, if it really was the Skusho.   I hope it was the Chagdso!

Nono Sonam Wangdus' lady keeps the great house, living in a small corner of it in inexpensive state.   You may remember she was an old love of Rasul's.   As befitted her state, she was not present at first, and message after message from Rasul went in to the great house praying her to come out and dance. "She is little big a lady, madam, therefore cannot come so quick."   At last with her handmaidens, she came, more splendid than any of the other queens, and danced alone before the Aqsaqal.

The crimson in the women's cheeks was more apparent at this festival than it had been the day before.   Rasul had told them that he was "'asham' before his Mem-Sahib" that she should see the women of his country with dirty faces. (The Naib had told me, among other startling things of his observing, that the religion of the country forbade a woman's ever washing after her first delivery!)

After some five hours, giving the tamasha time to get fairly under way, we took our leave and were conducted over the house by the great lady and the Aqsaqal.   A veritable old palace, stately chambers, spacious halls, wide balconies, locked storerooms, frescoed walls, carved pillars, private chapel, Merovingian kitchen—(is that early enough?)

Now don't take me to task if I confuse the doings at Hundar and Deskit.   The two towns vied with each other in this welcoming business.   I may have put the Deskit Lambardar's hat on Hundar's Zildar.   Deskit is the Lady Ba's province. It was there she got her thrill.

Yours,

BA

PART II

WINTER AND SPRING ON THE HERMIT'S CRAG

WINTER AND SPRING ON THE HERMIT'S CRAG

Gypsy Davy

LEH
DAK BANGLA
December 4

Dear DAVE,

We have your letter about pools, irises, tennis courts, vacations, Rabbit Companies and the like things that make a man's heart glad to think on. We judge from your comment on the length of our letter that you took up your pen in self-defence, lest your mother make you listen to the whole of it.

We crossed our last high pass for the winter, four days ago, the Khardung, seventeen thousand six hundred feet. The night before the crossing we camped at the last village on the north side, at thirteen or fourteen thousand. We were not in the village, of course. We were at least half a mile from its dirty skirts. Roger was with us. He had come over the Khardung to meet us. Of course, he poked his nose into the village. He said there was a serai there, piled high with several lakhs' worth of silks, namdas and charas from Chinese Turkistan, waiting for transport.

There were Turki haji resting there on their way to Mecca, come over I don't know how many dreadful passes (one of them well over eighteen thousand) in this bitter weather, and with some bad ones still to cross. Roger says he saw several of these fellows at the dispensary door in Leh waiting to have frozen toes cut off. Now and then one has to lose a foot, and sometimes one who refuses this sacrifice dies a little further on the road to Mecca which will help him to heaven, as you doubtless know, with much less trouble and expense than the whole journey to Mecca would entail.

To get back to that village: about the middle of the night we heard men whistling and calling on the trail, down below us, already under way for the pass. We were up, eating our breakfast by a hot brazier, hours and hours before the dawn.

The great arête across the valley rode down the sky. Your boiling point would give you twenty thousand feet everywhere

up there, and twenty-four and twenty-five thousand feet if
you climbed a bit. Spica flashed from behind a pinnacle
in the east, and in the west a big star suddenly went out.

We heard whistling and a curious sound like "pstuss!"
near at hand. The darkness took shape. Big, black shadowy
forms loomed before us. They moved right up to the tent
door. We saw them clearly in the starlight. Yak. Long
horns. Tails so bushy that all the Company's rabbits tied
by the ears would not make one of them. Fringes dragging
on the snow. High withers like bison's. Tails waving high
above their backs like skunks' tails. Much tugging at nose-
rings, and now and then a terrifying grunt.

I felt sure some nose-ring must break out, and a yak charge
the tent and overturn the brazier. Can't you see Lady Ba
and Roger trying to escape under the bottom of the tent,
between two rocks? (We keep her well anchored with big rocks,
—you can't drive pegs in this country.)

If you please, those wild yak bulls were saddled with our
riding-saddles! My knees were a bit wobbly, I can tell you, at
the prospect. I thought of Rasul's story of the cook who
got an inch of yak horn up his nose. I was much relieved
to find that Lady Ba's yak had lost his horns in a row, but
he made up for lack of horns, after she got on, by bristling
a great bunch of mane a full twelve inches straight up under
her nose. The man who was leading Roger's yak let go the
rope, and there was Roger, all alone in the Himalaya, astride
a great black, grunting brute, behind a pair of horns that
spread a good three feet!

A long line of these brutes trailed out ahead of us, and a
long line behind, under our loads. Our ponies travelled
light behind them.

My yak crawled over big boulders like a tank. His short
black legs looked to me, each one, as thick as two horse's legs.
He had more confidence in them on sloping ice than I have
ever had in mine. He ploughed through deep snow as
though there were no snow there. He panted like a dog,
and hung his tongue out, but kept steadily on, up the ever-
steepening grade. The snow on either side the trail was
all marked up where he and his fellows had been dragging
their black tongues, licking up snow the way the Limited
scoops water, only not quite so fast!

When the sun was well up, a good many hours later, we
reached the edge of the glacier that blankets the north side of
the pass, a huge thick thing. The summer trail runs high, off

to the east, along the base of an ice precipice, all scarred with avalanche tracks, for there have been heavy falls of snow this year already. But the yak of the haji and the traders have made a safe zigzag winter trail, right down, where they couldn't travel in summer on the bare ice but can now in deep snow.

Just before we left the last rocks we passed a horrid, bloody spot with lots of bird-dung on the boulders all about. Ugly gusts of wind swept down the slope, and made the snow drift fast. We knew if it but blew hard enough we could not make the pass. We zigzagged slowly up, and up, and up. Now and then we passed the carcass of a pony frozen stiff. That new snow hid bones enough to grow a million irises.

A strong wind swept the pass. The old yak ploughed through drifts there, up to their eyes, as fit at one in the afternoon as they had been at four in the morning.

We rested in the lee of some rocks. All the great ranges to the north were hidden in cloud. But Rasul's country lay in bright sunshine: "my friend mountains," Leh valley, the broad Indus and the high snowy range that walls off Hindustan.

My love to all of you.

GYPSY DAVY

Chhota Sahib

Dear DAVE,

The other night when I pushed and pulled myself up over the Khardung La, and started down the Shyok side to meet Sahb, I heard drum-beats ahead,—ravens tapping on empty carcasses, horses disembowelled by wolves. Twisted they were, mouths open, nostrils spread wide for that last gasp of thin air.

Pung! Pang! Peng! the ravens played. Gurgle! Gurgle! Gurgle!

Yours,

ROGER

DAK BANGLA COMPOUND
LEH

Lady Ba

December 4

Dear HARLAN,

We walked into Leh yesterday after resting for two days in the nala below the Khardung Pass. The pass was strenuous, and we rather dreaded so big a town as Leh, especially the complications which might attend selecting our winter quarters. It's rather a terrible thing for gypsies to feel obliged to stay anywhere and, with the passes closed, we've got to stay in the mountains somewhere till spring. (Roger had to lie snowbound five days in a hut on the way down to Srinagar to get the money, five days in one windowless, low-ceiled room, with the family, human and quadruped, in the next!)

The crossing of the Khardung into Leh valley was thrilling. We didn't get the view back into the Kara-koram country we had hoped for, but after a month in valley bottoms, with only one really high camp (the people of the Shyok valley would wonder what I call "high"! I suppose I mean high enough to look out) it was good to be for an hour on the top of the wall, even if one could only lie out of the wind, in a nest of blankets laid on snow, and drink fresh-made yak-milk chocolate.

I shall never forget that ride down, and I don't believe my littermen will, either. It was miles down, and the miles were steep and rough, and the darkness closed in early. After nine hours of sitting on a yak I wasn't very lively, and the Sahib was in a hurry to get his incumbrance deposited for the night. The horsemen had gone ahead to make camp. We raced down after them. The Sahib scolded the littermen to make them go faster, but as it didn't do any good he tried stimulating them by praise and offers of extra pay. He strode on ahead, and then came the litter with me, all bundled up in fur, lying in it. Roger ran alongside, sometimes above me, sometimes below, exhorting the men, singing their songs with them, or when their breath failed, singing Cornell songs alone, and shouting: "Shabash!" and "Bakhshish!" There were four in the shafts all the time, and the relief four ran alongside, ready to catch the shafts if one of the actual bearers stumbled. Now and then, one, or even two, fell, but they were always up in a jiffy, and the others were so quick to catch the load that I got no shaking-up. It was a good deal of fun, racing with the night.

Then a campfire in the distance, and then yak lying about outside our tent,—great horns and black bodies.

Next day we lay about all day and loafed. I sketched Chot and Gypsy Davy in their huge Yarkandi coats. And we slept.

Rasul had gone on into town and come out to meet us at the one little village on the way in. There, two women came to the trail-side to do us honour, wearing wonderful red and green capes and offering us: one, a bowl of milk with little dabs of butter on the edge, and one, a bowl of sage twigs burning. It wasn't far from the town but it seemed very remote. It was like an old ballad.

I was afraid Rasul would want us to put on a lot of side, in entering the town. He is Aqsaqal, and he has all along been rather desirous that we should appear "big." But to-day, in his happiness at bringing his friends to his home, he forgot everything foolish and was entirely natural and simple. He walked beside me and told me how, when he was only ten, he used to go with the other children into that valley and climb away up its steep sides, after the little bushes growing in cracks. He showed their halting-places, a big boulder, the broken corner of an old chorten just high enough to rest a basket on. At each, he said, they'd point out the next. " Is like march. In morning always thinking where will make camp at night-time." He sang the old songs, seemed to see himself with his heavy basket, seemed to think his old friends were following, —the boys, the girls: "Palket beautiful, Nome little beautiful, other girls not beautiful or ugly."

He said: "Then always sing-ing. Night-time plenty sleeping. Now I am Aqsaqal. Never singing. Night-time plenty not sleeping."

You remember? "We starting from home, early morning, about four o'clock, sometimes about five o'clock. Sometimes went to that valley west side Leh, called Chagda. There are each valleys different names. Sometimes went Laporma, some-times Seyuchan, sometimes Feynugla, sometimes Shongsha. That side do not find any water, but two places are little springs. In big valley is Leh. Branch valleys are all those names which I wrote. Sometimes we went two miles, sometimes three miles before we reached to the valley, about seven o'clock or eight o'clock. To that place we eat breakfast; eat all together; spread blanket for table. When eat, that time speak very nice matter and laugh very plenty. Half food eat that time; half keep for tiffin, under a stone. After breakfast, some climb up mountain, some other side valley, some this side valley. We don't take the burtsa close to each other, but what speak can hear, and what sing. All we hear from other side of valley to this side. When get hungry, then take that little piece, which keep in own pocket, and that eat. Some girls singing other side of valley, some singing this side of valley. Sometimes boys up the mountains sing, and from this side to other side said with singing plenty different matter, and what came into mouth that tell.

"Hussin and I climb very high place where we found the tsafat growing in cracks in rocks. We put in the cracks our pickaxe, and sometimes break a big piece of rock. When is ready to break, we call: 'Take care! Don't tell you heard or saw, and we will let fall this rock for your tamasha and ourselves wood!' When the big stone falls, it go from hill to hill, the noise, like cannon and gun. It go below very far. That was very good tamasha, and there was plenty dust. Sometimes we fall some stone, without wood. When big piece falls, breaks into plenty piece.

"When get enough wood, we put into baskets; tied with rope and carried on back; and came below. As we came down, we sang a song like this:

'Don't look up the mountains at the sun.
You will be cold; never be warm.
If look far away husband or wife,
Heart will be sorry, never be glad.
Come people, quickly down.'

"All came below to that place, where took breakfast in the morning-time. Then, that place, eat the tiffin all together. That time speak more nice matter than the morning-time with these girls, and sew the pabu. When we have thirst, we eat the snow. Sometimes very late afternoon we eat that tiffin. After that tiffin, carry load, each people's on back. Then one would say: 'Hadám malá hadámly' (what that means, I not know. I did ask other people; that not mean anything.) Then other one would say: 'Haslám boo nilály.' And there were always rest places by old buildings with stones. When reached to that place, one boy said: 'Take rest.' Others said and sang other things. What came into mouth that said. Sometimes we reached to home before evening; sometimes evening; sometimes after evening."

Yours,

Gypsy Davy   Tsam Skang
December

Dear Odo,

Living out in all weathers a year or two at a stretch seems a serious business to you, I suppose. But it isn't really, if you have a comfortable tent you can rely on. My old tent has made place at last for a better, after thirty years of service. Not the identical tent, of course, but re-built biennially like those thousand-year-old Japanese temples that have been re-built every twenty years all that time, exactly the same. I'm in a mood for eulogy, but my theme's the new tent and there's no least hint of the old in that.

The new tent's heavy by our standards. You'd not be wanting to carry it on your own back far, and there's ponies that would balk at carrying it on theirs, poles, pins, ground sheets, rain sheets, sun sheet and all, thrown on. And I can't pitch it in five minutes, but I can in ten, alone, and in a high wind, if I set it to cut the wind.

It's ten-ounce green flax, if you please, and eleven feet square, and nine feet high, not to mention big triangular end-flaps and doors and wide skirts and a multiplicity of guys for this and that ingenious purpose, and three poles and knobs on the pole-ends, but I can strike it and strap it into its valise in the same time it takes to pitch it.

The secret of its tractability lies in there being these three poles (high centre and low ends) and its being shaped, when pitched, something like the hull of a yacht upside down with a deep keel, so that it cleaves the wind neatly.

When I set out to pitch it I hook the doors together and so get a square to place my corner pins by. I might as easily get a parallelopiped with disastrous consequences, but I don't. That is, I never did but once. Having set the pins, I unhook the doors, slip the loop of a double tackle over the spike of each end pole, and raise those poles, leaving the tackles hanging loose. The poles stand of themselves and the tent is already two-thirds up. Then I raise the centre pole. (Of course, I am not writing of poles fresh from the tent loft, but poles repeatedly shortened a little until they are just the right length.) Then I stretch out a loose end-tackle, hook the corners of that pair of triangular end-flaps into a big hook at the far end of the tackle, draw out the flaps until they come fairly taut, and drive a pin. Then I draw the tackle taut and that end of the tent is up. This process repeated on the opposite end pitches the tent.

I can go on driving pins and stoning down the skirts if the weather demands it ad lib. And if I want more space inside, I can stretch a half-dozen guys that pull out the sides, and make a wall. But we rarely have a chance to drive even one pin. We have to use big rocks instead. And for that purpose, all the guys and tackles have six-foot rock-ropes extending out beyond their pin loops, and all the pin-loops along the tent sides have rock-rope extensions.

Suppose I have the tent set up in a north wind, with its long axis north and south, I close the north end-flaps, and sit in the south end with the doors and both flaps reefed back. If the wind shifts to the south-east I hook the flap on that side, leaving the other reefed, and remain sitting there. If I want more air I reef back one or both of the north flaps. There are large hooded ventilators on each side near the top, with flaps worked from below, to close them in very cold weather, and the sides can be made to clear the ground in hot, by reefing the skirts and drawing the rock-ropes there taut. (Angbo's idea, that.)

We can make wide porches at either end by stretching out the end-flaps, with a low pole holding up the outer corner of each, and roofing the gap between flaps with a triangular piece cut to fit. This makes a big airy tent that will need no fly in the hottest weather we are likely to see.

The tent has points in common with Ulysses' bow. Ten minutes, I say, will suffice for me to pitch it alone, but it takes six Ladakhis longer than that. And when it comes to levelling a platform on a mountain side and bringing the big rocks a little distance it often takes a crowd of men two hours and more. It takes time to sweep out the tent, too, and to lay the gay rugs neatly on the green ground sheet, and place the black tin boxes and tidy up generally.

We rarely make camp in an easy place where there is shelter and wood and water, for although our dwelling is but a tent, it is after all our only dwelling, and we nearly always manage to get it pitched, if even for a night only, in those high places where we would be. It is shelter enough in itself, and wood and water always find their way up on willing legs. The men camp lower in places more to their liking.

It's a far cry, this luxury, from a bachelor's bivouac, but I'll warrant you'll be deeply interested, once you've taken your lady out! Our salams to you and her!

Yours,

Gypsy Davy   Tsam Skang
                                      December 15

Dear Alice Annette,

I am wondering if you are still a queen, or if the rude years have deposed you.   Do you still sometimes sit on your throne-cloth? We rummaged America far and wide for a crown worthy so fair a queen, but there are no crowns in America, except play-actors' crowns set with false jewels.

There are real crowns enough down in India, of fine yellow gold set with wonderful jewels, that might be had up for the Lady Ba: crowns set with real rubies, red as pigeon's blood that shine in dark places, and with pink pearls that change their colour and their lustre in every changing light, and with the emeralds you love so.   But the Lady Ba wears no crown, no coronet even.   It's a red leather tam she wears, with a brooch of silver stag's horns, and high red leather boots, and a sky-blue broadcloth cloak between.

Sometimes she rides a milk-white palfrey, with trappings of silver, enamel and camel's hair.   The fringes almost sweep the ground.   Sometimes she rides a coal-black yak with scarlet saddle-rug and saddle inlaid with ivory.   His own black fringes sweep the snow on either side of him.   He waves a black tail high behind her ladyship, as bushy as all the plumes of the Round Table.   A black mane he waves before her.   A man almost as black and woolly leads him, and when the man pulls at the ring, the old yak's nose stretches and stretches until he gives a grunt and comes with it.   Sometimes she is borne in a green and scarlet litter by eight tall men in livery.

Her Ladyship is lonely to-day, sitting, snow-bound in these great mountains, by a glowing brazier in the door-way of her green pavilion.   She commands me to solicit tidings of your majesty.   The royal mails will reach her by His Highness the Maharaja's courier, at Tsam Skang, Ladakh, half-way round the world.

Your Majesty's most humble and obedient servant,

                                      Gypsy Davy

Lady Ba   Tsam Skang
                        Last Month of the Water Hog Year

Dear Stephanie,

I hope you haven't lost the lucky penny I gave you, and that
you are careful as ever to pick up pins when you see them
lying. I've found here in Ladakh that the children not only
know how to get good luck, but they know how to get rid of
bad luck. Listen to this:—

I made a storma yesterday:
Two sticks, crossed, you see, this way.
Then like a spider web I wound
Some new-spun sheep's wool round and round.
I took it to my corner dark,
And with my flint I struck a spark,
And then again, till it blazed up bright—
Then ran and threw it out to Night!

Bad Luck's gone. If it comes again
I'll borrow my father's iron pen
And write me a real true lama charm
To keep off every kind of harm.
I'll tie it with hairs of a dog and a sheep.
(I'll pull them out while they're asleep.)
In my mouse's skin I'll wrap it well,
And then—but the rest I may not tell.

This much I dare to tell you, though:
If Bad Luck comes, I can make it go.

                                        Yours,
                                        Lady Ba
                    (Our men call me "The Lucky Lady.")

Lady Ba   Tsam Skang
                                        December 20

Dear Win,

We've "settled in," as the English say. A settling quite
to the gypsy taste. A high, high cragtop, linked to the skirts
of the far-away village by a pony-trail looping slowly down and
down, and by a precipitous pak-dandi (foot-path); the pony-
trail built for us by singing pigtails, the pak-dandi a relic from
the days of a hermit, former incumbent.

Cragtop itself made habitable by days of labour of more pigtails (setting up little piles of stones to keep off lhas while they laboured), building a forty-foot platform, carrying rocks for a wall a man's height on the low side, bringing earth in back-baskets, spilling it out over their heads, then, corners of grey robes tucked into green girdles showing scarlet linings, dancing it down hard and solid.

While my rom and the native engineer Dorje, and the handsome old blacksmith and his son and his son's son contrive ways to combat cold promised in February, I bask in the sun at the door of the tent, and, greatly at leisure, turn to reading Francke's *History of Western Tibet*. Dr. Francke's a real historian, grubbing for his "mouldy foundations of hearsay" in Tibetan records, deciphering stone inscriptions, living among the people, noting and interpreting their customs, their songs, their traditions. I've gleaned from his pages various quaint-nesses which I think will please you if your mind, like mine, "lets go a thousand things, the dates of wars, the deaths of kings," and "yet recalls . . . two petals from a wild-rose tree."

Herodotus tells a story about this part of the world,—ants big as foxes digging up gold with their feet. They say he meant the marmots who do do it in making their holes, a misinterpretation of a Tibetan word. Perhaps both marmots and ants do it, and Herodotus' informant credited the ants with the marmots' size. Down Khalatse way, there's still a belief in ant gold-diggers, Dr. Francke says.

The first human beings to come here, they think, came from both east and west: Dards, from the west, farmers, ditch-makers, bringing water from mountain gorges for the little patches they could cultivate; nomads from Tibet, driving herds along to feed on wild grass,—or cultivated, I suppose, if they could get it. The grain-growers seem to have found that mutton was tasty, perhaps in an attempt to get their own grain back after conversion. And they in turn, taught the nomads the virtue of barley, parched and ground. They joined forces, and their descendants dwell here yet, eating both sattu and mutton, tilling the soil, and loving to wander.

It's peaceful errands they go on, trading, or serving travellers. They've never been very great fighters. Iba tells us there was a time when the Ladakhis were so very brave that their legs could not be broken,—an inverted expression, rather! But nowadays they don't think of scrapping, and they seem never to have been keen about starting trouble, or clever about handling scraps when forced into them. One king of theirs, called on

H

to help his Tibetan overlord against the Mongols, applied to the Kashmiris for forces, did everything they asked in return, changing his name and religion, promising yearly tribute (eighteen piebald ponies, eighteen pods of musk, eighteen white yak-tails and all the wool of his country to go to Kashmir for weaving)—and after all appears not to have got the help he was seeking.

They had fine names for their weapons, suggesting poetic temperament perhaps, rather than warlike.

> Three-Fingers-Long-for-Sinners
> Wild-Yak-Long-Point
> Killer-of-the-Red-Lightning-Flame
> Knife-of-the-Black-Devil.

Dr. Francke thinks there was a good deal of poetry in the people before the ruler of Tibet in 1300 turned every one Buddhist by royal edict. Their old folk religion, a jolly kind of mythology on the surface, full of gods and heroes and devils, was too vital to die out, so their Buddhism is a curious sort, having very little in common with Buddhism elsewhere. It seems to us that the poetic temperament is marked still. Our servants will sit up half the night after a twelve-hour work-day, singing and dancing. In Rasul's summary of the qualities of a servant, he always mentions his degree of skill in singing and dancing. The dancing is a very slow stately sort, with so little variety in it that we soon weary of watching it, but crowds will sit in silent rapture for hours, gazing and gazing. The women dance in one group, the men in another. The women make little slow gestures of hand and wrist,—only two that I've noticed, interpreted to mean plucking a flower and offering it to a divinity. The men get more vigour into their dances at times, but that may be when they are imitating a dance of some foreign country. They are great travellers, and it's a point of honour to learn the dances of the countries they visit and bring them back to show the people at home.

I didn't like their songs at first, but now I'm beginning to love them. That's fortunate because it's painful for my littermen to refrain from singing. These people do every kind of work to song. They say "Singing makes heavy loads light." Their Tibetan word for "working songs" Dr. Francke translates as "consolation du travail." I understand their scale has only five tones, but Europeans find it hard to sing them because the intervals are different from ours. The obvious characteristics are the great swell and the marked diminuendo in every line of a song,

and the plaintive quality. Their little wooden pipes are delightful,—each man carries one, stuck in the folds of his girdle
along with a knife and a drinking-cup, and rarely, a pen, just
above the flint-and-steel pouch.

In the Shyok Rasul would ride his pony up near my litter
and join the men in singing. One favourite was the song of
a man about to set out on a journey, bidding a sad farewell to
his wife. He tells her, "I put my foot out, but my heart is
ever to your side." And again, "As must want water when
thirsty, so I must want you." (I recall a line in English poetry:
"I know thee as water is known of thirst.")

Rasul has a song of his own, which he taught some of the
younger men on our rest-days. It's quite the thing, I should
judge, to have your own song, which you sing when called on
to add your bit to the entertainment, and which is sung by other
people, but always known as your song. Rasul's is very long.
He composed most of it on the journey to China. One part
describes his learning in China that his wife had died. "She
was a flower, and now the flower is dry and broken. She
was the mother bird, I was the father bird, going out to get food
for the little birds." He says, "I made it when my heart was
very broken." This is an attempt (not my own) at writing
down the music of it:

I suppose part of the apparent poetry in their speech is
nothing but translated metaphor. English might sound quite
as piquant if the figures of speech implied in some of our most
humdrum expressions could strike the ear freshly. Still it
is hard to conceive as everyday prose this, in a formal treaty
(I'm back at the *History* again), "tribute shall be paid" by one
king to another "so long as the glaciers of the Kailasa do not
melt, or the Lake of Manasarowar does not dry up." ("Till
all the seas gang dry, my dear, and the rocks melt with the sun"?)

One tradition describes an era when the people were so
rich that they always wore hats of gold, and their mouths were
continually full of tea and beer. There was some kind of
show in the bazar the other day, at which we saw the Raja

(deposed, but still allowed his title) wearing a tall hat of gold. And I should think every one's mouth was continually full of either tea or beer. The tea-kettle in our cook-tent is always on. Twenty cups at a sitting is not considered intemperate. And the chang goes 'round at a tamasha with never a pause. The precious chang! Chhota Padre Sahib Asboe tells us that barley is dearer than wheat, so much is beer prized beyond bread.

I'm outrunning the capacity of even the stout registry envelopes we use, but I must copy off two songs from the *History*. The first one was sung by a boy prince of Ladakh not long after Alfred burned the cakes in England; the other by the last real prince, when Maharaja's soldiers seized the big palace across the valley there, and the little prince Chogsprul fled to Spiti.

I.

"Oh Father Nyima gon,
Do not go a-hunting!
In my dream last night,
I saw something bad in my dream.
I, a boy, had to die.
I saw the colour of blood on my golden saddle.
I shall no more dance to the sound of the trumpets and
    clarinets.
O king, do not go a-hunting!
Thy son, Zlava gon, has to die."

II.

"The sun is rising, the warm sun of the east. . . . . .
When I, a boy, lived in my fatherland, I was surrounded by
    servants, inside and outside the palace.
When Chogsprul lived in the great town of Leh, the number
    of his servants was like the stars of heaven.
When I, a boy, went to a foreign country, I was alone with my
    horse.
When Chogsprul went to Spiti, we were only one man and
    one horse.
When we went across all the large and little plains, I was so
    thirsty that I humbly prayed for water.
When I, a boy, was still in my fatherland, I had always a
    pair of teapots, like the sun and the moon.
Then I, a boy, went to sleep under a cedar-tree . . . . . ."

Yours,
RI MEM-SAHIB

Lady Ba   TSAM SKANG
                                                 December 21

Dear DONALD,

Roger says he crossed a fine new bridge at Khalatse on the Treaty Road.   It's not a road, only a trail, but it has been used by traders for nearly fifteen hundred years.

The bridge was built for the traders, just like the one you took us to see them building over the Missouri.   There have been lots of bridges before it, probably.   The ends of one old one are sticking out yet, Roger says, and there is some very old carving in the rock near by, which the Historian Padre Sahib says means this:—

"Whoever thinks evil of this bridge in his heart,
    Let his heart rot.
Whoever stretches his hand toward it,
    Let his hand be cut off.
Whoever harms it with his eye,
    May his eye become blind.
Whoever does any harm to the bridge,
    May that creature be born in hell."

Gypsy Davy wrote Hal how Ibrahim protected our box of notes in the cairn at the Baltoro's snout, by a curse, you remember.

I suppose the Yankton bridge-owners have their bridge "protected" by insurance.

                                                 Yours,

                                                 LADY BA

Gypsy Davy   TSAM SKANG
                                                 Christian New Year's Day

Dear NORMAN,

We have your letter about the bird-table in the tree.   That was serious business,—the water freezing.   What did all the birds do?

We are perched like big birds ourselves, on a bird-table in these mountains.   It is a great bare rock, not smooth and slippery like your rocks in Kent, but rough and crumbly. The top of it wasn't big enough for us to perch on, so we had to build a rock platform for our gold-green Arab tent.   And every night when we go to sleep, we wonder if we shall fall off before morning, and go tumbling all the way down to the bottom.

There isn't a tree or a bush anywhere on the rock, but here and there there are tiny bunches of withered grass a long way apart. And there isn't a drop of water for the birds, except in a huge cauldron in the cook-tent, some distance down below us. (You might know the ogre and ogress would have a cauldron.) The birds could never get to it, for the suffocating smoke there is in the cook-tent, and if they did, they would burn their toes perching on the copper edges, because there is a hot fire under it all the time. And if they drank any of the water, they would get cooked inside, because it is boiling. That water has to come a long way on ponies' backs, up a steep zigzag trail from a little ice-bound river far below.

And such birds as there are, besides us! A great raven comes every day and perches close to the tent, and sits there, gurgling and croaking and pulling corks out of bottles, and presently his mate joins him, and croaks and gurgles and pulls corks out of bottles. They are shiny blue-black, the pair of them, and have ugly lumps on their beaks. Presently they soar off over the valley. Sometimes a lot of them get together and perch all over the side of the rock; great black ugly things, big enough to carry off your cat Diamond in their claws. There are a good many bones and teeth much bigger than Diamond's lying about. There are big black feathers, too— and once we saw a fox, and once we saw a wolf.

Sometimes a magpie, white and bottle-green and black, comes and takes the raven's perch, when he isn't there, and stays until the raven comes back. Then he leaves in a hurry, taking his long tail with him. I never saw one of them in such a hurry that he forgot his tail, although it is so long it must be a nuisance.

There are lots of crows, too, very big and black, and black choughs with yellow beaks. I think it would take four or five crows to make a raven, and two or three choughs to make a crow.

Sometimes when we are climbing up the trail, we hear a sudden whir of wings, and a hundred pigeons rise from the rocks about, and go dashing over our heads. Blue-grey they are.

Every day a big eagle comes sailing by, close to the tent. I can hear the rush of his wings through the air, now as I write. I think he is big enough to take you on his back. You'd have to hold on pretty tight, but you'd not be bothered with the flapping of his wings, for he never seems to flap them. He just sails like an aeroplane.

I think I saw him just now sailing under a sky as blue as a bluebell mist, with no hint of cloud anywhere in it. There was something that looked like golden-red hair standing pretty straight up, just abaft his neck. I wonder did the owner think the earth had dropped out from under him?

The eagle flew pretty close to a crag where an old hermit lives, and snatched off his yellow cap. Then he shot upward two or three hundred feet to where a boy was tending a flock of goats, and I thought surely he was going to carry one of them off, for the goats here are little bits of things. The boy stopped singing, but the eagle must have decided that you were load enough.

Then he wheeled and sailed out over the valley. You had got your heart back in its proper place by that time—it must have choked you, rather, when you had it in your mouth! You were looking about you. I suppose you saw all the tiny villages scattered about on the little scalloped terraces. The bottom of the valley must have looked like a long flight of scalloped steps, leading down to the Indus. The eagle sailed right over the king's castle, on a crag like ours, over there. Then he wheeled once more and sailed off westward over high snow mountains, eight or nine times as high as those soppy clouds that are always drifting between you in England and the blue-bell sky.

With that bonnet of yours, and the green kilt, and the sporran, he would never be setting you down in Kent. It's near Breadalbane he'd be sailing with you, and I suspect he'd loop the loop and let you dive into soft rain-wet heather, a mile or two down.

Yours,

GYPSY DAVY

Lady Ba   TSAM SKANG

January 5

Dear MARY,

I'm sending a bracelet to you, a heavy silver thing with thick ends, set with turquoise. It's a man's bracelet.

What I wanted to send was a woman's sweet flaring cuff of white sea-shell. A pair of them, between long red sleeves and shapely brown hands, clicked lightly together in greeting, first at the bowed forehead, and again a little lower are very dainty and effective. But the pretty Christian Chondzin, who can talk a bit of English, tells me that it was a painful process to get hers on, involving hand-bandaging, also that they're very cold in bed at night! So I'm letting you off and sending the man's kind instead.

Isn't it incredible that here, in a little pocket in these huge mountains away in the very innermost part of a great continent, the women should all wear sea-shells? They wear strings of small ones hanging from their sashes, too. And you'd think from their coral ornaments and the precious ear-rings of rows on rows of seed pearls, that they must live on the seashore.

It's only because Leh is a trading-post, of course. Not a woman here, except Chondzin, has ever seen the sea. I doubt whether any of them have even seen a lake. The only stretch of water they can know is the blue Indus far away down below their village. That they know rises in a lion's mouth in Lhasa-land, but I think they never wonder where it goes.

I wonder how you are liking your Quaker college. Will they let you wear a heathen bracelet there?

Yours,

LADY BA

Gypsy Davy   TSAM SKANG

January 12

Dear JACK,

We have just been reading Waddell's *Lhasa and its Mysteries*, which we commend to your attention. Rasul likes the pictures. He reminds me that the English expedition into Tibet happened when he and I were crossing the Tsaidam. We ran across large numbers of the Dalai Lama's camels in charge of servants there, in a dreadfully cold place. We had reports that the Dalai had fled to China.

Further east, we met more of his company, munshis and people of that rank. Still further east we met big Lhasa men with high combs in their back hair. I thought they were women until Rasul explained.

All these people were very friendly with Rasul, especially the big ones. The big ones had him to tea and asked him innumerable questions. He didn't know much, for we had been out over a year. We didn't even know the Dalai was running away, until we had it from his servants. They served the tea in an ante-chamber, opening into an apartment, decorated beyond belief gorgeously. Rasul is sure the Dalai was hid in there behind silken curtains, listening to every word, and it's quite likely he was.

Yours,

Lady Ba   TSAM SKANG
January 12

Dear IDA MARY,

That soft grey wool sheet you gave me is welcome these nights. I supplement it by a kapok mattress on the tent ground-sheet, a full complement of blankets, a "tigar skin for bed," a big namda (thick felt mat), and, before I insert myself I warm the nest with a copper pot of coals to which we had the blacksmith attach a long handle.

I might mention another smithy product, the neat little stove copied from a paper model Gypsy Davy made. That sits in a pit beside my bed. The stove-pipe of re-shaped Standard Oil tins worms its way out underground and stands erect at a safe distance in a sheath of juniper planks, adze-hewn. Through the long sunny day we don't need a fire, but towards evening it's agreeable to see and smell the thin blue smoke curling from the stove-pipe as one comes in from a climb. And in the cold starry dusk just before dawn, I like sleepily to watch I-she on his knees, opening the stove-lids with a clatter, taking out the ashes down to the rock bottom, banging his heavy bracelets or big turquoise rings against the sides as he does it, then starting a fire of apricot and precious tset, tossing his black plait out of the way of the flame. It wasn't so much fun before we took out the damper. He used to close it firmly, then blow amain with the goatskin bellows.

By the time I am dressed and combed, still using my bed as a day couch, Chot comes stamping up over a little knob on this spur between our tent and his, stuffs more wood into the stove and begins to take "Sahb's" dictation, blowing on his cold fingers. It's not so awfully cold, but Chot is so long that his blood can't reach his finger and toe-tips before sun-up.

"Sahb" lies on the terrace before the tent, encased in his bed and a bulky Esquimau garment. When he has delivered himself of the morning's first letters, arisen and arrayed himself, he tells Chot to bang the cymbals, and I-she appears with the ewer full of recently boiling water, and the big copper basin, into which he carefully pours a little stream over Sahb's and Chot's gingerly extended hands, and my wash-cloth. (We postpone the bath till noon-time! It's an affair of elaborate ritual then!)

I don't eat breakfast, not exercising enough at this height to want three meals. But Chot and Sahb cook themselves eggs on the little stove and eat them with chapatis and chocolate from the cook-tent, in the midst of dictating and writing. Then they study a bit of anatomy and are off down the pak-dandi to the hospital to observe, and probably obstruct in their efforts to help, Doctor Heber; back, hungry again, for luncheon.

There are religious limits to our diet. No bacon, for the cook is Mohammedan, and we all know the old tradition that if a pig-eating sahib insist on his pig-meat, the faithful serve it salivated. No beef, because the Maharaja in the far-off Vale of Kashmir is Hindu,—capital punishment for killing cattle. We can't even have a rabbit because our Buddhist neighbours say that that little beast, having ears like a donkey's and feet like a dog's, is by analogy inedible. Luckily the hen and the sheep are neither holy nor accursed, and though tiny, they are, in various guises, our mainstays, relieved, "ever & anone" by a fat partridge or pheasant from the Charas Officer's bag or a steak of shapu or ibex from the Doctor's.

The cook-tent's a long way down the hill, but we've burned our tongues more than once, and never had a Laodicean mouthful. We're too dignified to visit the cook-tent (too discreet, really), but Chot says there's a great to-do down there when it's time to serve dinner. Piping hot food comes off one or another of the little stone stoves, gets into dishes with tightly clamped covers, and is set carefully into a great basket lined with namda and covered. Basket heaved up, shoulder-straps adjusted, and I-she, bearing in his hands a tray with three covered bowls of soup on it, climbs nimbly. With trays for individual tables, and stove-top for warming-oven, we make comfortable efficient arrangements, and eat more co-ordinatedly than in houses understaffed with butlers, where one dish gets cold before its concomitants have been ceremonially offered.

We thought we should lack vegetables, but every little while some appear, on a plate with a note from the Tehsildar, in a basket with Mrs. Kunick's or Mrs. Heber's greetings, or tumbling out of Iba's kerchief, knotted at the corners, collected from Allah alone knows where: parsnips, turnips, toothsome carrots, beet-root, onions,—sweetest ever tasted. Rice Chot brought up from down country, long yellowy grains, Peshawar, the kind that's best for pilav. Raisins and pistachio nuts come with every caller. Dates were to be had in the bazar, but proved quite tasteless. Bread is beyond Samat, though the blacksmith made us a fireless cooker to keep the yeast warm and to bake in. The yeast comes from the baker's. He bakes a lot of flattish cakes every morning in a huge squat earthen vase, filling the whole corner of his shop. And at noon, when the last batch is out of the oven, he squats for a space over the open mouth to rest, and to conserve in his garments' folds the precious heat still lingering. Iba's wife and Mrs. Kunick are most generous with loaves of their own making. Mrs. Kunick even tried to teach our Samat her art, but for the most part we depend on our own version of the chapatis which "come more natural" to him. They're delicious, paper-thin, crisp and hot, with plenty of Danish butter and Holland cheese. We've no other tinned stores than those two, nor feel the need of any.

You see, we're warm and well-fed. And happy? Content, with a degree of contentment one never would have time to savour in the "torbellino del mundo," even if it were obtainable. And here, where we find life utterly desirable, the religion demands renunciation of all desiring.

Yours,

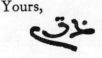

Lady Ba

Tsam Skang
January 15

Dear Stuart,

We're glad you and Jim are coming.

We're having a star atlas sent to the ship for you, so that you may learn some stars before you get here, for we three are all keen on them. You can usually find a darkish place somewhere on deck in the evening to get a look at the sky. I embroider the stars, as fast as I learn them, on a big chart I'm making.

You'll have to learn twenty Urdu words a day, from the list* I enclose. It's useful anywhere in the Indian Empire. Iba, our Karawan Bashi and Samat, our bewarchi, and a few of the ghora-walas know it, and the rest of the men are learning it. A munshi goes to the serai every day to teach them. None of them know any English. When Chot goes off by himself, as he will do very soon after convoying you up to us, you two will have to fill his place as karinda and munshi, so don't waste a day. It's a funny language, not a bit like Latin or French or Spanish,—more like a boys' gang code.

The Lascar crew on your ship will use some of the words. You'll hear the boatswain call out "ahsta" to them when they're hauling on ropes and singing. And you'll hear somebody telling them to work "jaldi jaldi" when they're squatting on the deck scouring it with half-cocoanuts. I never made out what the lookout's call is. It may have been "sab thik."

Our men,—your men—don't look like the Lascars. They are brown, but rosy-brown, and they're thicker-set and sturdier, and their faces are broader and jollier-looking, and they wear long wool robes, girt with gay sashes, and horned caps, and pigtails. Roger will meet you at the Bombay wharf with one of them. You must be able to say something to him when you see him. The usual Indian greeting is "Salam" but he'll be pleased if you say "Jhu," which is the proper Ladakhi greeting. He'll reply with "Jhule," in "respect language."

I'm running a few Ladakhi words into your list. Some things up here haven't any Urdu names. There may be a few Turki words, too, from Turkistan up north of us.

The grammar, so far as you need to learn it at the outset, is simple. No need of bothering with genders or declensions yet. There are no articles. Put your verb always at the sentence's end. (You must understand that this Urdu is only an artificial medium between us and our men. It's no more their native tongue than it is yours. Their Ladakhi you'd not learn quickly, as it has a Chinese quality, and uses different voice inflections.) The men get on with only a few verb forms. They drop the "na" of the infinitive, and add "ta hai" to the root. For the past they drop the "n" only of the infinitive. (I've indicated the few irregular cases.) For the future, they drop the "na" and substitute "ega." You'll want the imperative, which you'll form well enough by dropping the infinitive ending and substituting "o." You'll have plenty of time to develop your grammar properly later,

* See p. 271.

and plenty of incentive.   Iba is a delightful talker, and you'll
want to understand his stories.   But it is absolutely essential
that you learn enough at once to manage every-day situations.
I hope you'll find some kind Indian on the ship who'll give
you help with the pronunciation.   If you don't, just remember
that the consonants are pronounced about as in English, and
the vowels are all Italian, as you've learned them in your Latin
or Spanish.   You'll have to make a glossary for yourselves,
English-Urdu.   And of course you'll have to drill each other
in making simple sentences, using your vocabulary.

Yours,
MEM-SAHIB

Gypsy Davy   TSAM SKANG
January 31

Dear CLIFFORD,

We are camped on a bare cragtop in the midst of a wild
sea of mountains, high as the highest thunder-head that looms
up over your Lake.   On the other side of the world from you.

Roger and I took a look at you this morning, down through
the green ground-sheet, through the rock platform, through
eight thousand miles of rock, some of it pretty hot, I suspect
—out under smoky skies.   A wide plain by the lakeside,
bristling with tall buildings of iron and glass, a "bad lands"
spreading further than a man can see.   Boisterous rush of
wheels down the arroyos.   Big ungainly nervous beasts in
panicky flight, travelling on wheels, an endless herd of them,
bellowing and snorting.   And what a stench! Whirl of propellers churning the lake, driving big hulks about; churning
the air, dragging giant darning-needles at uproarious speed.
Din of wheels in the buildings themselves, wheels without
number, all going lickity-brindle.   Try as we may, we can't
believe our eyes and ears and noses.

If you were to look this way you'd see nothing but snow
and ice and bare rock peaks under the blue sky, and far down
below these, a bare crag set in a tawny waste, and on the cragtop, us: Lady Ba and Roger and me, in the door of our green
Arab tent, me dictating this letter to you, and Roger writing
it and Lady Ba studying Urdu.   The people in the village
down below us sleep till ten, and when they emerge from their
dens are none too conspicuous.   I imagine that unfamiliar

things as small as that must be in rapid motion for you city folk to see them, even near at hand.

Here things move slowly. Here there are no wheels. There's nothing whirling fast in all these mountains. There are slow little wooden turbines, not much bigger than boys make for play, that grind the grain. There are spindles tossed and caught back and tossed again. There are cylinders loaded with Lhasa prayers that the passer-by, with lives behind him and lives before him, sets slowly turning to pray for him. But there's not one wheel.

There's no road for a wheel to turn on. There's business enough here, but it's done on crooked narrow trails, done on legs—men's, ponies', donkeys', tall sheep's, yak's, dzo's, bullocks', camels'. Elephants might work in the lower valleys if they weren't so big. But Hannibal found it was necessary to drive them "with great leasure" in the Alps, "because through these narrow streights they were readie ever & anone to run on their noses." The trails up here are too narrow for them and they'd smash the bridges. Even camels are barred on the Treaty Road.

No plane dare venture over here, for there's no place where she could rest the sole of her foot, not to mention the dreadful shaking-up she'd get in the uneasy air over these mountains and valleys. And there's not a boat of any sort, since Sven Hedin's sectional wore out. The Indus water's well churned here, but not by propellers.

In this quite wheelless land, men still wear finery: long-eared hats, long crimson gowns, long blue sashes, sleeves to their knees, pigtails to their heels, silver loops in their ears, long rosaries—a dozen vulnerable points about them where a wheel could get them. You've had to cut off all your fringes. You'll come presently to union-suits, and airmen's helmets on shaven heads.

Yours,

GYPSY DAVY

Lady Ba   Tsam Skang
                                        February 1

Dear Rosalind,

We're in a land of folk-songs and folk-dancing.

It brings back memories of you three in Tanager House, taking down an old song from Lady May's little English mother,—little woman in the great peacock chair, singing shyly, Cynthia in the chimney corner softly touching her harp, you and Dorothy on the floor at her feet setting down words and music.

We can't write down the songs for you, alack! And we are slow to learn their dances, even Gypsy Davy.   Do you remember old Deacon Wark's saying of him when you were all learning a reel in the farmhouse kitchen? "You are doing it varra well, sir.   You are an intelligent mon!"

Does this give you a sense of the dance?

When I am a man, I shall learn to dance
    Slow and stately and slow.
While the trumpets snore and the little drums beat
And the jewelled pipes shrill high and sweet,
    Slow I shall dance and slow.

A long, long scarf I shall hold it out,
    Slow and stately and slow.
While the people sit and hold their breath
And watch me in silence as still as death,
    Slow I shall dance and slow.

A sword from its sheath I shall draw it out,
    Slow and stately and slow.
With fierce, firm step I shall stamp about.
When the drums beat fast I shall leap and shout.
    Then stately again and slow.

                              Your
                              "Lady Ba"

Lady Ba   *Nine o'clock this morning for me*
                               but nine o'clock last night for you

Dear JAMES,

I'm not quite sure what the date is. One New Year is just over, the proper Tibetan New Year, finishing the year of the Water Hog, and beginning the year of the Wood Mouse. Two months ago when we arrived at Leh, the year of the Wood Mouse had just come in in Ladakh only. You see, once the king of Ladakh wanted to make war a long way from home, but the army wouldn't go, probably because it couldn't bear to miss the New Year tamasha. So the king finished that year off two months early, and had the next year begin straight away. Ever since, Ladakh has been two months ahead of Tibet. A month ago the eighty odd Christians celebrated the beginning of Anno Domini 1924. For our Mussulman caravan bashi, the year 1342 began back in the summer sometime. And the Hindus in the bazar would tell you that this is the tenth month of the 5026th year of the Black Age.

It's not the simplest thing in the world to head a letter as to place, either. It's easy enough to write "Tsam Skang, Ladakh" but I'm sure you'll not find it easy to read nor to understand, unless at least I tell you that Tsam Skang means "hermitage," and that we are on a crag a long way above Leh, the capital of Ladakh,—Leh is such an important town that the people usually call it "Ladakh" as if it were the whole of the province. I told our friend Rasul Galwan that many people in America had never heard of Ladakh, and he replied politely: "Does no matter, madam. In Ladakh many people not knowing where is America."

Well, even if you don't know where to find Ladakh on the map, I'm sure you'd feel at home here, because there's music. Every single person sings and pipes or drums. There is not one village in these wild mountains that has not a band of at least kettle-drums and flageolets. Often the players are boys. The instruments are generally home-made, and sometimes very much the worse for wear. In one village we passed through, the drummer was blind and his drum-head had a big tear in it, but that didn't stop his playing. The great brass and copper telescoping trumpets, twelve feet long, are so astonishing they ought to have a letter all to themselves.

But of course, you are saying impatiently: "All very well, but what about the fiddles?" And that makes me hesitate. You'd maybe not feel at home here after all. All day long the drums beat, beat, beat, down in the village, for a "borning birth" party or a wedding or some other kind of tamasha, and often the sound of the pipes comes to us.   And mornings and evenings we hear the lamas' cymbals and trumpets,—but never a sound of fiddling.

I had told Iba I wanted to hear a fiddle, and today he brought up the hill to me the only fiddle left in all Ladakh, if I understood him, and the only fiddler.   The fiddle was a curious thing, and the strings were mostly gone, but the fiddler knew how to get a little sound out of it, and he sang an old song that has come down from very long ago:—

> "Do not think that my fiddle called Trashi Wanggyal
> Does not possess a great father.
> If the divine wood of the pencil-cedar
> Is not its great father, what else?
>
> "Do not think that my fiddle called Trashi Wanggyal
> Does not possess a little mother.
> If the strings from the goat
> Are not its little mother, what else?
>
> "Do not think that my fiddle called Trashi Wanggyal
> Does not possess any brothers.
> If the ten fingers of my hands
> Are not its brothers, what else?
>
> "Do not think that my fiddle called Trashi Wanggyal
> Does not possess any friends.
> If the sweet sounds of its own mouth
> Are not its friends, what else?"

As I write the little song down, in Francke Padre Sahib's translation, I wonder if the Ladakhi people have always rather looked down on the fiddle.   The fiddler's song is surely defending his fiddle.   I believe he is of a foreign race.   I am sure now you'd not feel at home here, and that you will never hunt out Ladakh on the map to come to: a land of pipes and tamtams!

Yours,

LADY BA

I

Gypsy Davy   TSAM SKANG
                                              February 2

DEAR WIN,

It's long between mails here. Two carriers have been lost already. I wonder, do your letters and mine lie coldly waiting the spring, beside grey-robed figures, stiff and stark under one avalanche? Rasul says to the Mem-Sahib, "Does no matter, madam. In summer will come the letters."

We love our hilltop. It's a stiff climb up, and few make it. We have it all to ourselves, with the doves and the crows and the choughs and the ravens and the magpies and the lammergeier, and the wolves o' nights, howling. What is it, I wonder, running for its life before them? A hunter killed the lammergeier's mate the other day. She gave him her wings for brooms, stuffed his pillow for him and feathered his arrows.

We sit in our open door-way and watch Winter draw his snowy pall across the face of things. Slowly the brown valley bottom whitens, and the long fans, sweeping down between spurs, and the precipitous spurs themselves, descending from the old King's domain of everlasting snow and ice. Vainly the thirsty air and the warm sun strive to withdraw the pall. They thin it, and here and there on southern slopes my lord Sun rends it. In all this time, it is only inches deep down here, not over two.

Every few days high cirrus mounts the southern sky, and at its heels follows a storm, a feeble shattered thing, drifting over the snowy ramparts, all its fury spent. Little flurries of snow fall through still air, glancing in sunlight. Some lies from storm to storm, but the most is licked up by the thirsty air under a clear blue sky, wherein a bright sun rides, unveiled by any vapour from morning to night.

The nights are cold, much colder in the valley than up here. The valley folk are prone to lie abed until the sun's well up. Leh wakes late in winter with a feeble voice. The people are lively enough when they're awake, but they leave their housetops promptly with the sun. And the shepherds leave the crags above us long before they lose the sun, and come down singing, urging their flocks on, to get them safely folded in the village before dark. They pass close below our crag, and we hear the sound of many little hoofs upon the scree as of rain pattering on leaves.

Yours,

Lady Ba   TSAM SKANG
                                            February 4

Dear LITTLEJOHN,

If you lived here, you'd play on the roof on winter days.

> High on the roof of the house are we,
> Mother and Granddam, the he-goat and me.
>
> Granddam's fingers pull and pull
> Fluffs and fluffs of our old sheep's wool.
>
> Mother's spindle twirls and twirls,
> Dresses for boys, dresses for girls.
>
> Sweet is the air up here in the sun.
> I dance and play.   I shout and run.
>
> Khabardar! But you cannot fall.
> Winter's grass makes a solid wall.
>
> Billy-goat slept.   I pulled at his beard,
> Then scuttled away before he reared.
>
> Up by the ramp come little hoofs.
> Donkeys, too, like the sun on roofs.
>
> Mother's and Granddam's turquoises shine.
> I pat their lappets of lamb's wool fine.
>
> The sun shines hot.   I fall asleep
> Between the goat and a soft old sheep.

                                            Yours,
                                            LADY BA

Gypsy Davy   TSAM SKANG
                                            February 10

Dear ROLAND,

Did Rasul ever talk to you about his fakir? He has been
showing me to-day the room where he died, corner of an old
disused masjid, walled off for him by the Wazir's orders.

He used to pick up dead twigs under the trees in the court
for firewood. He slept on a plank laid over the place where
he had cooked in the day. Rasul says he kept himself and
the place immaculate. If they brought him more food than
he needed for the day he always gave away the excess, and took
his chance for the next day.

He had a considerable reputation for holiness and for second sight. Was much sought after by the great and wicked, but was loth to give audience to such. Persistently refused for some time to see one very bara Maulvi, in Leh on tour. When he did finally, he rebuked him ruthlessly for his many sins.

Rasul must have known his fakir for many years, long before he came to Leh. I think he first met him on his way back from Srinagar, after the journey when he and Kalam Rasul spent all their pay on clothes,—"on all body was like English, but in pocket not one rupees." He paid a visit to the fakir on that occasion, but was not very kindly received.

In Leh the fakir lived on a roof near the bazar at first, where Rasul's mother, that "very old wise woman," came to think highly of him. He taught that lovely daughter of Rasul's to read Urdu and read the Qoran with her there.

When Rasul was away on safar his fakir's face used to come before his eyes, and keep him straight in time of temptation. "It is no order of my fakir," was his reply to tempters. The fakir stood out stiffly against whoring, murder and theft. He used to say: "Keep own body clean. Then dreams will come true." It was mindful of this advice that Rasul washed his hands with sand in default of water that "darkness night" on the hill with me in Turkistan, when the dream decided him to stay with me all the way.

Rasul is unusually broad-minded, you know, even to the extent of eating sahibs' food. The fakir seems to have been so, too, saying that God does not look at a man's religion, but at his way of life.

If Rasul had not behaved himself while away on a journey, he used to feel very nervous about meeting the fakir again. The fakir always knew what he had done, and would refuse to see him until he had taken steps to atone for his offences.

He lost his eyesight by cataract eventually. Refused to let Heber operate, saying: "Allah gave. Allah has taken away. Who are you to interfere?"

As Rasul prospered and the fakir grew feebler, Rasul wanted to provide a servant for him, but he would not accept of one. One morning Rasul came to visit him, bringing sattu for the day. The fakir went to the ditch outside to wash before eating, came back in, staggered a bit, and fell, dead, into Rasul's arms. The room was so clean, Rasul said, that there was nothing for anyone to do to put it in order.

Rasul has missed him sorely. As a great man he meets with flattery and servility or hostility, none of the "tonic criticism" he needs. Clever enough to solve any problem for a sahib whose work he is upon, he is, like any artist, absurdly easily imposed upon in his own affairs.

He said sadly to the Mem-Sahib: "When I am little man, get little enemies. Get more big, that finish, get enemies more big. Now I am little big man, finish all those little enemies, get big enemies."

The Tehsildar, schooled at a Mission down country, told me the other day that Rasul had never accepted a bribe. "Living in a little house. Why be honest?"

By the way, Iba says that a man's honesty depends on his wife. His own wife Amina is honest, therefore, he says, he is!

Yours,

Lady Ba   TSAM SKANG
                                         February 15

MOTHER dear,

The women here don't know how to knit! Only a few who have learned from the missionaries. I once set seven young German girls off into giggles by saying I couldn't knit. I'd like to get them into this place. The only need there is for knitting, where people don't wear socks or mittens or sweaters, is for making shoes, and the men do that. You often meet a man with a half-knit pabu on his hand, knitting as he walks, black and white yak-hair in a herring-bone pattern. The women do the spinning, but they can't sew,—the men do that, too. It really is quite my kind of a land.

The Sahib Bahadur needed a warm coat for the winter. Of course the longest coat in the bazar was too short, so one had to be made. Ibrahim bought a piece of dark-blue Turkistan silk for the outside and some very superior lamb's wool for the inside, with yards and yards of plum-colour silk for the girdle (long in proportion to one's importance, and the Sahib is very bara) and plenty of little gilt buttons from China. This took several days. When everything was ready the funny old tailor came up to us in the bazar where we were walking, followed by the usual little crowd, and stopped us. Then he walked once, slowly, all around the Presence, looking him carefully up and down. And that was all there ever was for measurement or fitting!

It's a handsome coat, too, warm and light, and its lines are agreeable. I insist there's a style and grace to the Ladakhi garments. And their comfort is obvious. The sleeves are long enough to cover your hands completely, if you want the warmth. You can put on an indefinite number of coats, one over another, to suit the season. In fact they speak of the temperature in numbers of coats required—far more personal and expressive than degrees marked on a glass tube. It's three coats cold this morning!

Sahib wears the local cap, blue and gold brocade outside, curly black wool inside, showing at the edges and where the elf's horns turn up. Chot wears a scarlet one above his big Yarkandi mantle, brown and blue cloth, striped. He doesn't care for a coat to his ankles. The Kalon, man of wealth and prestige, undertook to have "our both Sahibs" shod properly. His personal bootmaker came to the tent and drew patterns, but seemed to doubt them later—it was New Year, and much chang was flowing. He's making his third attempt now to get them big enough.

We're all fairly picturesque. I wear a scarlet tam or a Wild West Stetson and sometimes tall red boots with my fox-lined postin of turquoise-blue broadcloth (from Russian Turkistan, perhaps from Samarqand!) and flourish, as I ride, a whip of ibex horn decorated with silver dragons, jewel-eyed.

The Ladies' Aid of the Mission is making me a set of doll-clothes. I suspect Mrs. Kunick must be doing most of the work, as so few of the women know how to use a needle. They're all keenly interested, however, and every Wednesday afternoon they gather at Mission House, leaving their goatskin capes in the porch—just a plain goat with tie-strings at two of his corners, not fitting very closely around the neck, but that's convenient because it allows room for the baby. I go in sometimes to see them, all sitting on the dining-room floor, some spinning the woollen thread they sew the clothes with, others cutting out patterns, or sewing clumsily, and all discussing just how to make the things, and how to get the best materials. Mrs. Kunick's man goes to the bazar for samples, which they consider and often reject. They bring some things from their own treasures. The bits of turquoise matrix for the cobra head-dress are real, and so are the corals, and the seed pearls for the ear-rings. The silversmith is going to make a little necklace of silver and coral drops, and they've even turned up a miniature vanity kit,—silver tweezers and cleaners for ears and nose and teeth, all dangling on tiny silver chains, worn at the right shoulder. (Not just a lady's frivolity. Iba wears one and so does Roger!)

One of the dresses is to be a spotted one, such as used to be indispensable to a bride's outfit—rather gone out in Leh, though still de rigueur in the country. Most amazing spots. They wrap a piece of the cloth tightly around a stick with four peas at its base and dip the whole in blue dye. That keeps a bit clear of blue. Then they dye yellow the part where the peas were, and the stick's place comes out red finally. Very elaborate, and I confess I don't understand it altogether, as my explanation suggests, though Mrs. Burroughs explained it carefully. We had to send to Khalatse for the spotted cloth.

I'm learning a lot about customs. An unmarried girl wears white yak-hair plaits in with her own hair, and also white drawers. When she marries she leaves off white and puts on black. Country girls wear broad drawers, while city girls (Leh's a city!) wear theirs very scant but very long, so that they crumple up into a great many little ruffly folds. Nobody wears stockings, and handkerchiefs are always raw-edged, stuck in the folds of the long sash, for show only.

It must take real grace to be a Christian, because the Christians don't wear the thrilling Bod head-dress. It has a heathen savour, looking like a cobra, and associated with snake-worship historically. It was a royal prerogative, till some queen or other was deposed, when the common women seized upon it. The broad elephant's ears of black lamb's wool which seem to go with it are a later addition, dating from a time when another queen had chronic earache. The native Christian pastor told me these things. He must know, I should think. Royalty now wears ears of sable.

You take off the cobra at night, but you sleep wearing the elephant's ears and the long plaits far down below your waist. Of course you can't wear all that wool and greased hair day and night in a house never entered by sun nor soap, without getting vermin, so once a month the beauty-parlour lady comes and cleans you up. She charges a man's full daily wage for her work, and you have to feed her besides, knowing that she will tell the next client what you gave her. That's a good bit for upkeep. As for initial outlay, you may have inherited a cobra from someone, and it's not expensive to provide a new red cotton or felt base, but of course, you can't help wanting to add a turquoise. I'm sure one's secret ambition must be to have every inch of red covered. The Christian elders, as I said, think one can't easily wear a perag and be sure of salvation.

I should think there'd be the same danger about the ear-rings. They really are lovely things,—parallel hoops of seed pearls. I wanted to send one to each of my belles-soeurs for bracelets, but they cost too much. You should hear Rasul tell the story of how his "hoping wife" cozened him into giving her a pair that cost a thousand rupees and then decided that she couldn't marry him after all. "I said to her, 'In my young time my mother was very poor. She winnowing wheat at your house. I watching when some time your mother giving my mother little bread at your door. I thinking in my head: 'We am very little people.' Now you saying you want marry with me. Then not want. Does no matter. And for that thousand rupees pearl things, the poor wheat-winnowing woman's son is very glad to give. You keeping them. Does no matter.'" With a lordly gesture he told me coming up the path to the cragtop!

He had to marry some one though. He overheard his brother and sister-in-law planning what they would do with his property after his death. "That night I praying said to God, 'God, you give me more children, or else you take away my goods things before I die!' And next day I go out in the street and I meet one young girl, carrying water. Now I have Mohammed Rasul and little Bulla." This wife has all her teeth and all her hair, too, though she's not so "high stylish" as his hoping wife was. By the way, Mrs. Burroughs tells me he asked the missionaries to send to England to get a wig for that lady, suggesting that they get a blonde one, while they were about it. He has always been experimentally minded. He told me he had once put on a sahib's evening togs. "I wear this thing, madam. In front, here—" patting his breast, "I am all hard. I try turn my head, this way, other way. Not will turn. In China I see punish-thing like this thing. Madam, why sahibs wear this thing?" (He went to Western China, you know, with my rom,—that journey when the Chinese dubbed his sahib "Ba," source of my ballad "title.")

But I must stop. If I get to talking about Rasul I'm as bad as a mother quoting her children. And it's not altogether unlike. All these servants of ours say we are to them as their father and their mother, and we do grow fond of them and feel responsible for them in a manner not far from parental.

Yours filially (does that make you grandmother to all these pagris and pigtails?)

خدا قسم

P.S.—Tell Dad that Rasul says his mother could remember the days before law came to Ladakh. "Before law come to Ladakh, not was so much the matter. Law teaching make the matter. My court [he has jurisdiction in quarrels between traders] is little court. They ask to me: 'Is law this?' I say: 'No. I no have law. What is right, you people I tell you'."

Gypsy Davy   TSAM SKANG
                                  LADAKH
                                        February 15

Dear JANET,

It is very odd that you should call yourself the daughter of a sea captain. It's a farmer's daughter you really are. I should like to see your stables now. I remember when I saw them last, they were rather small. I believe one of the carts was out of repair, and several of the horses needed shoeing. You might say those stables of yours were leprechaun stables.

Do you know, sometimes I feel as if we were camped in the country of the leprechauns: the mountains are so huge, and the people and their stock and their fields and their houses and all their things are so little. We are camped on a great rock high above them, and that makes them look even smaller than they really are. The fields are very little scalloped terraces, long flights of them, thousands of steps. It never rains, and they have to bring water to the fields in little ditches from the little river that flows down the valley. It must be no end of fun doing this, always building little dams to turn the water this way and that, and get it to each of those many little scallops.

There are tiny donkeys wandering about on some of the scallops, digging up roots and ploughed-under stubble with their hoofs. The last bit of stubble was long ago cropped short by the other stock before the donkeys were turned out. There isn't a blade of grass to be seen anywhere in the bottom of the valley. There is a thin sprinkling of snow, but it isn't deep enough to cover a blade an inch high. Broad trails, brown in the snow, run out in all directions up the little side valleys where the tiny sheep and goats are driven out every morning, after the sun comes up; what for, you could not imagine if you sat in our tent door-way and watched them. You would say to yourself: "They are no bigger than rabbits, and they won't need much, but I can't see enough for even a rabbit.   I can't see anything but crumbly brown crags."   And presently you would see them climbing up among the crags, and wandering off in all directions with their noses to the ground. You would never see two close together.   If you were to go over there, you would find little bunches of yellow withered grass, each growing quite a long way apart from its fellows, and perhaps one or two other unsociable plants, very tiny.

I think you would like the singing shepherd boys.   They forgot one of their goats the other day, a very little black one that had strayed a bit.   I wonder if the wolves got him during the night.   If they didn't I am sure the big eagle scared him out of his wits.   He gives us a start every morning, that eagle, when he sails by our tent door.   We can hear the rush of his wings through the air before he gets to us, and by the time we get out to look, he's away up!

There isn't a tree or a bush anywhere to be seen, except for little clumps of poplars, planted about the tiny villages among the scallops.   On the mountain slopes and above the terraces there are odd-looking black spots, but these aren't bushes. They are yak, looking after themselves.   The yak would continue to look like black spots until you got pretty close to them, for their long skirts hide their short legs, and their horns are so slender that they do not show at a distance.

The villages must be leprechaun villages, little bits of houses with windows scarcely big enough to put your head out of. You can imagine how much air and light they let into the little dingy gloomy rooms, with mud floors, and mud walls, and ceilings of poplar poles and willow withes all shiny black with the smoke of burning dung.   It's only the wealthy leprechauns that burn wood, and it's precious little that even they burn.   And when they do get a little heat in a room they are very careful all winter not to let it out.   They depend on sheepskin coats instead of fire and two or three woollen gowns under or over the sheepskin.   It helps, too, to have the family and the sheep and the goats and the yak and the dzo and the chickens and the ponies and the donkeys all living in the same house.

The old yak has to go in, one horn foremost.   If you call unexpectedly you are almost as likely to find him in the living-room, as you are to find the master of the house.   He doesn't belong there, of course.   He has his own quarters, but if you were to go into one of these houses, I don't think you would blame him in the least.   He may be a very polite old yak, who wouldn't have made the mistake for the world.   Every house we have gone into has had dung and straw in the front hall, and in the house of a friend of ours who is a high official, a calf strolled into the second floor living-room one day when Roger was making a call.

There is one part of the house that I think you would really like, the roof. It is a flat mud roof, with parapets built of braids of grass. You get up to it through a hatch, by a ladder. The leprechauns sit there all the short winter day, in the sun, carding and spinning and weaving, and doing all kinds of work. But when the big snow mountains on the west come sweeping up across the sky, pretty close to the sun, you can see them scurry down the ladder.

These leprechauns are very superstitious folk. I wonder if they think that some great glacier dragon has clapped his jaws over the sun, and keeps him in his belly all night, and belches him forth in the east, an hour or two after daybreak?

On a high crag just above the biggest village, stands a castle, where the king lives. Sometimes he calls for his pipe and he calls for his bowl, and he calls for his fiddlers three. Only they aren't fiddlers. They beat drums and blow horns and oboes, and clash cymbals. The sound of them comes faintly to us, across the valley, on our crag, as we sit in the tent door-way, in the moonlight.

Yours,

Gypsy Davy

Gypsy Davy   Tsam Skang
Ladakh

February 16

Dear Sandy,

We haven't seen a sail for moons and moons. The nearest way to water is by the Zoji La, a long month, the furthest, out by China, the better part of a year, and a fair chance of being shot up with poisoned arrows, or decapitated, or seized and weighted with rocks and dropped into a river. It would take almost as long to reach the Arctic, and you would stand an equal chance of being bled to death by mosquitoes, or hugged by Siberian bear on the way, and if you should reach the coast, I'm thinking you'd look long and vainly for a sail. I expect there would be ice thirty or forty feet thick, out as far as you could see.

This old Asia (which really takes in Europe, doesn't it?) is such an immense patch of land, holding the sea far off at all points of the compass, that most of the people who live here don't know there is any sea, and the few who have heard of it don't believe the idle tale. But all the same, there wouldn't be a man jack here to believe or disbelieve, if there were no sea out there. The country would be as dry as a bone, every inch of it. I suppose almost every drop of water or flake of snow that falls on Asia anywhere comes from the sea.

On the high mountains hereabouts a lot of snow falls, but almost none falls in the valleys, and no rain falls there at all. The inch or two of snow that does fall in the valleys quickly goes, but all that falls, with hardly anyone's seeing it, on the high mountains stays, and piles up and packs down into thick heavy ice, that squeezes out on all sides, and creeps down the valleys. That ice must seem always to have been there like the rocks, piled up against the sky, a mile or two or three straight up above the villages. It melts a little in the valleys in the summer sun, and the people catch the water and lead it in ditches onto their little terraces on barren fans in barren valley bottoms, thankful for every sunny day. That drop or two of water, added to thin soil from time to time to make a little wheat and barley grow, comes plainly from the melting ice mysteriously replenished. The ice moves so slowly that they can no more see it move than they can see a plant grow. But some years the glaciers lengthen. Perhaps then they think they grow as plants do. The old men say if you want to cultivate a fan at the mouth of a dry nala, you must cut a large block from a live glacier and plant it in the gravel at the nala's head where it will last over from year to year, growing larger and larger until it becomes quite a respectable glacier, capable of furnishing all the water the little terraces need. Rasul says: "It come all time in my head: that big glaciers country, many glaciers, one side come water to all Ladakh, one side come water to all Baltistan. I thinking making food for many people, those glaciers. If not be those glaciers mountains, must to die these people." But whatever any one thinks, no one suspects the sea.

I wonder if you have any idea, yourself, how much the sea has to do with watering the land? The Pacific and the Arctic doubtless have hand enough in watering vast stretches of Asia, but I think they have little hand in watering this highland, this roof of the world. The Atlantic and the Mediterranean may help a little, part of the year, but the Indian Ocean and

the Bay of Bengal seem to do the bulk of the business.   One
or the other of them is hard at it when the monsoons blow,
and both of them lend a hand from time to time when some
wide-spreading cyclone comes slowly circling up across the
lowland.   All through the rainy season, great banks of sodden
cloud come charging up the high southern barrier.   Rain falls in
torrents on the lower slopes and makes dense jungle grow there,
full of venomous snakes and blood-thirsty animals.   Snow
falls deep on the upper slopes.   On the barrier's crest some of
it stays, and gradually packs down into ice, that squeezes out
in glaciers as it does in Ladakh.

The clouds that win their way across the barrier are no
longer sodden.   They are like squeezed sponges, but there
is enough snow left in them and carried on across the dry
valleys, to make wider and deeper snowfields and immense
glaciers on the next big range to the north, so high and cold
that most of the snow that falls there stays.   There is still a
little snow left for the next range, but for the country farther
north there is none.   That is the great desert of Taklamakan
and the Gobi.

We see very little of all this, camped in behind that huge
southern barrier, except for some of the panoply.   We see
storm signals flung across our sky from horizon to horizon,
those long mares' tails that make you sailormen take in your
sails.   We know a storm's abroad.   We even see thin ragged
bits of lower cloud come flying over the big barrier, and now
and then one showers a handful of snow on us, glancing down
in sunlight.   Sometimes we see as many as three strong winds.
at once, one above the other, up under the mares' tails, blowing
light clouds this way and that, though about our tent, pitched
on a cragtop, twelve thousand feet above the sea, and some
eight thousand or so below the crest of the barrier, we have had
scarcely a breath of wind all winter.   Light dry stratus now
and then forms in battle array on the south, and charges well
up toward the zenith.   Once in a long while a thin sheet of
grey nimbus with snow in it covers our sky and lets fall an inch
or two even on the valley bottom, to vanish shortly, scarcely
wetting the bare earth.

The India weather man says enough rain falls in one part
down there on the southern slopes of the barrier to make a
sheet of water four hundred inches deep each year.   Up here,
if all the snow that falls in the valleys were melted, it would
make a sheet not three inches deep most years, and some years
not over one inch.

There is a breach in the barrier through which some dak
runner will carry this letter out, at the risk of his life.   There
sodden clouds break through and bury the Dras valley on this
side, deep in snow.   I have seen the snow in April there ten
feet above flat dobe roofs.   The people had shovelled it off
and were sitting in the sun, carding and weaving and spinning,
and the goats and sheep and dzo were up there with them.

What news of the Sea Mew?

Gypsy Davy

Gypsy Davy   Tsam Skang

February 18

Dear Harlan,

The Doctor got an ibex yesterday, about a mile from our
camp, thirty-six-inch horns, four-hundred-yard shot.   They
are so numerous around here that he deliberately passed this
one at fifty yards, thinking he'd find a better pair of horns
above.

There are lots of shapu about, too.   He got one the same
day, twenty-eight-inch spread, still nearer at hand.   There are
many wolves and some foxes (there's a funny old stone fox-
trap on our hill).   And there is a snow leopard about with an
unmistakable howl.

That shapu meat, by the way, was delicious but the ibex
was tougher than mule.

The only shot-gun in the valley, outside the Doctor's gun-
room and the Charas Officer's, is a rickety old single-barrel
I brought out twenty years ago, and gave Khalik as bakhshish
when he left me in China.   Khalik was imprisoned when the
gun was found in his possession some years after he got back
to Leh.   His companion, "that old cook," had persuaded
him to hide it, although he had credentials which would have
enabled him to keep it, I think, had he declared it.

Our ponies are lodging with a wealthy old Bod at the foot
of the hill (a mile away) paying their rent in fuel.

Yours,

Gypsy Davy

Gypsy Davy   Tsam Skang
First month of the Wood Mouse Year
(February 21)

Dear Will Scarlet,

I remember a certain night in The House on Weir Hill. The Weir young had all retired. We supposed them snugly tucked in and fast asleep. There was a sound of thunder on the stairs as of elephants descending. The whole band burst into the living-room, the leader leaping up and down, and yelling at the top of his lungs. His father gagged him, while his mother interpreted: "Something's happening to the moon!" We saw the band back to their sleeping porch, and sure enough there was a big nick in the moon.

Last night the full moon was riding high. Yonton was gathering up the dinner things. The dogs all up and down the valley were howling, or rather barking. Suddenly Yonton said: "Kala! Dark!" and we looked. And the moon wasn't full any more. Roger ran down to the cook-tent. The cook was shaking his head and saying: "Jinn! Jinn! Jinn! Bara afsos! Very sorry!"

Presently the lamas on the crag opposite began to blow their big horns. One after another all the horns in the valley set to work. There was a most dreadful braying. But the Jinn kept steadily on, like a snake swallowing a toad. The lamas laid down their horns, and took to drums. The thunder of big drums rolled up and down the valley. I think they were even beating their huge pendent drums, and there was wailing as of frightened men and women, and whistling. Of a sudden the thunder of the drums, and the howling of the dogs, and the wailing and the whistling stopped. And the few lights set burning this last night of the New Year festival went out. The Jinn's jaws closed over the moon. The worst had happened. She still shone so that you could see her there, a bit silvery near her upper rim, deep golden-brown below. As she sank lower down his gullet, she got a deep golden-brown all over.

We fell to thinking how we might be suspect, living in this outlandish way apart on a high crag, always studying stars. The Mem-Sahib got out her gun.

We thought when the Jinn began to let go the moon, there would be great rejoicing, or at least efforts to help her out. But there wasn't a sound. It looked as if lamas and people alike were terrified lest the Jinn get them next, and were hiding in their dark cells of houses.

The six men and a boy, who had just finished, thick with dust from head to foot, three days of measuring their length like inch-worms around a gompa-crowned crag, must thereby have gained so much merit that they had little to fear from any Jinn, but the fellows who ought to have been doing this, and hadn't done it, must have been shivering in their pabu.

Perhaps the reason that the braying and the drumming stopped was that all the lamas were in demand at all the houses to keep devils out.   All the devils in the mountains must have been at large last night, especially the great she-devil whose name they never dare to mention, who lets loose the demons of disease. She rides in the midst of flames, on a white-faced mule, on a saddle of her own son's skin, flayed by herself.   She is clad in human skins, eats human brains, and drinks blood from a skull.   When they want to coax her not to send a plague, they offer her a cake made of blood, wine, flour, butter and the fat of a blue goat, serving it in a skull, of course.   There must have been a run on blue goats last night.

Love to all the Weir young.

Gypsy Davy

P.S.—Should that pestilence break out in spite of the blue goats, the lamas will be busy writing charms on paper, for the sufferers to eat.   I don't think they use the ℞ your father uses on his charms.   I suppose he has given up the practice of letting his patients eat them, but I'm not sure they've given it up all over Europe yet.   By the way, the Jinn didn't let go last night till Saturn cleared the horizon.   I wonder did he have anything to do with it.   If it had been Jupiter, he might have.   They think the ℞ has to do with Jupiter or Mars.

P.S.2.—Great Heavens, Bill! Iba has just told us that the Jinn used to eat the people on the earth, and had a mind to this time, but the lamas, foreknowing his intent, persuaded some divinity to throw him the living moon as a sop. When they and the people and the dogs saw the Jinn slowly swallowing the moon, they were sorry for her, and tried to attract his attention toward the earth, to give her a little respite. Today the Hindus eat no food for sorrow, but the Bods aren't quite that sorry.   The Mussulmans, Iba says, think it is all nonsense—and yet Samat is a Mussulman, and he believes it.   It is a wicked Jinn and I doubt not the lamas were busy for a month at least, at heavy charges to the public, to make the exchange.   The people, Iba says, were no longer afraid when the Jinn had appeased his appetite, and probably went to bed in peace. And the moon came alive again.

P.S. 3.—Rasul has just been up. He says that the people think it is lucky for the valley that we are camping in the neighbourhood this winter. There have been no deaths (only a Christian's) and no sickness. Last year there was a smallpox epidemic. And the prices of wood and food have gone down. All this they have set to our credit. The Mem-Sahib needn't have got her gun out.

P.S. 4.—The Mem-Sahib's made a cinquain of it:
> The Jinn
> Is eating the Moon.
> Bay, dogs! Beat, drums! Horns, bray!
> All ye compassionate people, come forth
> And wail!

Gypsy Davy   TSAM SKANG
February 22

Dear ADELA,

A sunny windless winter, clear nights of stars. A sculptor's winter. A block of Parian marble stretching from horizon to horizon, carved deep, with feeling for light and shade and colour. At dawn, at dusk, under a blazing noonday sun, under grey clouds, under a full moon, veiled by most lovely mists.

Yours,

ᘯ

Gypsy Davy   TSAM SKANG
February 22

Dear PAT,

If I recall your last letter correctly, you criticized the way my eagle trimmed his beard and his toe-nails, or was it the way he arranged his primaries? Perhaps he is a vulture for you scientific fellows, but he's got to look a lot more like one before we three laymen give him up. I can't believe he has anything in common with those revolting creatures down country. Would you accept him as a lammergeier?

Samdu certainly can't suspect his being a vulture. He shot the bird's mate the other day, and Samdu's much-cherished, hard-won wife is still a Bod, if he isn't one himself for the

K

moment. Samdu knows that the Tibetan vultures feed on lamas. All Tibetan lamas, except the Dalai and a Skusho or two are eventually butchered and fed by hand to vultures. And the bird Samdu shot, if he were a vulture, must have been here on a visit for change of diet, with a good safe-conduct for such lama essence as he had with him.

The bird would have to change his diet here, for there is no Ladakhi lama or Ladakhi flesh of any sort to be had. It's all burned. There is wood enough to char even a moderately poor man, not easily to be had, but still to be had. Charges for a burning appeared in Rasul's account the other day. "To taking dead servant's body and four maunds of wood for burn him." The Kalon thinks that an excessive allowance for burning a servant.

This burning is a gruesome business. There are little open stone furnaces on the skirts of our hill, belonging to the nearest village. I suppose nearly every family has one.

There are rude little piles of stone on the saddle, back of our tent which you might mistake for furnaces, but they are not that. They were built over the corpses of smallpox victims which lay for months before burning, well weighted down to keep the wolves off. If those bodies had been burned before the smallpox demons had left, the demons might have got singed, and then they would have wiped out a whole village in revenge for such indignity.

When a man dies, they break his neck, jack-knife his body, fold it in three, I mean, truss him up so to speak, sew him up in a bag, and set him in a corner of the living-room. They keep the body a long time in the house, for religious reasons, but I suspect partly, too, to let it dry out a bit so that the burning will be less expensive. Meat will dry and powder on the bone up here.

Chot and Angbo have gone to a burning to-day. They are real travellers, out to see what there may be to see. Angbo comes from a village far down the river, and he is "seeing Leh" this winter. We older folk contented ourselves with watching the little procession wind across the valley. There was a red spot in the centre which we knew to be the hearse. We could see the smoke of the fire for a long time. If Chot comes in before dark, I'll get him to tell you what it was like, closer to. —Here he is now, with a letter on the burning, to Dave. You'll have to apply to Dave for that.

Yours,
GYPSY DAVY

Dear DAVE,

There was a big celebration down in the village to-day: a cremation. So I went along to help. Down the hill and across the terraced fields I went; here, a starved donkey vainly trying to dig up ploughed-under stubble, a raven lazily gurgling near by on a terrace edge, there, a dog slinking behind a house,—no other life. The people were all at Chogspit's house.

When I arrived, the last wailing session was over, the last chang being drunk. In front of the house stood the hearse, a box covered with red and yellow silk, fastened on two poles. In a small lightless room the lamas were ending their work of exhorting Chogspit's soul to come out of him. Hard work it was,—ringing of bells, chanting of chants, and swaying of bodies.

Then we started, Chogspit in his little box, all the men taking turns at carrying him,—even Angbo who came along with me took a hand and came back telling how "halka" he was. Ahead of Chogspit walked the lama band, each trumpeter blowing when he had the breath, each drummer beating when he felt like it. Chungduk led the procession, wood-bearer by appointment from the stars, proud of his office and of the two six-inch logs he carried like a baby. He walked with head erect, and pigtail swinging. I expected him to burst into "Ha *dam* ma la! Ha *dam* zer!"

So we wended up the mountain side to the family oven and rolled Chogspit into it. The men circled round him, prostrating themselves, foreheads to the ground, again and again. When one dropped out, another took his place, until all had paid their respects. Then they left.

The lamas put in their last licks while the fire was being kindled, chanting, strewing barley grains and peacock feathers and pouring apricot oil into the oven. Then they picked up their tools and left.

Chungduk, his helper and I, were alone with Chogspit, a delicate piece of work ahead of us. The astrologer had read the horoscope as foretelling that the worst that could happen to Chogspit would be for his elbows to burn first. He would lose ground in the cycle of re-births and run the risk of getting stalled in a cold hell. So we had a look in, and lo and behold!

his elbows were the only part toasting. Much talk and excitement. We pried him round (I hope in time) with a pole to a better position. His head began to sizzle, and fat sputtered. If you look close some day you may see where a bit of it burned my face.

Chungduk lamented the scarcity of fat on Chogspit's body. It meant an all-night session for him.

I pulled out down the mountain across the terraces. A raven flew up before me with a red mess in his beak. Another step and I saw that starved donkey, down on the terrace below mine, fallen from weakness, feebly struggling to get up, blood welling from an empty eye-socket. I took my chance on a Bod hell forever and helped him into his next life with a rock.

Yours in Three-Corner Round,

ROGER

Gypsy Davy   TSAM SKANG
February 23

Dear BARRETT,

Wintering on the tiptop of a bare gneiss crag, twelve thousand feet above the sea, in latitude thirty-four or thereabouts. An old decrepit couple, long past the age limit for the natives of the place. A man is tottering to the grave at fifty here, and a woman doubtless much earlier. We climb up the long spur behind us, higher and higher daily, but we rarely venture down into the valley where the people and the cattle swarm in dirty spots among the terraces that nourish them.

In spite of tales about a dead line at twelve thousand for the cat, the cat does live a short life down there, but the real family pet's the louse. The people, old and young, cherish the louse, and the louse reciprocates with so hearty an appetite as sometimes, it is said, to kill his host. Can't you see him waving his plumes on the horns of a jaunty fur cap, or marching up and down the labyrinthine lines of gold brocade upon the scarlet crown of one, or crouching on a blue turquoise strung on a silver ring hung in a dark ear, or on the turquoise eye of one head of a thick silver snake glaring at the other head across a dark wrist, or dancing on the wide turquoise on a dark finger, or climbing up a long black pigtail, or playing hide-and-seek among the fringes of a dark-blue girdle? Can't you imagine whole families asleep in the heavy folds of a crimson gown or at dinner on the dark body under it?

The Bara Sahib borrowed one last summer from a coolie who carried our coats in the Braldoh, or rather the louse borrowed the Bara Sahib. There was hell to pay in three camps, up and down that valley. The long train of coolies stood in fear of their lives. The servants trembled whenever they came into The Presence,—storming up and down, cursing and hunting, hunting, hunting. The Mem-Sahib and the Chhota Sahib looked on in silent awe. At every friendly move on the part of the louse, the sahib stripped, and all hands searched his clothes and body with microscopes.

Well, he was found at last and slain. Then we built a great fire in a pit, and piled in rocks, and built a wickiup above it, and made a tent of all the clothes and all the blankets of all the sahib log, and heated them up to such a heat as to discourage the most persistent egg. No coat or blanket since has gone to a coolie's hands, except in a heavy canvas bag, with throat tied tight, and mouth securely locked.

Bara Sahib Bahadur ke hukm!

Yours,

GYPSY DAVY

Gypsy Davy   TSAM SKANG

February 23

Dear NORMAN,

The postman brought a lovely butterfly from you to-day, and bluebells in a greenwood,—up to the top of this crag where no bluebells are, and no butterflies, and no greenwood, but only bare dark gneiss with lichens on it, golden-brown, and in a cranny here and there a spear of winter grass, and on the north slopes winter snow, fast thinning now, slaking the thirst of the dry air.

At the very edge of the crag, by Roger's tent, there are a dozen bare willow shoots, thrust into a pile of rocks, bending this way and that. A month since, they were white with paper prayer-flags, sometimes fluttering but usually hanging stiffly. The ravens came and plucked them, one by one, until the other day I saw two great black fellows tearing the last to shreds, to weave into their nest.

When the flags were planted there, the people sprinkled

beer and grain and flesh and flour about them, and called on the genii of the crag to take these and spare the flags. I don't believe the genii got either food or flags. The ravens took them all. They take bits of the Mem-Sahib's silk threads, too, the gold and green and scarlet she embroiders stars with on a wide strip of dark blue cloth.

I never got Jimmy's letter. I am afraid it was buried under an avalanche on the Zoji La, and will lie there till summer, in the dak bag, by the body of the poor black man who carried it.

Yours,

GYPSY DAVY

Lady Ba   THE HERMIT'S CRAG
February 23

WILL SCARLET,

There is a hero-tale of Ladakh! Minstrels recite it at feasts, recite it all night long to grown-up men and women, laughing and crying while they listen.

Ibrahim told me about it quite casually, as though that kind of thing might be common anywhere. He knows a lot of the story by heart, and told me bits of it, chuckling. And Angbo and old Tundup the tailor, who were patching the tent, listened, and laughed and forgot to sew, and kept on laughing when they went back to their sewing.

I found out that a wise missionary, Dr. Francke, who wrote the history of this part of the world, has translated part of the hero tale, which he calls the Kesar Saga, into German. I have got it from the Mission library, and translated it for you into English. I wish you could read German because I can't put it into English as sturdy and mouthfilling as the Padre Sahib's German, but I shall have to do the best I can. You must know the story of Kesar, without further delay.

Here's the first part. There will be more as I get it translated.

Yours,

LADY BA

Kesar's Fight with Kurulugu

The Vision in the Hermitage.

Kesar the god-king of Gling-land, in the third month of the third year, to hermitage betook him. Two months he abode there.

Then to Ane-kur-manmo, the goddess, came dreams of misfortune. To the door of the hermitage came she, and thus she lamented:

"Oh child of mine, hark to my speaking!
Sleeping lad, waken and hearken!
Three nights long have my dreams been troubled.
A flood I saw sweep the high valley.
The castle of kings saw I ruined.
Kurulugu the fiend saw I heavenward flying,
And Kesar the king on earth grovelling.
O, child of mine, princeling, hear me!"

Then Kesar made answer:—

"Dear goddess-mother, hear thou me for a moment.
Ane-kur-manmo, hear me, I pray thee.
On the hill to the right, a cake, so big, built I.
On the hill to the left, one, so little.
Flowers I made, butter-flowers, like the sun and the moon
    at their rising.
I painted them all with the rainbow's five colours.
Grain and bread I brought in great masses.
A lake I filled with pure water.
A holy lamp I lighted, shining in darkness.
Therefore, if thou canst, for three years give me respite.
If that be too much, for seven months I beseech thee.
Or, if more be not granted, let me have a week only."

And Ane-kur-manmo reflected:—

"Now is my Kesar waxed fat in religion!" and for a space left him.

The Setting Out.

Now spake the crystal consort, Bruguma, thus to her handmaid:—

"Food heap up like the ice of a glacier.
Strong drink like the waters of Maphong make ready.
Heaps of the strongest yak-meat prepare thou,
And meat of the fattest she-yak fetch likewise.
Also goat's flesh, in the mouth sweetly melting.

And the flesh of sheep, the strength of the eater increasing:
A good sheep, young and well nurtured.   Now go thou
Panting for breath with thy haste, and humble in spirit."

When all the food was made ready, sang Bruguma to Kesar:

"If Kesar the king of the gods, tarry not,
    But northward betake him,
Who is the hope of Bruguma, his loving spouse then?

If he tarry not in the blue light of heaven,
    But northward betake him,
Who is the hope of the sun and the moon then?

If he tarry not by the high glacier,
    But northward betake him,
Who is the hope of the white she-lion then?

If by the high crags he tarry no longer,
    But northward betake him,
Who then is the hope of the eagle?

If in the deep lake he tarry not,
    But northward betake him,
Who is the hope of Gold-Eye, the small fish then?

If on the high meadow he tarry not,
    But northward betake him,
Who is the hope of the wild yak, then?"

Because the loving spouse Bruguma could not tear herself
from the king's side, a month long she held him.

But one night at midnight came Ane-kur-manmo, the goddess saying:—

"He who was wise has lost his wisdom,
    He who was prudent is prudent no longer.
Kesar, King Kesar, when wilt thou travel?"

Thus she reproached him.

When the next day was dawning, Kesar woke full of fear
and misgiving, doubt-beset and unquiet.   With the sun he
arose and fetching his foal, Kyang-god-byerpa, from the marigold garden, set a saddle upon him.

Then came the loving consort Bruguma, with all her maids
and the neighbouring maidens, bearing sweet-scented cedar
twigs burning, and jugs full of beer, brims decked with butter,
and all did escort him.

A half-day's march on his way did they go thus, then turned
homeward, and a half-day's march came Kesar back with them.
Then fell the evening.   And lo! a black dzomo thrust sharp

horns into the flank of Kesar's foal, Kyang-god-byerpa.   Then
waxed Kesar wroth, and he shouted: "Why dost thou, dzomo,
at my journey's beginning, attack my kyang?" and a quiverful
of arrows shot he.   But never one hit the dzomo, the goddess
Ane-kur-manmo, come in this guise to warn him.

Down sank the sun.   Vanished the dzomo.   And Bruguma
and her maidens bade farewell to the god-king.

Of course, it can't be as exciting to you as it is to me.   Why,
Will Scarlet, this story is as old as the mountains nearly, and
yet it's full of things that are happening to-day.   We're living
on a hill that used to be a hermitage, and we can see a little
hermitage on the mountain side above us, where a real hermit's
living.

Ane-kur-manmo dreamed of a flood—no wonder.   We've
seen many a ruined stretch where once there were villages.
And as for the cakes with butter-flowers, and the rainbow's
five colours, and offerings of grain and water and holy lamps
at altars, we've seen them ever since we crossed the Ladakh line!

"Heap up food like the ice of a glacier!"   It may not mean
much to the Ohioan now, but if you had been born in Ohio
some years back or been born recently anywhere in this part
of the world, you'd know no better way of expressing a quantity.
The one thing that never gives out in Ladakh is the ice of the
glaciers.

I love Bruguma's song.   How a woman must hate to see her
lord start northward over those terrible passes!

The name of Kesar's mount, Kyang, makes me think he was
one of the wild asses Iba promises we shall see on our summer's
safar further up the Indus, toward the Tibetan border.   Even
the marigold garden is modern, for marigolds are the flowers
people love best in this part of the world.   We saw lots of them
in the Shyok, and Kunick Sahib, who helped me most kindly
with the translation, tells me that they grow them here in Leh
in the summer in little gardens on their flat earth roofs.

As for the escort with cedar twigs burning and jugs full of
beer, with butter-flowers on the brim, that's as regular a pro-
ceeding here as, say, sending steamer letters, or going to the
train to see a guest off.   We've nothing so accepted, or so
pretty, in our customs.

Even the shooting a quiverful of arrows without hitting
seems natural.   We went to a festival on the edge of the village
last week where the soldiers shot for hours at a cow's horn filled

with blood, but couldn't hit it, at very close quarters, because it was enchanted.   They had guns, funny old guns that they loaded with powder and ball, but the arrow shooting we saw at another festival wasn't much more accurate.

I met an old dzomo in a lane between high walls by Kalon's house the other day, and I turned back, I can assure you. Her horn-spread left no room for passing.

Do you know Stevenson's "Davie an' Donal' an' Charley an' a' "—seeing each other home?

"Ane went hame wi' the ither and then
The ither went hame wi' the ither twa men
An' baith wad return him the service again
An' the mune was shinin' clearly!"

Partings are as old as folk-songs and as modern as to-day's sunrise.

If you don't want more Kesar, cable!

Yours,

LADY BA

Gypsy Davy   TSAM SKANG

February 25

Dear DAVE,

Wolves on the mountain behind us.   Lots of them. Howling in the late afternoon.   We raked the snow-flecked ledges with our glasses, but in vain.   We could see nor hide nor hair of them.

Then they were silent for awhile.

Just as night fell, they began again, louder and closer than before.   It sounded as if they were running.   The men who came up with wood for the stove looked scared and asked if we had a gun.

Then there was silence again.

We thought maybe they had got the old hermit on the ledges above us, and were pulling him to pieces.   He wasn't near enough for us to hear the chattering of his teeth as he sat in his little stone hut, waiting for them.   Nor to hear the crunching of his bones.

Then they began close at hand.

Mem-Sahib got out her shooting-iron and loaded it.

Chhota Sahib was shivering in his tent, in spite of his little stove and a teething temperature—for, would you believe it,

Chhota Sahib is actually at last cutting his teeth! By to-morrow or the next day he may have an extra one to chatter. We were expecting the Doctor Sahib up to have a look at him.

Suddenly the howling ceased.

The Doctor did not come. And did not come. We waited. And we waited. And at last we decided the wolves must have got him. We were expecting him up the pony trail, right through the midst of the howls.

But they didn't get him, after all. He came up the pak-dandi. He saw only one, about five yards off. He says it's he will get the wolves, not they him.

GYPSY DAVY

Lady Ba   THE HERMIT'S CRÀG
                            The Wood Mouse Spring

Dear DOROTHY,

Rasul dined with us last night. He sang us a song. I can't give you the music, but here is his English version of the words.

It's a musician's daughter singing of her lover, the Raja. The musician is a lowly person in these parts, though music is the breath of life here.

I'm sending you a square silver "good luck ornament" such as the Raja might have given the musician's daughter to wear in her black hair.

"The Raja's love is like a good-luck ornament.
In my breast comes hope like water.
In my breast is like water from many ditches, join-ed.

Talking is like ravens' croaking.
Talking is like writing in water.
But what in heart hidden is safe, no one can talking."

Has Carol begun to appreciate folk-song yet? Our salams to your Man John.

Your
"LADY BA"

Gypsy Davy   Tsam Skang
                               Spring, Year of the Wood Mouse

Dear Odo,

We saw some shooting the other day, by Maharaja's sepoys.

It seems that once a year, not punctually at the return of Sun, but at the proper time, the lamas have a grand tamasha, gathering from far and near to hurl old Winter out, and let the Spring come on. There's a lot of reading of the great book, which I believe it takes a pack train of a dozen yak (one man told me a hundred) to carry, not so much because of the volume of the matter as of the volume of the timber and parchment. There is incantation, investing of certain butter images with the sins and vicious traits of the winter demons, and finally, a grand shooting up with flaming arrows of all the evil, in the midst of a crowd of the simple folk who inhabit these parts.

But as the Hindus who govern have one calendar, the British who help them another, the Mohammedans, who do much of the business, another, and the Buddhists who really belong here still another; and as the calendar of the Buddhists themselves is somewhat confused, there seems to be a curious tendency to repetition of the tamashas when Maharaja butts in as he does now and then, in pursuit of a policy of fostering the customs of the conquered. At any rate, all I could make out of the affair I am about to write you of was that it seemed to be a repetition of that grand spontaneous one.

A desolate place: a barren fan, at the foot of barren mountains, —chortens and mani walls; two small cannon firing blanks; some fifty rifles, heavy old muzzle-loaders; a tall slender sepoy from Kashmir under each, now for the first time this year, got up in regimentals, cotton khaki from pagri to puttees; a big leather bag of powder, and another of ball.

Everybody falls out and helps himself. In capping, hammers at full cock. Guns always held horizontal, pointing at some part of the crowd, or at us in the Tehsildar's tent.

A cow-horn filled with blood hangs at some fifty yards. Firing begins. Explosions varying from the cap alone to a tremendous bang, enough to burst the barrel. Much firing, but no hits. A layman or two in long crimson robe and horned fur cap borrows a rifle and tries his hand without success.

The little captain calls his men off and marches them up in front of a fat lay figure set on the mountain side at about the distance of the firing squad at an execution, and they all set to work on that.

Meanwhile a rabble stones the horn.   No hit among them even at six feet.   Finally a burly fellow kicks down the supports.

The lay figure bears as charmed a life as the bloody horn. The Tehsildar, whose troops they are, tells me the lamas have worked hard to cast a spell against Maharaja's bullets.   The Church sits a little to one side of the State, calmly confident, the highest personage present wearing on his head a tiara of ivory, carved into graduated skulls.   (Ivory, is it, or human bone?)

At length the Captain orders: "Cease firing," draws his sabre and at the figure single-handed.   He slashes off its head, and the rabble falls upon the body, first with stones, and then with hands.

Do you remember, when you and I were trying out your Luger, how the Mem-Sahib broke the spell on which your bullets and mine had all glanced off?

Yours,

Gypsy Davy

Lady Ba   Tsam Skang

March 2

Dear Melvin,

I've just been down to the Padre Sahib's for tea.   Kunick Sahib and Mem-Sahib have dwelt among these Ladakhis for many years now, have cast in their lot with their people for ever.   I love to sit in their sunny living-room and hear their affectionate discerning talk.

Today they've been telling me how debts are collected. If you owe a man money, which you are reluctant to pay, he comes and dwells with you.   If he is a grandee, he sends his agent, but in any case you, as debtor, are never alone.   He walks with you, or behind you, through the bazar.   If you stop to buy something at one of the little wide-open shops, he tells the merchant that you are making the purchase with money you owe him.   If you pause to greet a friend in one of the twisty lanes of the village, he tells your friend why he is there.   He follows you into your house, squatting on the namda near you while you smoke your huqa.   When your food is brought, he takes a big kulcha out of his bosom and eats it comfortably.   To casual callers he tells his story.   Of course, at odd times he mentions the debt to you yourself.   Perhaps he may choose to sleep alongside you, his quarry. In any case, he bores you so fearfully that at last you open your strong box, the curiously-wrought key of which hangs from your girdle all the while, and count him out the rupees, the annas and the paisa.   Or, if the strong box is empty, you call on a friend in whose hand you have placed some of your funds for safekeeping, asking for them again. Probably your friend has been speculating with your money and has none at hand to pay back.   So you go into the bazar and pause before the shop of one of the old Hindus, Shiv Ram, for example, and negotiate a loan, with which to buy yourself a bit of solitude.

Later on Shiv Ram will want his money back. You will bring it to him if you can get it, because he charges twenty per cent. interest ("interax" Rasul calls it, combining the two most inexorable consumers of cash). He will be squatting among his goods. You will tell him you have come to pay. A crowd will gather. Shiv Ram will open a box and take out his book, and tell you how much you owe. You will count it out in silver. Shiv Ram does accept paper money, but his customers generally don't trust it. "How could paper be money?" the people say. "Barley, turquoises, wool have value, and silver coins are conceivable, but dirty bits of paper? Bah!" The Grand Khan's paper money didn't reach as far as this. When you have counted out almost the full amount you will begin explaining to the crowd that you are a poor man, that you have had bad luck, and that Shiv Ram's rates of interest are exorbitant. Then Shiv Ram will tell the crowd he was not obliged to lend you the money, that if he had not come to your aid, you would have been in a desperate condition, that he needs his money, etc., etc., showing your note and signature. The crowd will take sides. There will be a good deal of discussion. At last you will count out a little more, and then Shiv Ram, with a grand air, will forgive you the very last paisa, put the coins into a leather bag and lock it up in his box, and the crowd will move off, talking it over, and shaking heads.

I wanted to ask the missionaries if the tale were true that a big yak-owner had arranged with the lamas to foster a superstitious fear of a certain safe pass in order that caravans might avoid it, taking instead one where they must trans-ship to his animals. But looking into those clear eyes I recalled Iba's comment: "Kunick Sahib log think no evil," and the gossip died in me, for the moment. It's not alone to the natives that these missionaries, by their practising, preach !

At five o'clock the littermen called for me, one making correct announcement at the door, while the others pressed noses against the window-panes! Mrs. Kunick (the Madre Sahib, I think we should call her) made up a little packet of cakes for the Ri Sahib who rarely leaves his "ri," the Padre Sahib got his hat and stick to escort me a little way, and off I set for the cragtop.

Near Kalon's house, on the way back, I saw Ibrahim standing very close to a Lhasa man. The Lhasa men dress more jauntily than the Ladakhis. They wear their long robes pulled up under their belts, so that they come only to the knee, showing their high boots, and almost always they keep their right arms outside their sleeves. Iba saw me and came across the little bridge to meet me, with beautiful politeness as he always does. I asked him what he was doing, holding hands with the Lhasa man. He said he was bargaining for horses for the caravan. The Lhasa man had squeezed Iba's thumb three times up under his sleeve, and then all five fingers together, once. That meant he would sell the horses for three hundreds and one fifty. Iba had squeezed the Lhasa man's thumb once, and after some deliberation, once more, meaning two hundreds. The Lhasa man had withdrawn his hand. Iba says tomorrow or next day or perhaps next week, he will squeeze the Lhasa man's thumb twice, and then add the all-finger squeeze, and he thinks that will be final. He may have to squeeze the index finger for an extra ten, but he hopes not.

Business awaited me on the hill-top—Rasul's account for three months, on big sheets, ruled inkily by hand, with a heading showing the "Graend Ballance, Total."

Here are a few items which may interest you:

Telegramps all differin places
Lamp sheep skin for coat
Tigar skin for bed (really snow leopard)
To the dead servant taking his body and 4 maunds of wood
    for burn him
2 empty tins of oil
Cook cloth cooking-time wearing (I am attempting to
    introduce aprons)
Apricot rocks (delicious nuts, in puddings, or salted like
    almonds)
Goat grazing two mans
To poor people little etc. things
To one poor cannot speak

To one sickness coolie to riding to home him
To make horses shoes, iron-bringing man wages
To winnowing barley grain three womens
2 wooding boxes
5 bundles wishing soup (washing soap)
12 mens on hill water and wood carrying
1 iron like stick (crow-bar)
1 new birth child good wishes
1 water-putting-thing for hands-washing (we've adopted
   the Mussulman custom)
To eggins and chickens

Gypsy Davy   TSAM SKANG
                                                  March 2

DEAR DAVE,

I wonder how you'd like to stand in the pabu of one of these shepherd boys up the mountains after winter pasture, always two together with a band of a hundred sheep and some goats. All day listening and watching for the wolves, with no dogs to help. And sooner or later the wolves come. They don't attack the band and try to scatter it. They couldn't do that with the goats there. The sheep wouldn't scatter. They'd just crowd round the goats. But the sheep have to separate a good deal hunting feed, and some stray too far. It's these the wolves pull down. The boys throw rocks, of course, but they're not dead shots like Barrett. Why don't they use slings?

I wonder if the wolves respect consecrated sheep with red paint and ribbons on them.

There is probably a good pinching at the hands of their mothers awaiting the boys whose tallies are short. The wolves nearly always hunt in little packs. The Charas Officer says only once in a great while has he met a wolf hunting alone, and he doesn't remember seeing a pack bigger than seven. The other night he came on a pack in the moonlight, eating a dead donkey.

Yours,
GYPSY DAVY

Roger's off to meet Jim and Stuart.

Gypsy Davy   TSAM SKANG
                                                March 3

Dear DAVID,

A long time ago, when you were very young, I think about
a month old, Lady Ba and I set out to visit you.   We travelled
all day over the hills and through the wood.   In a little glade
in the wood we found a big turtle which we thought would
make a fine birthday present for you.   We didn't realize how
very young one month is, and were surprised to find you sound
asleep in a darkened chamber.   Your mother let us in on
tiptoe to look at you, but when we brought forth our gift,
she was horrified and bade us take it quickly out of doors.
Perhaps you never knew about your turtle.

In this country babies don't lie in cradles hung with pink
silk curtains like yours.   They lie in a sort of pit in the dirt
floor, in nice warm powdered dry sheep's dung close to a warm
fire of another kind of dung in another pit.   Their mothers
think this makes much stronger men of them than swad-
dling clothes.   If you had had your birthday in Ladakh
you might perfectly well have had the turtle in bed with you,
unless your mother had been afraid lest he cast the evil eye.
She would never have let us or any one else look at you, for
fear of that terrible evil eye.

Your room in Chevy Chase was dimly lighted while you
slept, but I imagine your mother raised a curtain a little when
you waked.   Your room here would have been as dimly lighted
all the time.   If the tiny window had been wide open at high
noon, there would not have been light enough to save
me from bumping my head on the low lintel of the door-way
and smirching my bald pate on the shiny black ceiling beams.

What do you think makes them black? Smoke, if you please!
They build their fires in the middle of the floor and say to the
smoke, "Find your way out if you can."   It has a hard enough
time finding its way out, and some of it never does.   The
room is as thick with it as your living-room when your father
is burning tobacco freely, but it wouldn't bother you and the
turtle down there on the floor.

When you had got a little older, say a year or two, and
had grown a proper pigtail and had it lengthened out with
yak-hair, and had a proper pair of silver rings with turquoise
beads strung on them in your ears, and heavy silver bracelets
on your wrists, and a long red woollen gown like a bath robe,

L

or rather two or three of them, one above the other, to keep you warm, and the jauntiest fur cap you can imagine, and pointed shoes of yak-hair and gay Lhasa cloth, and a charm or two to "fend from Sathanas,"—when all this had happened to you, you would be allowed to play by yourself upon the flat roof on sunny days.

The wind doesn't blow here in winter, and the sun is wondrous warm on the coldest days. You would climb to the roof by a ladder sticking up through a hatch. There would be a parapet of grass, long braids of it, neatly piled, to keep you from falling off. Maybe some of the goats would follow you up, if your brother had overlooked any when he drove the flock out to pasture. The people of your family wouldn't have a separate house all to themselves the way they did in Chevy Chase, of course. The goats and the sheep and the donkeys and the ponies and the yak and the hens would all share it with you, and some night a snow leopard might get in, and then there would be such a commotion among the animals as you'd not soon forget.

I hope you would keep your turtle in bed with you every night, for the leopard might get him. You would have to watch him pretty carefully when you had him on the roof, for a pair of big black ravens would come regularly to perch on your parapet, croaking and gurgling and pretending to pull corks out of bottles and cocking their heads to look at him. And if you turned your back for a minute, one of them would be off with him.

Yours,

GYPSY DAVY

Lady Ba   *March* 4

Dear WILL SCARLET,

Here's more of the Kesar story.

The Journey.

That night the god-king and his horse dwelt at the entrance to three valleys.

In the night-time Ane-kur-manmo showed them a monstrous vision. In the upper valley wolves howling. In the lower valley foxes yapping. Before them, the reed, without lungs, piping. The round dung, without feet, dancing. Then a fearful storm on the pass.

It was to try the god-king's courage that the goddess after this fashion alarmed him. She would know, had he the spirit to carry through the journey to the northland. Sorely he suffered but he turned not back.

In the morning all was quiet, and Ane-kur-manmo put into his hand a nutshell of flour and a nutshell of beer, saying: "If you pray to the gods, from these nutshells you will get savoury food beyond man's imagining." Then she gave him for the foal a saddle-cloth, a mat of woven grass.

Last she brought a pearl-white she-fox and thus she warned Kesar:

"If the little fox glide slowly slowly forward,
Steal you, horse and man, slowly slowly after.

If the little fox fly swiftly swiftly forward,
Haste you, horse and king, swiftly swiftly after.

If the little fox by zigzag winding make its track,
Do you, horse and king, do likewise after.

If the little fox lie down to slumber,
Sleep you, horse and king, too, tranquil.

If the little fox from sleep spring sudden,
Up, you, horse and king, and speed you."

Now travelled they, horse and king, the little white fox preceding, over a plain, up over a mountain's back, through a river. At sunset in a desolate empty place they made halt.

Now was Kesar an-hungered, and his thoughts were of food only. But food there was none, save in that wee nutshell. "Of what use is so little?" sighed Kesar. "There's not so much as a bite and a gulp there."

But the foal set to eating the grass mat, his saddle-cloth. The whole night long, "churum, churum" went he. And when the king lifted his head in the early light of the morning, lo! the foal was content, and much heavy dung lay about him, yet the grass mat was as if unnibbled. Then said Kesar, reflecting: "Who knows? What might happen if I ate?" So he ate and drank from the nutshells, and sweet of taste he found the food, and the drink was like buttermeal, sugar and syrup. The more he ate, the more was created.

"This is my good goddess," he thought, and took courage.

Now over nine passes they travelled, and through nine valleys and over nine high plains. On three passes stood three altars, one red, one white, one blue. At the red did Kesar make offering, saying:—

> "On a red pass stands a red altar.
> A red altar has been built there.
> Let me offer a red cloth there.
> For the sake of Gling-land's altars
> Grant me my heart's desires.
> Hold me in mind, ye god-kings."

On the blue altar he placed a blue banner and on the white, a white one, and a prayer like to this prayer at each he offered.

Then over a black valley they travelled and over a black plain. On a black pass stood a great black altar. "The demon-king's altar is this one," thought Kesar, and he overturned it. Its stones he cast into the river. The dust he gave to the winds. Not a trace left he.

Near by, the demon-king's goat-herd tended the demon-king's goats in the valleys on this side and on that. Kesar asked the herd for news of his master. The herd said rudely: "Who art thou? What art thou?" And the truth he spoke not.

Then Kesar seized the man by the throat and smote him three times on the cheek. "O gracious King," cried the goat-herd. "I knew not that thou wert Kesar, god-king of Glingland. I pray thee give me release in this life and in my next birth. I will tell thee all thou wouldst know of the fiend Kurulugu. Now he is afar, gone westward. The Dzemo, his lady, sits at home in a cage of iron. If you go to the castle you will see, in the gates to the north and the south and the east and the westward, giants sitting on horses and elephants, with swords in their hands. But fear them not. They are dead, without power."

Thus he told him and Kesar went forward, but none the less fear went with him. As he rode he shot arrows to cheer him. And he watched how the dust rose where the arrows bit the earth.

Doesn't that last remind you of Cuchulain tossing his ball and dart ahead of him as he went? Only Cuchulain was never afraid. I like Kesar better because he needed cheering sometimes. Ladakhis aren't much ashamed of being afraid.

The old story is older than the Buddhist religion here, but I suppose some good Buddhist put in that bit about the "next birth." This folk-tale is a living thing. It could put out a new shoot at any time,—this week perhaps, if the Kalon or some other big man (like Iba's friend the Lhasa trader, who gave me the velvet slippers) should have a party and invite people to hear the minstrels.   The minstrels might be inspired to add a new bit, and it might so take the people's fancy that they'd demand it every time.   Iba says, by the way, that he will get the minstrels for our men sometime, and let us come and hear.

Those altars we see on every pass.   We took my litter out the other day to start the new crew practising for the summer's safar, up to the little saddle behind our camp.   There was a cairn there with a pair of shapu horns, and some crooked sticks and faded red cloth strips.   And the men all shouted strange words, that thrilled me to hear.   Francke Padre Sahib says the words are "Lhala sollo lhala mchoddo" meaning "given to the gods, offered to the gods."

Lady Ba   TSAM SKANG
                                                 March 5

ALICE dear,

I send you a copper bowl which Rasul and his wife let me take from their kitchen shelves.   A dim room with one wee window, that kitchen, and smoked beams like polished ebony. In its darkness the jewelled women of the household tend dung fires in a big clay stove all shiny black, watch over the pot of rice, stir stews with great brass ladles, churn butter tea, spin or gossip, or sleep on piles of felts in corners.   And the children and their cats race about, in and out, to and from the street, the roof, the room of state upstairs.

This is the way Rasul used to feel about the kitchen, tell Littlejohn.

> The kitchen beams are shiny black.
> The smoke goes up, but comes curling back.
> It likes the kitchen, the friendly smoke.
> I like it too, with all the folk,
> The cozy warmth, the fire that glows,
> The copper plates and pots in rows,
> The tea that bubbles and boils and sings,
> My sattu cup and all our things.
> No wonder the smoke is loth to go
> Out to the cold and lonely snow.
>   LADY BA

Gypsy Davy   Tsam Skang
                                            March 10

Dear Marion,

Was it tales of ghosts and tappings on the window-pane
in the dark? Terrifying things, surely, but not half so dreadful
as what befell us on a day.

About noon you might have seen us climbing the bleak
snowy slopes back of Leh, on ponyback: the Aqsaqal in camel's
hair, Lady Ba in pale blue, the Bara Sahib in dark blue, the
Chhota Sahib in stripes of blue and tan, pigtailed fellows at
our horses' heads, the jauntiest of them all at mine, a Lhasa-
wala. Lady Ba is envious of every stitch of his clothing, and
all his ornaments, ivory, turquoise and coral, and the long red
tassel at his pigtail's end.

The trail wound up and up among big white chortens like
giant flower-pots on six-stepped pedestals with bare stone
stalks in them, all flowering at the top. The Chhota Sahib
found little figures in niches in the sides of them, made of the
dust of dead men's bones.

After a while the Raja's castle loomed ahead. The parapets
of the castle and the temple roofs about it were all crimson
with people in their best. We rode into a great crowd in a
wide place before the castle. A lama led us through a temple
gateway down among some strange masked people, and then
up a ladder, through a hatchway and we came out upon
a loggia. There was a big courtyard down below us,
where a gay company sat and stood, banked ten deep about
high walls. The tops of the walls were crowded, and the
little roofs adjoining. So was the bare crag above the courtyard, wherever the slopes were gentle enough to sit on without sliding, and there were boys on steeper slopes, clinging to
narrow ledges. Above the boys perched ravens. And for
crown on its head the great rock wore a ruined castle.

There was glitter of silver and gold in the sunlight. Big
turquoise-studded cobras on the women's heads said to the
sky: "What is your blue to ours?" And coral about their necks
said: "You cannot vie with us till sunset." There were pearls
too, and there was ivory and their robes were a dark wine-red.
There were women from distant villages with unkempt hair
hanging in dull matted cords like oakum. There were nomad
women with shiny hair well kempt, and silver bars across
their foreheads, and silver pendants hanging nearly to their
eyebrows.

I suppose you must be saying by now: "But, Gypsy Davy,

this isn't dreadful!" No, it isn't, but if I hadn't told you this, you might have thought the dreadful thing befell a Cleveland crowd. You must have one picture more to quite prepare you. The crowd right under our loggia parted. Everybody looked that way. Out came marching a band of lamas, in long wine-red robes, and crimson headgear, tall crested caps like Roman soldiers', and double pointed ones like bishops' mitres. The first two carried thin drums, held high by handles, and beat them with curved irons. The next two carried jewelled oboes. The next two long trumpets, so long that little boy lamas had to hold the ends up. The next two, tall jugs of beer. They marched slowly round a tall prayer flag, long narrow strip of cloth nailed lengthwise of a mast, and sat down near the throne of the Skusho.

And then the dreadful thing befell. A dozen demons burst whirling into the court yard. Not slender and sprightly and clothed in scarlet tights like our devil, but tall clumsy giants, big with flying silken robes in the five Buddhist colours, embroidered and brocaded. Little aprons at their waists, worked with death's heads, flapped as they whirled. Their necklaces were strings of dead men's teeth. Rings of little grinning skulls crowned their heads; huge ugly heads bobbing and whirling. Horrible faces of men and animals, green, red, blue, grinned at us, lowered at us, fixed grins, fixed frowns that never changed. And out of each head three great eyes stared, one where the Cyclops' was.

They danced fiercely, stamping and whirling, and brandishing sabre and cutlass. The crowd shrank back from sabre points. I was sure I saw an eye on one, but perhaps I dreamed it. We might, any of us, have dreamed worse things than that, for we were nigh swooning.

And all of a sudden we were dragged back from the gates of hell—if it was the pit actually yawning there. But I have a notion these were really friendly demons, come to fend baleful ones. All of a sudden we were dragged back out of the nightmare. A door opened behind us, and in stepped the postman, a lame bundle of grey rags and a big brass badge, with the English mail, just in, three weeks late, and handed us your letter!

Which reminds me I set out to answer that letter. There were lots of things in it besides ghosts, but I have fetched so wide a circuit that the rest will have to wait.

> Yours,
>
> GYPSY DAVY

Lady Ba

Dear MARION,

On another day those demons danced again, down the bazar this time, and if you had seen them, this is what I think you'd have said.

Yours,

LADY BA

Down the long bazar the demons come:
Loud snoring trumpet, high-handled drum!

Taller than giants they twirl and they prance,
Horribly, terribly, fiendishly dance.

One has a head of a bright, bright blue,
And his eyes they are three instead of just two.
And the one behind him has horns!

The next has wee skulls in a ring 'round his head,
And the devil behind him is blazing red.

Gorgeous their silks with broideries grim.
A tiger-head's coming,—and look! Behind him—!

I'm glad I don't sleep in a four-legged bed.
I should never climb up in the dark for dread
Of those terrible ones with the horns!

Lady Ba   TSAM SKANG

March 11

Dear ROLAND,

Rasul's book has come. The Great Myth has turned out a fact. Leh is awestruck.

He sits in his big room by his "glasses window," using a finger to keep his place, slowly reading. The village climbs the wide lighted staircase ("like on ship," evidence of his travels) enters the room, looks at his picture and facsimile autograph, and listens while he translates a page or two into Ladakhi.

He wrote the publisher: "It was a glading day in my life when got me my book. I have been much busy and happy in reading my book. God will bless you and your sons."

All that month in the Shyok he was thinking about it.

"When will come my book, sir? What colour will be my book? Will be mop in my book, madam? Myself am very hurry for read my book." I showed him in the atlas all the places in the world where copies were to be sent. He was so pleased that I wished I knew someone in Greenland or Patagonia. That night he meditated on his own mortality, as contrasted with the immortality of the book. "Must to die, sir—must to die. If I am King, must to die, and become silt. But will live my book in the world. Many time, sir, I thinking, in writing, must to be true my book."

I had supposed I was doing all the editing ("Madam, what is Editor?") but I find that he was not so undiscriminating as I supposed. More than one delectable tale he tells us he omitted from the book as "asham' matter, good for telling, not good for book." I remember, too, in cutting, I was always finding that I had cut out something essential, and having to reinstate it. His sense of structure is conscious. When one of his stories appeared so rambling that the Sahib grew restless, he said: "Sir, you stay. After, come very sweet this story. But in story coming many branch."

When my Hindustani dictionary arrived after we got to Leh, he saw it and said eagerly: "Is my book, madam?" You remember the size of Forbes? Well, I suppose his manuscript would have run to more than that in bulk without the intervention of an editor. I explained steadily that only a little of his story was to be printed. He struggled with the idea, but couldn't quite take it in. It only made him suspicious. He would start: "That man, Khalik Hussein, who was cook for Himbro Sahib,—" breaking off, watching my unresponsive face "is in my book, madam." A pause. "Is in my book, madam?" Insistently: "Is in my book, madam. Must to be in my book." He approves the title: "I thinking, madam, is right, my book and title. I was 'Servant of Sahibs.' Is right matter."

I got him to tell me how he wrote the book. It seems that for two years, out of the fifteen he was at it off and on, it was his sole occupation. Every day when he rose, he said his prayers, took a little food, and then spent the whole morning in his big quiet room, writing. He never went out to the bazar, and no one came in. His good daughter Daulat protected his privacy. He writes very, very carefully, forming each letter with pains, leaving neat margins and wide spaces between lines, slowly as a child in dame-school. He says he was writing English so constantly at that time that he thought and dreamed in it, "into my style, my breaking English, my crooked spoon English!"

The post in the Commissioner's office spoiled that, but much of the story was safely down by that time. In the office the babus were glib with phrases like "your favour of the 12th ult." One of them, "that pandit who was my enemy," made a mock of Rasul's English. "I say: 'Yes, is very bad, my English. Why you keeping in your files my letters? Throw away my English!'" Of course his experience, his acquaintance with people in all the surrounding country, his resource, made him invaluable as Aqsaqal.

He keeps repeating to me stories which I know by heart. He can hardly believe that I know them as well as he does. I try to get him on new ground. I want more, much more. Sahib got him started on De Filippi's campaign. He is in very good form on that. You can see De Filippi in some crisis over the coolies. "Sahib moved his both hands, made like a dance. Then I did say: 'Sir, you don't fall into sorrow. Is my work'." And you can feel the load, that one load, dropping off the Chief's shoulders, on to Rasul's. "Not came any matter in my head, what shall I do. At night thinking plenty."

It's an amazing story, the getting of all those loads up on to the Depsang, coaxing coolies to do double and twice double work, settling quarrels, discovering resources—such as hiring the coolies to make themselves footgear from the hides of dead horses and camels up there on the high plain, incidentally interpreting for eleven sahibs. De Filippi took him aside sometimes and made him rest.

You must read it some time. He sends an instalment up to me occasionally, but he is not well this winter, and writes rarely.

He has written a letter to Sir Francis thanking him for his foreword: "Now with your name must come my name far way in world. Where head go, tail must follow."

He sends you his salams. The beautiful bracelet you sent his wife, her successor wears as an ear-ring!

Later.

A note just arrived from R. In it he says: "Sir, on pag 198 of my book you will find ——" Is this on the head of

The Editor?

Gypsy Davy   Tsam Skang
                                                   March 13

Dear Dave,

   Did I say the wolves ran, howling?
   It was the howl that ran!
   I listened very attentively this morning about 4.30.   That
howl ran faster than any wolf ever ran; down the spur, across
the saddle, well up toward the tent,—then off across the valley,
clear to the further side.
   A bucket-line of wolves, sitting properly on their haunches,
with muzzles pointed at the low moon?

                                                   Gypsy Davy

Lady Ba   Tsam Skang
                                                   March 13

Dear Carlisle,

   That was a good letter you wrote us.   It made everything
of your world seem quick and real again.   I'd been rather
doubting—or perhaps I had almost forgotten the existence
of any other world than this.
   Shut in here by snow on the passes in all directions we've
been living in the sunny present, or remembering the months
just past.   Today I've been recalling, in all its detail, a visit
to a monastery at Deskit in the Shyok.   I wonder if I could
make it live for you,—with only leaping sympathy of
imagination on your part, to help me?   Don't try to read it down
town, but some quiet Sunday afternoon looking out over those
wooded hills of yours, where our caravan would not seem such
an utter anomaly.
   We were making camp only halfway to the sky that day,
because the site of sites was occupied by a monastery.   We had
hardly got settled when three red-robed lamas came down to
our camp to greet us.   They put loose-woven silk scarves
around our necks and invited us to come up to their abode.
I was a little sad.   I'd been riding a long time and was ready
for rest.   But it was the only courteous thing to do, so I got me
once more on Tomar's thickly-padded back and suffered myself
to be guided up and up and up—the lamas always choose
sites like those we love for our camps.

We wound up nearer and nearer the buildings piled one above the other among the crags, high walls leaning inward, many loggias. We rode in through the outer gate, the horses' hoofs clattering on the stones of the courtyard. A little group of lamas and women and children gathered to look.

At the inner gate I must dismount. Leaving Tomar with a sais, we climbed an enclosed cobblestone stairway with treads so narrow there was room only for our toes, and so steep my breath was scarcely adequate. Out upon a roof. Below us, parapets set with poles from which great yak-tails waved, and prayer-banners streamed out on the breeze. On our roof a row of wooden barrels filled with printed prayers, to be set in motion, effective motion, by a touch in passing. Everywhere monks twirling little prayer cylinders as they watched us. The whole object of the establishment is the repetition of that prayer, "Om Mani Padme Hung!" over and over and over, millions and millions and millions of times. The monks own lands, they sell seed, they serve the folk by burning holes in their scalps when they are ill, by carrying the sacred books on their heads around the fields to bless the harvest, by exorcising or propitiating devils, by making predictions from horoscopes, by bestowing names on the newly-born, and guiding the souls of the newly-dead into the proper paths. But the real reason of their existence is the murmuring, the chanting, the fluttering, the whirling, of the "Om Mani Padme Hung!" The traditional interpretation is: "O Thou Jewel Flower of the Lotus, Hung!" the "Hung" having no more meaning than the "O," but Rasul says he has never found a lama who knew the meaning of the words. All the more effective, I should say, if one didn't know!

At the top of another flight of stairs they gave us seats on a dais before three low tables and administered tea in pretty cups with silver standards, and pointed silver covers. There was a copy of Kim's lama's Wheel of Life on the wall. Rasul explained it. He is a Mussulman, but many of his friends are Buddhists and he knows a lot about their "tamashas" and their pictures.

After tea they unlocked the huge door of an inner room— an amazing place. They wouldn't let a woman come very far in, but I saw a plenty: colossal bright blue devils, with many heads and many hands, and horrible expressions: and lurking behind the door a big hobby-goat painted in bright colours.

When Gypsy Davy and Roger had been shown the mysteries,

they led us to the door of the great central room, where the monks were assembling for service. It was a shadowy cavernous place, hung with banners and silken Chinese paintings. In the dimness, far back, a huge golden Buddha loomed. Near him sat the head lama, yellow-robed. Red-clad men slipped past us and sat down cross-legged on cushions, in a long double row lengthwise of the room. Then the space filled with a great humming, and droning, swelling slowly, falling, rising. Sweet-toned bells mingled with it; then the high sweet pipes. At crises the long trumpets brayed their one sustained note, and from the lifted cymbals "the East leaped out, snarling," while once, only once, a tall priest, standing, raised a curved iron rod and smote a huge suspended drum, that it thundered. All the while the chanting.

Stupid faces, vicious faces, coarse faces, here and there a kindly or intelligent face. My mind struggled to remember how the wise and gentle Gautama, who hated idols and emptiness of ceremonial, spent his life in protest against the very sort of thing that has grown up about his name. I tried to think of these men as devil-worshippers. But that music, that grave chanting, those marvellous bells and pipes, those clashing cymbals and that once-heard Olympian drum! I forgot the wide blue sky outside, and the sweet clean air. I felt that I could bow my head forever to that mystic chanting. Om Mani Padme Hung!

Next morning before the dawn, as we lay watching the stars, there came far and faint and very sweet, the sound of the pipes. High on the roof against the paling sky we made out long-robed figures with slender flaring oboes.

I've heard them often since, those pipes above the snoring trumpets, the clashing cymbals, and the throbbing drums, and I know, that wherever I may be, as long as I live, there will be a little ache in my heart of longing to hear them again, "faint and far and very far, faint and very sweet." They are playing now,—now, as I write, and they'll be playing as you read. Always somewhere, among these stupendous mountain ranges, high upon crags, hidden in shadowy rooms, or clear upon roofs, long-robed men drumming, chanting, piping,— Om Mani Padme Hung!

Your sister,

Gypsy Davy   TSAM SKANG

Wood Mouse Year, Spring Time

Dear NORMAN,

Lady Ba and I were at dinner last night, not sitting on chairs at a mahogany table, but sensibly, on the floor of our tent in the open door-way, Lady Ba on her Lhasa saddle-rug on her side the tent, I on mine, on my side. The little stove roared in the stone pit between us. Two candles burning in big tin lanterns dimmed the stars a bit. I couldn't find the Bull for a long time, and when I did find him, there was the young moon sitting on his nose and shedding such a bright light about her that the Bull's head was all but invisible.

I was carving a shoulder of lamb. (A shoulder of lamb here is about as big as a shoulder of rabbit in Kent.) There was a big pile of chapatis behind me, on a cloth. I heard a rustling there, and I looked, and lo and behold! one of the chapatis was running off into the dark as fast as its legs could carry it. I grabbed it, and it stopped trying to get away.

Then I went on carving that shoulder. The slices were each about big enough to cover one back tooth. I heard a little clatter in front of me. I looked, and there was a mouse, sitting on the edge of my empty soup-bowl. I asked him sharply what he was doing there, and he jumped straight up into the air eight inches. I thought he would land in the bowl, but he didn't. He landed outside, and made off into the woodpile.

Yours,

LONG-BEARD

P.S.—This is a Buddhist crag. There's the ruin of a hermitage on it, a bas-relief of Buddha on a rock, Buddhist prayer flags, ruins of temporary graves in which Buddhists have waited while the evil spirits that killed them were going out of them, furnaces for burning the bodies of Buddhists who have parted with their spirits, bones of dead Buddhists lying about. But I verily believe that's a Mussulman mouse! This is the month of Ramzan and he's taking all his meals after sunset.

Lady Ba   TSAM SKANG
                                             March 20
Dear CLARA,

We went down to Leh yesterday.   It's only a mile or two
away, but we never go down unless we must.   We've barely
seen the great bazar.   I visit my dear Mrs. Kunick occasionally
at the Mission compound just outside the city.   I climb down
the foot-path, with I-she to carry my coats, and when I am ready
to come back, I find Tomar waiting, all saddled, or eight
cheerful pigtails with the litter.   They take me up the winding
pony trail, with the moon or stars rising over the mountains,
up and up and up to the cragtop and the tent and Gypsy Davy,
and happy though the afternoon has been, I'm always so glad
to be back that I don't lightly start down again.

But this day we had promised Rasul that we would come
and see some of his "young time" haunts.   He met us, looking
very nice in his small fur-trimmed cap and neat long dress with
folds of soft white at the sleeve-ends, by the tall leafless poplars
of the Residency compound, black and creaking with crows
and choughs and ravens.   He showed us the terrace where
he was playing when his brother came after him, the time the
tailor-man's roof fell in.   Then he led us through the twisty
streets, past the serai, through a little bazar, under the great
old tree the Buddhists hold sacred, across the running ditch,
to the little house in the alley where he used to live.   A crowd
was following us curiously, as always, but he seemed quite
oblivious.   He was thinking, I am sure, of nothing but that
long-ago day.   He pointed out the roofless part of the house.
No one has dared rebuild that roof.   In the wall we could see
"my happy hole."   There was the tiny door, in the latch of
which he found the jadu, and the tinier window beside it from
which his mother scolded him.   Mrs. Heber says his mother
was known as "a woman strong in wrath."   I could imagine an
angry face in the Mussulman white head-dress with a turquoise
brooch in the centre (I've seen the brooch), quite filling that
window and overawing the naughty small boy in the street
outside.   The kindly neighbour, who took him in, lived in
a large balconied house, overshadowing the little one.   I've
seen the woman who made the jadu, a sparkling, birdlike little
old creature, with at least four rows of seed pearls in the big
hoops in her ears.

He read the story aloud to us afterward in his big room,

following the lines with a finger, pronouncing carefully and laughing gleefully at the funny bits.

THE WIFE OF THE POOR SAHIB

HOW WE LOST OUR BREAD AND FOUND JADU.

"One time I saw a boy play with a banjo, that had made himself, with own hand. His father was banjo-man in Leh.

"That banjo look me very wonderful one thing for my play. But he not could give me. That was a spoon of wood, which the Ladakhi people use for cook.

"When I came home, I did find one old spoon which we had, and I did make me a banjo, with own hand. But was little hard work: could not ready it in that day. I did keep it into hole where I keep all my playthings all the time.

"The following day I went to the meat-seller place, and bought a little piece of stomach of goat, and some horsehair of tail. I did find that all thing. And I was very busy near the happy hole, in the work of my banjo.

"That day was nearly done, but could not get dry the skin. In that time, Mother came from the winnowing-place to home. Mother called to me. I put the banjo quickly into the hole; came to Mother. She bade me mix the wheat flour for chapatis. When I done the flour, I gave to Mother. She did cook the bread. That time I could not cook the bread. Mother herself did; and then bade me other work which were in house, which I can do. All that I did, but my feel was to that hole, where was my banjo. And said myself: 'When Mother goes out room, I will do my own good work.'

"When Mother done her bread, then said me: 'Take care, Rasul, don't let the goats eat the bread.' Then Mother went out room. I found time for own work, and thought that: 'It it a long time now, would not come goats from hill. Until, do my own work. After, then will take the bread, and will shut the door of room.' In this thinking, went to that hole where was the nice banjo, and made it. In this business I did forget the bread and door and goats.

"One time I heard the noise of goats from our room. I did came down into room. There were all our goats. They had reached, while before, and had gone the bread, all. These our goats were robber, like our grandfather. I found very bad luck for me. Now what shall I do? Anyway, I beat to those goat with a big stick, and myself said: 'What do?'

"And those day were Ramzan, the Mohammedans' one month we not eat anything daytime. We eat evening and middle-night. Those bread were for evening, and for half-night. Mother and I were both very hungry. Why? We had not eat anything in daytime, and it was nearly evening for the dinner. Mother must surely beat me today. That time came in head a lie-matter. Must need tell her that the door was shut and that goats opened it they-selves.

"While after, Mother came in room, and she not knew what fault I had done. When Mother get in room, I went nearly the door, and said to Mother that lie-matter. Mother not believe for my lie. She got very angry, came toward me for beat me. I ran away out the house. Mother could not catch to me.

"Then I wait an hour in bazar, and said myself: 'What do?' One thing, that time was very hungry, and where sleep? Now must need go back at home. Maybe Mother forget that angry, I will find good luck. I did come home. When I reached the door, that was shut inside. Then I beat the door. Mother came on the window, and said with very angry: 'You don't come my home. Where you like, there go. I don't want you any more. I am a poor woman in this country. Got little to earn living. With that brought up you children. You don't thinking I am poor. You play like a rich man's son. Today you did this fault. Next time, when you would be older, you must rob. Then will take me the court-place. That time what do the poor woman?' And said many matter. I could not remember that all.

"When Mother said all that matter, my feel got very sorry. Myself said: 'Why I did make the banjo? If not did, was not so much bad luck.' And I said many times to Mother: 'Please, Mother, you forget this my fault, and let me come in, and don't beat me today. I shall not do like this fault, never. If you see any my fault, future, then you must need beat me very hard. Let me come in, and give something for eat.'

"Mother said: 'I don't open the door. If you find food and clothes, where you like, go there. Your brothers went, I could not catch to them. You do same them.' I said: 'I never do like them. I am like your servant. What you like, that you do to me. If you want sell my body, you sell me, for your expense. You are my mother.'

"Mother did not give any answer. The window shut, went to bed. I left out the door. I did sleep by the our door on ground, in the hoping maybe I will get in, at half-night, when Mother take food. That time was feel very sleepy and hungry, but were many play in my head: with that, feel was happy. Sleep a little, but not much sleep in the sorry.

M

"One time I try open the door: could not open it. But I got one thing from a hole up side our door. That was a pieces cloth, one inches wide and long, like a bag. In that was a piece paper. I looked it in the moonshine. There on was wrote some thing. I do not know what it is, but it was nice one thing for play. I tied it in my belt, and sleep again.

"In the sleep I heard the calling for eating-time. Then got up all Mohammedi people for eating. My mother got up, too, but not take me in. But there was near our home good one woman. She was a very good friend with my mother. She and her husband came their door and said me: 'Rasul, come here, take food, and you sleep here. You is good boy and hard-working boy. Your mother does not see that all. She sees the little fault, which to-day you done. Come in.' I did went to their home, and they gave me bread, meat and tea. I got happy, and they ask some question: 'How the goat eat the bread?' I told all the banjo matter: what I did, that all. They laughed very plenty. After, I did show that thing, which I found, which was in my belt. When they see it, they said: 'It is jadu. It was made one woman for bad luck to your mother. You are lucky boy, for this you found it.' That time they called to my mother. Mother came there; see it, said: 'Lucky boy.' Mother forgot that my fault at all. And said: 'I want read what is wrote on it.' That thing were very bad one thing, but for me it came very lucky thing. With that mother let go me. She did not beat to me.

"In the morning mother went to a mullah to learn what was on the jadu. The writing was Arabic. Mullah said: 'If was left at your door this thing, then will the husband of your daughter not like your daughter any more. You must wash it in milk, and throw in river.'

"Afterwards my mother went many times and fought with that woman, who had done the bad thing. They not fight with hand, but with mouth; said many bad matter, both my mother and that woman too.

"Myself got good luck; made the banjo well, and got the skin dry. The good woman friend of my mother said to Mother: 'Don't tell anything. You look what he has done.' My mother said to me: 'Let show us.' I did show Mother the banjo. Then Mother laughed very plenty, and it showed to many people and said: 'That lose bread, but found the bad-woman thing.' All people laugh who seen my banjo.

"After several days I found a next play, forget that one."

Lady Ba   TSAM SKANG

March 28

Dear DAVE,

Roger is on his way to Bombay to meet Jim and Stuart. He had to start from here just about the time they left New York. That gave him a week's margin, in case of bad weather. (When he went down to Srinagar last autumn to get our winter supplies, he was snowed in on this side of the Zoji for five days.) The pass isn't officially open till June, but the traders use it constantly, and Chot is as competent a mountaineer certainly as any portly Hindu merchant. The heaviest of them all recently had himself carried over the Pass on coolies' backs.

The Sahib talked with Roger, or rather telegraphed to him and got instant answers the day after he crossed the La. Roger came into the office at Sonamarg at the very minute the Sahib was in the office at Leh. It was rather exciting. One doesn't think in terms of long distance telephones here.

Now today has come the first letter. I'm copying it for you. Chot has some ripe old Viking blood in him, you know, and though we tried to hedge him about with prohibitions and cautions, he got an adventure. You can't hedge a fellow in who tries to catch wolves in his hands. (That was an earlier adventure.) Perhaps it's just as well his mother should not see this letter—or Jim's or Stuart's.

Yours,

LADY BA

Chhota Sahib   BALTAL

March 12

Dear SAHIB AND MEM-SAHIB,

The Zoji La is passed. I can't go, or send a man ahead, to Sonamarg with a telegram, because of the deep snow, snowstorm and avalanches, so I am writing you, hoping that if I concentrate hard enough one of you will get a feeling that everything is all right.

By working twelve, fourteen and twenty hour days, we reached Kargil in four days. Band-o-basted for a day, reached Dras in three more, waited a day for the coolies to get ready, got to Mechoi in two more, and reached Baltal today.

From Kargil to Baltal the new snow was anywhere from our knees to our hips, except near villages and where avalanches had swept it off.

The men wouldn't do the La at night because of the wind. My head man, the "twenty-year veteran," who is the dak overseer of this district, says they very seldom do it at night.

My coolies, and the overseer with his dak coolies, wouldn't start until eight, but I got impatient, and went on at seven.

The day was like most of the others since Kargil, cloudy and threatening. The night had been fairly clear. I kept the trail fairly easily, and waited for the others after a dak and a half.

The clouds came low like a thick fog, and it began to snow a little. The overseer said a little snow didn't matter, and the coolies said nothing, so we went on.

At the top of the La, it began to snow harder.

We met thirty dak coolies here, coming up with a month's mail. They had been waiting because they were afraid. So the overseer began giving their leader a beating with his stick. I was so engrossed in seeing such an amount of mail accumulated that I didn't pay much attention to the beating.

Soon we started on again, and it began to snow harder. We crossed some old avalanche snow, under which are the two dak coolies killed this winter. (My youngest coolie was a brother of one of these men.) A little farther on they showed me where seven Kashmiris were killed last winter.

We hurried, then stopped while a little avalanche came down from far above, a short distance ahead. It was now snowing in earnest, and we could see only a few hundred feet.

The men began plunging in snow up to their hips. I found a harder place where I sat down and slid several hundred feet.

Yonton looked unhappy, but I, to my surprise, felt a strange exhilaration most of the time. I must say that when I looked up and saw one wide avalanche track after another, with hardly a breathing space between, my heart climbed a bit.

We finally reached an open space at the bottom, where I waited for four of my coolies who were several hundred yards behind. One of them had been covered to the hips by the spent part of an avalanche, and the others had pulled him out. When I showed astonishment he said: "Kya karega?" They all thanked me a lot at Baltal when I gave them a maund of wood, and some tea and tobacco.

While waiting two minutes I had heard seven avalanches in

Roger in charge, an old hand now, having crossed the Zoji five times, and Jim and Stuart, new to it all, with who knows what adventures, behind and before them!

Yours,

ذق

Gypsy Davy   TSAM SKANG

May 1

Dear ADELA,

The Parian marble mountains I wrote you of were lovely in their season, loveliest in the light and shadow of the rising or the setting moon.   But I welcome back the warm brown tints of the naked rock.   I love them best.

What an immense block old Nature found here, ready to that sculptress' hand of hers! How many many thousand years has she plied her chisel and her hammer! How the chips have flown, and still fly! Here and there great piles of them, forever sliding down, down, to the bottoms of the valleys, half bury the vast forms she chisels out.   Her sculptures seem to rise from ruins much vaster than they.

But it needs only her great ice tool, set with hard cutting points and continually washed with fine quartz flour, to sweep their bases clear of ruin, and carve and polish them as she would have it done.

The mightiest of her works, though, is but a short-lived thing, starting to crumble ere she's done with it.   Tomorrow these Himalayas will have crumbled down to a tame lowland.   Now God walks alone among austere peaks under the stars.   Presently the rabble will swarm in fetid lowland air, unconscious of any star. .

BA

Lady Ba   TSAM SKANG

May 3

Dear JULIET,

Our men are in deep gloom today.

A man in one of the villages is keen to go with us on our summer safar.   All the men want him.   They say he is excellent company and a fine singer.   Iba wants him.   He says he is a good worker and a carpenter,—and Iba has to discover a carpenter in every village to carry out some of the sahib's inventions.

But he can't go.

His wife won't let him.

She says both her other husbands are away, and she can't give leave to this one.

There's nothing to do about it.

Yours,

Gypsy Davy   TSAM SKANG
May 10

Dear NORMAN,

We have your letter with your drawing of the locomotive. It came last night. We haven't seen a locomotive for so long we had forgotten what they look like. I think the yak's the nearest thing we have to one up here, but he doesn't look very much like one, and he doesn't pull anything but a very little plough.

We have been watching a sandy strip of desert three or four miles off, down toward the Indus, all day, for the three young sahibs. Iba went to meet them yesterday, with fresh horses, and an escort of men in new gowns and red caps with gold embroidery in front like the rim of the rising sun, and red girdles and red charoq. He should have met them last night.

The boys will find the irises out, and apricot blossoms and a tiny yellow flower, and the pussy-willows, and some of the leaves on the willows. Lady Ba saw a soft silky little donkey today, all grey, not much bigger than your cat,—just out! They'll find our dog looking pretty ragged. He's shedding his hair.

Ramzan is over, but Abdullah still obdurately refuses to break his fast before dark. Maybe he didn't see the new moon on the eve of the Id. I don't see how he could know what time to come out and look for it, living down there in the dark crevices among the rocks in our platform.

Abdullah's table manners are still bad. He grabs a chapati from the pile when my back is turned, and hurries off with it to a dark narrow space there is between two iron boxes behind me. He backs into this space and tries to pull the chapati in after him, but of course it won't come, so he sits there and nibbles it. Just his nose is in the light. All the rest of him is in the dark. He nibbles such a lot that I'm sure he can't eat it all. I think he takes what-he-can't-eat home with him.

That is really very good manners in Ladakh, but we haven't got used to it, yet. If we had learned Ladakhi manners before we went to see you, we should certainly have taken some of those little buns home with us,—all we could stuff into our pockets. My! wouldn't we like some of that salad of yours that you were growing on the front doorstep!

My love to you, and Lady Ba's.

GYPSY DAVY

P.S.—Here they are at last, safe and sound.

Jim Sahib   TSAM SKANG
                                                May 13

DEAREST MOTHER,

Here we are in Leh at last.

Ibrahim, our picturesque caravan bashi, whose face is made up of myriads of wrinkles from smiling so much, grew somewhat stubborn and insisted that we take to our horses, after we had walked all but this last march from Srinagar. He also pointed out gently but firmly that it wasn't proper for us to enter Leh in old khaki trousers and disreputable chapli. Riding pants and high Cutter boots were the order of the day.

The main bazar at Leh, unlike most bazars, is very wide. It was full of all sorts of people, unkempt visitors from Changthang, Hindu merchants squatting in front of their shops, and the smiling rosy-cheeked women of Ladakh with their striking turquoise head-dresses and heavy purple gowns. As we rode along, people greeted Roger from all sides. He is a great favourite with them.

The top of Tsam Skang is gay with green tents: the Ri Sahib's on a stone platform on the very top, Chot's on a saddle lower down, mine and Stu's on platforms lower still, the smoky cook-tent and the blacksmith's below us, and below them the guest-tent at the head of the trail. Our big brown blankets, hanging to air every morning on yak-hair ropes stretched between poles, must make the crag look as though it were flying extra large prayer-flags.

It's a busy place, unpacking all the stuff we brought, and packing and balancing for the spring safar. We're going into the nomad country, where the wild asses are. I may bring home a mate for Chicken Little.

The men are delightful, so simple and genuine after those slippery gentlemen of India and Kashmir. When we rode past the serai, Iba blew on his little hunting horn that Chot had brought him, and they all came tumbling out in their new clothes and red hats, with the Three-Corner Round on their sleeves. Stu and I each have one to help us in our packing and balancing. I don't know much more than "here" and "good" and "come" and "get out," but it's surprising how much you can make them understand with a few well-chosen gestures. To get a man to come you must motion him away with your fingers crooked down. If you crook them up and beckon, he just stares at you or goes in the opposite direction.

Early this morning before dawn as the tattered masses of mist were climbing our hill, the lamas began blowing their huge horns and clear sweet pipes. You have no idea how beautiful it was.

Yours affectionately,

JIM

Chhota Sahib   TSAM SKANG

May 20

Dearest FATHER,

The caravan has gone and I am taking my last look, for a long time. The hill is devoid of tents, their platforms bare, with "dead" stones on them. A smelly fire is burning on the kitchen platform, finishing off unsightly rubbish. Two little girls are gathering wood chips into their skirts as nimbly as goats nibbling grass. It is a beautiful morning. The sun coming through a thin haze gives a softer light. A raven is pulling at his soft-sounding bottle. Lazy Hamra is panting on a rock. Two brilliant magpies are noisily giving the cleaners advice.

I want to take a long last look, for perhaps ten or twenty years from now when I come again, the people won't be this same care-free singing people and I may not be the same.

In the valley the terraces falling gently away toward the Indus are as entrancing as ever: green, grey-green, brown and grey-brown, grain well up, grain just appearing, fields newly ploughed and fields yet untouched after the winter. A disorderly string of stones marks the little Jhangspa creek as it comes down just changed from the ice and snow of the white mountains about the Khardung. Jhangspa village, the Kalon's big old white-washed red-trimmed house, with the others descending from it, seems to fit into a half stockade of bare grey poplars. A little garden around the stone mill is full of green willows. Just to the north is an immense chorten with its symbolical steps, wedging into more grey poplars.

I can see Leh, grey and white, peering through more naked trees. The Raja's castle above it looks small and deserted. Black dzo are grazing in a swampy field below the castle. Villages, fields and rocks stretch up the closing valley and down the opening bay to the braiding Indus, a dark green strip, between dark brown mountains. . . . . .

With love,

Your ROGER

PART III

SUMMER AND AUTUMN ON THE TRAIL AGAIN

SUMMER AND AUTUMN ON THE TRAIL AGAIN

Gypsy Davy   CAMP 66
                                    CHIMRE

May 25

Dear ROLAND,

We struck our tents on Tsam Skang some days since. Left all the platforms empty, save for the big rocks that pinned the tents down. We've never found soil enough in any of our high camps to drive a pin in. For all the use we've made of our duralumin pins we might have left them in the tent loft. They're wonderful pins, though, for all that, and such fortunate Ladakhis as have seen them know them to be solid silver.

The caravan is well and gaily appointed for the spring safar, as gay, or, at any rate, as proud a caravan as ever passed down the long bazar en route to the Chang La. Most of the men are Bods this time, young zamindars from distant villages, out for a lark, all bubbling over with good spirits. The rest are Mussulman Arguns for butchering and horseshoeing and the like; as fine young fellows as the Bods and much better horsemen. Most of the Arguns in Leh seem to be professional caravan men, apt to be a bit rough and quarrelsome, like packers and teamsters in other countries, but ours are picked men.

Iba and the Mem-Sahib and I were troubled. Rasul is very ill and has been for some time. The Mem-Sahib and I went down ahead to say good-bye and found him very low in his mind. He has been thinking a good deal about death on and off all winter. He told the Mem-Sahib recently that he had seen in a dream that it was not to be yet, but he seems to be losing faith in the dream.

However, there was nothing troubling the men that day in spite of this and all the head-shaking there had been in Leh about attempting the Chang La at this time. Iba's friends and enemies have all assured him that we can't make it. We've had to put off our departure twice in order to hit on a day propitious for both Bods and Mussulmans.

The safar promises to be one long tamasha for the men. We had a taste of their humour the second day out. There was something of a stir in their camp a long way below us, and presently an odd-looking red stick appeared bobbing along behind a stone wall down there. A big black monkey climbed the wall, and came laboriously up the fan, on all fours, holding his stiff tail high. I think I'll have to quote Jim here:—

"When it got within a couple of hundred feet the Sahib picked up a big stick and pointed it like a gun. As the report sounded, down went the monkey as if dead. Then Roger and I investigated. When we got within a few feet the thing jumped up and we ran for our lives to the shrieks of amusement of the men. Next we sighted a human goat jumping about on the rocks near us. Sahib shot at it also and it promptly died, dramatically. Then a party of singers arrived with one of our donkeys all decked out in gorgeous trappings. Roger got on the poor thing, levelled a stick like a lance and charged the monkey. The donkey stopped about ten feet from the enemy and looked him over suspiciously. The monkey came to life quite suddenly. Aqboz fled braying. A fight between the monkey and the goat ended the show."

We made short marches, pitching our tents high, near the heads of steep fans or on high spurs or cragtops, remote from villages. Always there was a train of men from the last village, armed with wooden shovels and wooden hoes and a rude mattock or two to level the site. Of course, we carry a sapper's kit of our own with shovels and picks and bars. The sapper pony always leads off and has his tools handy for bad stretches on the trail.

I love those feudal crags on the right bank, the little flat-roofed village clustered at the foot, the stately buildings of the gompa climbing to the very top.

It was the morning of the fifth day when we turned up Chimre Nala and began to climb. I think the Chimre people were scandalized by our electing to camp on an impossible spur instead of in their hospitable village. But they forgave us when they saw Iba's tents going up in their midst, and Iba himself presently withdraw his men from the cragtop and come down to them.

Iba seems to be very well known through here, and much respected. He comes into this district almost every year on business of his own. (His wife will do it for him this spring.) He was here when Rasul was getting the De Filippi expedition ready, and Rasul sent a thousand advance pony loads to him.

"Ibrahim was an honest man. And what things, rice, tea, flour, sugar and stores boxes, many wooding boxes, what I sending, all that I wrote to Ibrahim each things name. When the people came back they bring receipt from Ibrahim and we paid them. Then Ibrahim made clean the barley. There was much stones and sand. I said: 'Keep them one side for show Sahib.' Then I said to Dr. Filippi: 'Sir, I made clean all the barley which came from Kargil. Sahib said: 'It made good your cleaning them.' Then I said: 'From the barley get much sand and stones. I have kept all them one side to show you.' When Sahib hear-ed this matter, he get angry and said to me: 'Why you kept them? If I not believe to you, then how shall I make you my agent? You look my work. If you like, the things and money throw in river, does no matter.' I said: 'Yes, sir'." I have treated him in the same way more than once and always found him rise to the challenge. De Filippi wrote him a chit after the journey was over, which any man might treasure.

Ibrahim keeps his accounts most carefully in beautiful Ladakhi script. Once a week Karinda Stuart has a session with him. Ibrahim translates the account, which he has kept day by day, into Urdu, and Stuart makes a classified account in English for us. Rasul and I proved out Iba's honesty years ago. We chose him to get our year's supply of money from Kashgar and bring it to us in silver bars in the mountains back of Keriya. This is the largest expedition he has ever handled. He must feel like a quarter-master-general. I understand that he has something like four tons of grain to get across that pass, besides all our other stuff. He loves to tease the Mem-Sahib by telling her that when I travelled single I needed barely twenty ponies, but now I need a hundred! I notice we have no goats of our own as yet. Evidently Iba has enough on his hands to make the pass without goats. Goats can be bought on the other side, if grain cannot.

Here's Iba with grave news from Leh. Rasul's dream failed him this time. He is dead.

May 29 Camp 68 Tsultak

We passed through Sakti early next morning and found the village full of yak got together for our business. We camped that night and the next at Zingral, "under the pass," as Rasul used to say. Now we're over, bag and baggage. Iba put fifty of his yak across light, the day before we started up, with orders to come back in the night to better break the trail. Jim again:

"Ibrahim decided that it would be necessary to send about fifty yak over and back again to break the trail, so Stu and I thought it would be fun to go also and wait for the rest of the caravan on the other side. We started out walking, but a few hundred yards was enough. We were ready to drop. It is funny how sometimes high altitudes don't affect us at all and other times each step requires great physical exertion. The saddle yaks which Ibrahim had insisted on our having, soon came along and we mounted.

" They pushed on through the snow sometimes up to their stomachs with the slow but sure gait of a ten-ton truck in low gear. You didn't think it was possible for them to get tired. As we ascended I got sleepier and sleepier. The only thing that kept me from falling into deep slumber was the fact that my feet got cold. As we reached the top it started to snow and a cold wind sprang up which luckily was on our backs and not our faces. At the top was a cairn with several tattered prayer flags flapping around. The men gave a yell and Angbo started to sing for us. Stu and I got off and walked the rest of the way. It was far too cold to ride, and also travelling down hill isn't so hard. We pushed on through the driving snow for hours, the poor yak often 'way above their stomachs. The leading animal would rear up and then fall down into the snow to make the path when he came to a bad place.

" Along about sunset it stopped snowing and we saw a small patch of blue sky. It was nine o'clock before we reached the hut. We waited around till about ten when the main body of yak showed up with our bedding."

The headman disobeyed orders. The yak did not come back. Our chaprasi gave him a beating for it later, but that was doubtless much less uncomfortable than the return trip would have been. Iba ordered the ponies and the remaining yak over, anyway, with light loads.

The trail was pretty bad in places, and where foolish ponies tried to go round such they got stalled in the snow, and had to be unpacked and most laboriously got back. The Chang La's over eighteen thousand, you know. There was so much trouble among the hired ponies all along the line that their owners got discouraged. They told Iba that they and their ponies would die if they went on! Iba replied: "Ham mar-dalega agar ni jaega"—I'll kill you if you don't—beat up a few of them and then showed them how to do it. He and Chot and our men led some of the hired ponies carefully over one of the worst places, light, and made their owners bring on the loads. He saw to it that they led the loaded ponies carefully, after that, in the trail. And so he eventually made the pass without any serious mishap—got the whole outfit into camp by four in the afternoon.

The Mem-Sahib and I rode yak, crossing without adventure. Two dandymen ran alongside her yak, steadying her at places where wreck seemed imminent, patting and rubbing her big stiff boots with their bare hands from time to time, lest her feet be cold.

We made a comfortable camp at the first opportunity that offered, and are staying a day to rest up.

May 31 CAMP 69 TANKSE

It was amusing to see the men dance down a frozen river with the dandy—a bit risky, I thought. They think it a huge joke, the Mem-Sahib says, to try to take my stride when I am out of sight, stepping in my footprints. One of the songs they sing is about the way 'Johnsing Sahibi' used to walk, and how the little sheep-and-goat-herds mimicked him. How long ago was it that Johnson was B.J.C.? Or was it Governor that Johnson was?

The value of one needle in these parts, or one pin with a bead of coloured glass on the head of it, awes us. Have you fellows ever worked out a scale of values among primitive peoples? Buttons are the thing. The Mem-Sahib's mother sent her a collection which she and Iba dole out parsimoniously. Iba prized certain clear red glass ones so highly that she had to bestow them on him. At each village he comes to the tent, to her "dukan" as they call tin box No. 6. He sorts over penknives and tweezers and silver pencils and goggles and steel mirrors and the like, deciding what to give each of the dignitaries. The fact that the gifts come from America adds greatly to their preciousness, by the way. Iba spends a good bit of energy explaining how remote America is from England. I believe this is partly due to the fact that his bara Maulvi who lives up at the mouth of the Braldoh is anti-English and Iba feels obliged to assert our essential difference. Our head-gear makes this difference patent. No English sahib ever wore a tam like mine, a cowboy sombrero like the Mem-Sahib's, a pagri like Chot's, a soft felt shapeless, like Jim's or a real darkey bandanna such as Stuart fancies along with his

o

big ear-rings. Iba says, besides, that Englishmen shave. The younger boys are proud that he has noticed this distinction! Most interesting is his assertion that we don't speak the same language. He says we understand each other, but that the languages are very different, he knows by the sound. We upset him somewhat by proclaiming our friendship with the English at every opportunity. Iba himself appreciates and really likes the English. He says: "The English are just." You remember how Rasul used to brag of "The justful and lighted Government of English." Iba has a claim against an estate in Leh which he will present if the British Joint Commissioner has the settling of the estate. Otherwise not,—futile for a poor man to present a claim in a Wazir's court.

Iba is sending a messenger back to Leh with mail to-night. After that we shall not have an opportunity to communicate with any one for a long time. We have our eye on the Lingzi-thang if we can make it.

Yours,

Lady Ba

CAMP 69
TANKSE

May 31

Dear DAD,

You remember Mother's prejudice against birthday parties? How the only one we ever had was of your arranging? Perhaps you'd better not tell her, but on this, my five-and-fortieth, I've had one!

In my litter-and-eight (or my four-in-hand) I rode to my birthday party, Iba leading the way, his dress red side out, my sahibs four escorting. Half-way to the village the litter-men shifted, just to show off—they can make the shift without stopping the litter now. And on with a fresh burst of "*Ha* dam ma la! *Ha* dam zer" to where the Mayor and Council of Tankse and the Municipal Band were drawn up to salute us. Then our own pony men, camped in the village, fell into column of two behind us and the whole procession swept superbly into a stone-walled poplar bagh, the City Park of Tankse. Litter legs go firmly down. I behold the world from my green throne. The sahibs four diplomatically dodge various rich rugs placed for them, choosing to stand, or to perch on exposed rock surfaces.   And the party begins.

The Lady Mayoress brings me a plate of nuts and sweet-meats (don't tell Mother) and Iba gives her a necklace for me. We smile at each other, I wondering if she is wondering what I think of her.   When I come here next I shall learn Tibetan. There is no telling what I may have missed by not being able to talk with women.   Old Galton says in his *Art of Travel* (always in our book-box when not in our hands for perusal) that women, among their other uses, bring a caravan all the gossip, sometimes of rare value.   And if he found that true, what wouldn't I have found?   For though a woman may tell part of what she knows to men, it's nothing compared to what she might tell another woman.

The party was very different from those we didn't have in our childhood: no playing of Needle's Eye or King William. But it was so much like several parties I have attended since my last birthday that I soon got bored watching.   Of course if I had known more, I'd have been more interested.   For instance, since I did know that spotted dresses were once the height of fashion in the capital but have rather gone out there, within the last half century, I was interested to see that they were still gala wear out here.   I wondered how long it would take for the country girls to feel ashamed of them.   Styles in jewelry change, too.   Iba's wife sold me for a few pence a queer old necklace much handsomer than any of the four or five she wears.   She didn't care for it because it was out of style.   The new style came in about thirty years ago.   I wonder how long it will last.   Coral has been le dernier cri ever since Marco Polo.

I've no doubt the dances have as much history and romance in them as even our old "King William," but upon me who can't copy their slow hesitating step or feel the rhythm to which they dance it, hours of it pall, and I found myself looking artificially polite, and watching our funny travelled chickens, out of their coops for exercise and choosing the centre of the dirt stage to scratch in.

They seemed to suggest ideas to our men, for suddenly there stalked, somewhat disjointedly, out to the centre a rooster almost big enough for the one in the Mohammedan heaven who crows the sun up daily.   The crowd giggled, and Angbo whispered to me that it was Samat and Yonton, and then the great joke came off.   The rooster laid a ten-pound egg and then another and another.   Huge applause, and on the top of the wave of it, Chot dashed out and did halal to that rooster, planting one foot on the body and smirking at everybody. Applause redoubled.

Rather sporting of Chot to help the show along if he is half as sorry to part from us as we are to see him go.   He's leaving tomorrow.   Iba kept him for tea in his tent after the rest of us went back to our camp. Iba was very gloomy. Of course, it's the thing for the boy to be off on his own, and the dream he has of the northern route, Yarkand, Andijan and Samarqand makes one gasp with delight to think of.   Even if the Foreign Office can't get him the permit from the Russian Government they have applied for, he'll still have adventures, for he'll go south over the main range, and then across Persia. Baghdad and Tehran aren't names to mention lightly.   He has both routes plotted out in detail.   All this last month he has been poring over Stieler's *Atlas*.   He had long conferences with Iba on his roof-top in Leh.   Iba has travelled a great deal, keeping note-books of all his travels.   He has been telling Chot the stages of the northern journey as far as he has taken it, with hints as to horses and prices and feed and all that.   By the way Iba once spent a week in Rudok as the guest of the Jongpen telling the great man all about the countries he has visited.   He says his host took no interest in the wealth or importance of any of the "big men" in Yarkand or Khotan or Kashgar, but wanted to know what grew in those countries, what the people did, what they looked like, how they dressed, and what were their customs.   He gave Iba such a beautiful breast-collar for his horse that I feel envy whenever I behold it.   That and his orange namaz rug!   And his bell from Lhasa, all chased with Buddhas.   I think Iba knows I covet them. He has given me a ring, a great piece of turquoise, the good kind that won't fade, from China, not from Persia, in a silver setting he had copied from a Lhasa ring.   It is so big that it blisters my little finger when I wear it on the next one.   He says it's a sure preventive of the evil eye.

Father dear, do I hear you remarking something about "streams of chatter?"   I'm afraid I must have been thinking I was really talking with the Lady Mayoress. You may come to agree with mother and her Quaker forebears about the pernicious effects of birthday parties.

Your affectionate daughter,

P.S.—I've really stopped, but a runner from Leh has just brought Chot a wire, from the F.O. in Delhi, saying he can't go by Yarkand. Great excitement. We all love plans changing. Samat had made a Three-Corner Round cake for a farewell supper. And now Chot will have to go by Simla, and will stay with us till the Pangkong. He's not too disappointed, for the Simla trail bristles with high passes and wild rivers with devices for crossing them that would do credit to Barnum's circus, Gypsy Davy says.

Lady Ba

CAMP 71
BY THE MARBLE CLIFFS
June 3

Dear MINA,

The shore of the Pangkong Lake. The Sahib and Stuart have gone on ahead to find a camp on the farther side. Roger, Jim and I, with the main caravan have come more slowly through a valley beyond Tankse between marble cliffs, and here at this point we see the Lake.

Forty miles of land-locked blue; indigo in bays, emerald over sand bars, cloud-shadowed, sun-sparkled, wind-ruffled through turquoise to sapphire; silver-shot; at the far end, between Scylla and Charybdis, a streak of sheer light; beyond, dim mauve of distance, snow-crowned against a sky of robin's egg.

My litter's four stout legs let down upon the sand, I lie at gaze. The littermen in their new liveries of blue and grey, sleeves marked with the ⚡, squat about, to look also, from under rakish caps of scarlet and gold, Sawang piping quaintly on his pair of wooden pipes.

The loaded yak come lumbering up, swaying their ample tails: grain and grass for the beasts of the caravan. The load-ponies come next, under balanced packs, bags of Willesden green, boxes of scarred black iron. Our sheep arrive, our goats, our hens in coops, Ibrahim on a beautiful horse, decked out in fine harness.

I tell Iba camp must be here, not one step farther will I go till I have in some measure assimilated the beauty before me. Above the trail he points out a terrace. Yes, there!

Water, I wonder? That exquisite expanse is salt and soda.

Not a sprig of green on its borders anywhere, to indicate a fresh
spring.   Iba and Roger laugh at my question, and point to
the two Aqboz jingling up.   Our twin donkeys, lucky above
other donkeys in being chosen for this khush qismat caravan;
small donkeys; colour white grey, hence their Turki names:
Aqboz One and Aqboz Two; foreheads hidden behind red
white and blue insignia, through which grave eyes peer out;
necks encircled with scarlet bands and strings of coloured wooden
beads;—asses fit for Maharani's caravan.   But it is to their
loads that Iba and Roger call my attention.   Big demijohns
of water, from a spring miles down the trail.   Water from
a spring too clear for filtering.

Mem-Sahib's camp may be made at once, up on the terrace,
facing straight into that rippling, glancing, restless blue.
Blessings on the Aqboz! (And on Iba and Roger!)

Yours,

"THE LUCKY LADY BA"

Lady Ba   CAMP 72
                               PANGKONG LAKE

June 7

Dear CHARLOTTE,

That was a pretty poem you sent me.   Isn't it fun writing
them? Send me some more.

I've been trying to do a rondeau about this incredible Lake,
at the edge of Tibet.   It's only a rondeau manqué, so far,
lacking four whole lines, and its French descent shows in
rime riche, but I like it so well, myself, as far as it goes, that
I go about singing it aloud! See if you can finish it for me.

You know the lakes, "linkéd adown her giant glacial stairs,"
are the glory of your great range.   I didn't know how I had
missed them here till we came to this—this fjord, miles higher
than the seas, and months of patient travel from any coast.

> Earth's caught the sky from heaven down
> To clothe her sides of weathered brown.
>   Her talus grey, her copper green,
>   Dark shale and schist of mica's sheen
> She's clothéd in an azure gown.
>   Earth's caught the sky!

In bluest deeps gaunt shoulders drown.
White peaks sway softly, further down.
One rippling stretch of blue serene:
Sapphire, turquoise, ultra-marine.
Earth's caught the sky!

Yours,

LADY BA.

Roger will post this at Simla a month or so from now.
We're trying to get further north.

Gypsy Davy   CAMP 73
SHIP'S PROW CAMP
PANGKONG LAKE
June 9

Dear GEORGE,

We think you would enjoy this lake,—if you could feel at
ease at the height of the Matterhorn, with an army of Matterhörner towering above you.   I don't mean for fear of falling
off, for this particular Matterhorn, along with many thousand
others, is still in the block, waiting to be carved out.   You
would have to travel a long hard trail to get any lower down.

There's clear blue sky above our black rock prow thrust out
a mile into a sapphire lake, a stretch of twenty miles of sapphire,
turquoise-bordered, set among dark mountains, a thin white
sinuous strand between.

The southern shore looks curiously straight and uninviting.
Tawny and brown fans slope up from it a weary way save
where one dark hill at the water's edge breaks the monotony.
Tawny and grey moraines pile cumbrously up on the fans.   Crags
tower above moraines, dark ends of sharp arêtes that buttress
a tall range of Matterhörner and Dents Blanches.   Long
glaciers creep down between arêtes to brinks of precipices
where they end in high unstable walls of green ice that now
and then fall thunderously.   Snow still lies deep on the crest
of the range.   Long fringes of it reach down over the moraines,
all of a glistening whiteness as if it were new-fallen.

The north shore's beautifully sinuous,—deep embayments
filled with turquoise and sapphire, wide grey-floored valleys
with many tributaries, winding back between high scree-
mantled ridges to passes still deep in snow.   There's a faint

green fringe of widely-spaced grasses just springing along the
margins of embayment heads.   The rocks are dark, dark shale
and schist for the most part, but the schist has a silvery sheen in
bright sunlight.   And here and there there's a marble cliff with
a long scree below it, weathered the colour of some ancient
Zeus, glowing at night when all the rest is vague, as if the moon
shone on it.   Not far ahead on either shore, there are spur-
noses of bright green and copper-red, and on beyond, at what
seems the lake's head, there's a sober mountain-side whence
the sweet blue turquoise comes that all the men and women
of these mountains love so.   A water-rim hides the white
strand and the sea-cliffs above it at the mountain's base.

It's a low mountain with gentle slopes leading down to a
broad valley on the right, where there's a glorious opening-out
to the south-eastward.   Out through the gap, across a low pass
in that broad valley, high snowy summits lie lower and lower
still in our line of sight, as they step down the curve of the earth.
It is looking over the rim of the earth we are, that way.

A moody lake, unruffled in the morning, mirroring all this
beauty, but boisterous in the afternoon when the monsoon
wins over the high barrier ranges.   Scattered white fluffy
clouds of the van come sailing overhead before mid-day.   Toward
evening the "sullen rear comes labouring up," its "storéd
thunder" and "forkéd lightning" spent.   The whole sky is
darkly overcast.   Snow falls a little way and hangs in fringes,
caught in mid-air.

All our heavy impedimenta lie a long day's march behind
us in a gloomy wind-swept valley where a few half-starved
men and animals make shift to live the year round, quite out
of sight of the lake.   There Iba and most of the men are camped.
Here at the lakeside, on the very prow of a rock-hewn ship
we have pitched our little forester's tent of thin green sea-island
cotton, wide open to the south-east.   The great rocks of the
hull fend off the boisterous wind.   Our ponies feed in quiet
air along the grassy margin of the bay that lies between
our prow and them.   The cook's tent is well out of sight and
sound, above us on the hull, save that a high note of song floats
down to us now and then.   In some mysterious way that tent
emits rich milk, fresh eggs, juicy chickens and mutton roasts,
delicious puddings, macaroni au gratin, sweet butter, new
Holland cheese, and much besides.

You'd search in vain for Grand Hotels, or villas, or dak
banglas, along this lake.   In vain you'd look for floating
craft of any kind.   Ducks beat their way arduously above it,

or float near shore.   Long-legged cranes sail over it, and stalk about in shallows.   Gulls skim over it, and lammergeiers soar. Wild asses, antelope, big mountain sheep, Tibetan hares feed high up valley sides where you'd swear there was no feed nor water.

The Mem-Sahib's beautiful white Tomar ran off with a herd of kyang the other day.   Over two mountains and across three valleys the men said he ran.   He was gone three days with six men camping on his trail.   Adventure enough, Iba said, to kill any horse.   But Tomar came galloping into camp this morning, holding his head high, seven years younger than he went out on shikar.

Yours,

Lady Ba   Camp 77
                                                            June 24

Dear Constance,

In your next incarnation, do acclimatize early in high altitudes, and don't forget what you've learned in this life about painting.   Don't linger too long, either, in any of the thirty-two places of delight and the rest, because in a million years or more there may not be any mountains about any Pang-kong.   I want these mountains and this Pangkong painted. If you see a little wild ass pointing ears at your easel, don't drive him off.   It'll just be me, looking at the pictures.   I'm going to be a kyang and race about over these mountains where now perforce I crawl.

I can't paint, and the colour here has driven me to overhaul the *Concise Oxford*, *Petit Larousse*, Dana's *Mineralogy* and *The Revelation of St. John*, the only apposite reference books in tin box 14, for words to describe it and my emotions.

You see, I didn't expect such beauty.   The few books I had read about the country had all called it "bleak," "desolate," "arid," "barren."   I almost dreaded coming.   Even the appreciative Drew says that if there were verdure this lake might be as pretty as Killarney.   Bless his heart!

Verdure?   My dear, such greens as there are in the rocks themselves, and in the water shallows!   And as for bleakness, "wind-swept," yes, but "wanting colour," not these mountains of russet, tawny, golden marble. Broken bits on the trail as pure as Phidias' Venus when he first unveiled her. Desolate,—yes, the C.O. says that means "left alone"—I'll grant Drew that adjective. Part of the beauty of this long, strait, cliff-encompassed lake, with waters of every blue in or out of Heaven, is its exquisite aloneness. You feel as if you had intruded, with your train of ponies and your big black yak, into a palace of the gods while the gods themselves were elsewhere for the moment.

On my first march by the Lake, my rom had gone on ahead to find a fitting camp. He sent a messenger back to me with orders to leave the lakeside trail at a certain point and climb inland. I obeyed, of course, but reluctantly. Who could wish to leave that sparkling, lovely, moving thing? We climbed slowly, slowly, the littermen puffing a bit. We saw a bharal once, but nothing else compensatory. Quite suddenly we came up to a little saddle.

Dear—below us, far below us, was a bay, of the deepest blue, lapis lazuli, "the blue from beyond the sea." At the edges shading into clear "azure sheen of turkis blew," then into jade, against a white as of coral sand. I could feel you reaching for your brushes. The littermen stopped. One spoke. Another pitched a bit of rock at him to hush him. We looked and looked, as if that were to be our only chance to see it. Big Sawang released us from the spell gently with plaintive pipes.

Well, a long dip down and a long lift up and a long dip down again,—and camp fairly on the shingle where the Lake is narrow, the men bivouacking and the wee forester's pitched for me where I could hear "lake water lapping."

Next day Stuart and I wrestled with those books for colour words for that "arid" "barren" rock, for the bronze, the copper, the jasper, the jacynth, the heliotrope, the amethyst, the chrysolite, the chrysoprase, changing as the planet turned them slowly before the sun to show us their full range. The blues of the water changed in more than changing lights. They "sang in melody of motion to the sight." A faintest breeze, a wing shadow altered them.

At the next camp we were thrust far out into the Lake at its widest. It was like being on a sea-coast headland. You looked forward, thinking of the stretch of twenty more miles beyond the far-away bend.

A week flew by there, and then we turned back to the Lake's head and moved slowly along the other bank, making one camp high on a hill over there where we could see both up and down

the Lake, and deep down into it. A shining yellow spit plunged
under the blue water right below us, and sank to hazy depths
where we could no longer see it.

Again, camping low once more, in sight of "wet glistening
beaches," and marshes, not desolate, because the wild ducks
make their home there.

> " 'Chakwa, shall I come?'
> 'Nay, come not, Chakwi'.
> 'Chakwi, shall I come?'
> 'Nay, come not, Chakwa'."

(Got that from Forbes' *Hindustani Dictionary*, a treasure chest.)

And now the Gypsy Davy, whose own especial art is that
of camp choosing, who can make a camp of distinction anywhere,
has led us to a spot so high that I can do little more than lie
in the tent door-way and look—down, down, upon a bay of our
precious Lake, where for a final touch of grace we are today
being given a storm to watch.

> Storm-clouded, steel-blue, blue of burnished blade,
> Windy, dusky, arabesque-inlaid.

Your sister,

Gypsy Davy   Camp 77
                               Pangkong

June 24

Dear George,

We have spent three weeks on the Pangkong. This is
our second high camp above it, right at the elbow, of which
we have given you no hint so far. There's another twenty
miles of sapphire 'round the bend.

There is a high ridge rising abruptly from the lake-shore
on the south side here, between the lake and that broad valley.
I found an easy approach from the west and got the sahibian
part of the caravan up. We climbed higher and higher until,
when we had got up well over sixteen thousand, the ridge
fell away to a col some hundreds of feet below. A broad
nala plunged steeply down there a short course to the head of
a bay.

We descended a little way towards the col and made out toward the lake on the side of the nala. The surface of the slope was wasted into such fine material for the most part, that, although the nala side was fairly steep, it was possible to follow a contour with little deviation and very little work by the sappers. This shortly led us out on the northern brow of the ridge where there were good camp sites, and where we could command both reaches of the lake. But the west wind raked that side, drove cloud shreds flying up the pale sky, and lashed the deep blue liquor of the gods below us until it was all white with foam. The lake lay well down below us, a good two thousand feet. The mountains ranging up and down its sides assumed huge bulk and height.

It was a keen wind that blew there. We turned tail hunting a lee. We found one a little way back on our tracks where we could still command a glorious view. But it was a fairly steep slope, and the men were hard put to it to make a platform for the big tent. They made it, though, and found easier places for the cook's and for the boys'. (All our tents are that green Arab model. We make a gay encampment.)

Iba camped down at Shushal across the wide valley where there was grass of a sort for the ponies, and chang for the men after a long drought, and new company. He was fourteen miles away and the climb up to us was a stiff one, but wood, water, milk, eggs, meat, everything came up as regularly as if he had us at arm's length.

Jim is munshi now and has learned to write rather well. That is, his correspondent can read him easily, but he himself has even more trouble to read his own writing, let alone Iba's, than he had to make it. I found him in his blankets this morning, wrestling with a chit from Iba, by candlelight. Iba's chits arrive at unconscionable hours. My munshi confided in me that he has learned that the first two or three lines and the last one at least are always only "slush," salams and the like of that, to our graduated highnesses, so he risks a dive to the centre.

The centre of the chit in question, stated in reply to a query on Jim's part, that the Shushal grass would hold the animals for a few days longer, and that the men would be up by daylight to make a pony trail for the Mem-Sahib up the steep slopes beyond the col, to the highest part of this ridge right on the Tibetan march.

We had a clear day up there after storm. The wide setting that we saw our sapphire in became it well. The south side had a cold look, from grey moraines, up dark cliffs to snow and ice, on up snowily to that tumultuous skyline.   But the fans below all this were warm brown and wore a broad belt of yellow green across their middles where they oozed icy water. And reedy deltas below them marched out into the lake against militant waves.   That wide deep sculptured desert on the north wore all warm tints, high colour even.   (The snow on that side lies a long way back.)   No deltas there, but deep embayments at the dead valley mouths where waves meet no resistance.

We were high, nearly nineteen thousand feet, but not high enough to see across eastward to the green meadows Iba is always telling us about.   He resents our having given our word to keep to the Ladakh side.   He says three days' travel would take us clear of the desert and put us on rich feed.

Yours,

Lady Ba   CAMP 79
JUST OVER THE TSAKA LA
June 26

Dear ELLIS and MALCOLM,

If it had been the "foreign field" instead of "home" missions that had called your family, it might have been one of you we'd have met yesterday within an arrow's flight of the Tibetan border, instead of a young Dane, brought up in Labrador by his West Indies-born mother.   The Moravian Christian Brotherhood goes literally "into all the world."

We were far up above the valley-bottom trail, following our Bara Sahib who was picking out a way among rocks of red sandstone and blue limestone.   My littermen love following the Sahib Bahadur where no trail is.   They are proud of their ability to carry me up slopes so steep that I am almost standing in the litter facing backwards, clinging to its sides with both hands.

Suddenly one said: "Shikar sahib!" pointing down to the trail.   I suppose in New Mexico you used to get out your field-glasses to look at a stranger.   We hadn't seen anyone outside our own caravan for weeks.   Down we went to the trail, and lo! it was no hunter, but Asboe Sahib, our good

friend of the winter out "on tour," with a native Christian
pastor and a servant. He was less surprised to meet us, for
he says the nomads in the Rupshu and the villagers along the
Indus are expecting us, and that piles of firewood and even
bowls of milk are being hoarded against our coming. He
brings news of Chot, too, from some nomad who saw him and
Yonton laying siege to a snow pass a good way out on the
Simla road.

We made our camps adjoining, and the boys cooked dinner
for our guest in the pressure cooker (too precious to be used
by the servants).

We found that Asboe Sahib had a magic lantern, so we bade
Iba get the horsemen's tent ready for a tamasha and drum
up an audience. He is a good Mussulman, is Iba, but respects
Mem-Sahib's hukm, respected it to such an extent in this case
that he sent messengers out to nomad encampments to proclaim
that there was to be a tamasha in our camp, and that his Mem-
Sahib "commanded" the presence of every man, woman and
infant, at the tamasha. He got a good crowd together, and
Asboe Sahib and his assistant preached the word right vigorously,
the native evangelist making gestures with a pair of tongs which
he carries in his girdle against the needs of toothache patients
who may unwittingly appeal to him instead of Asboe Sahib.
These Moravian missionaries are much more than believers
in the word. They are diligent doers, and serve their neighbour effectively.

Iba seems bent on showing me that one of the "faithful"
can also be a broad-minded man of the world. He has just
brought us a beautiful piece of silver and gold work, made by
the Shushal smith. It is one of those frames for an image of
Buddha, done in high relief repoussé, eight scenes from the
Life, around the opening, overlaid with gold. The smith has
a reputation on both sides of the border, his father and his
grandfather before him, having worked in silver and gold in
that outpost of a village at fourteen thousand.

The three great missionary religions have met below this
little pass today. They all seem venerable to us. But I
wonder if old Earth is really aware of any of them, their lives
must seem so very short in terms of her thinking. I suppose
this pass itself is an upstart in her view, since the other day
when the Indus flowed this way out to the Shyok, as Dainelli
says.

Yours,

RI MEM-SAHIB

Lady Ba   CAMP 80
                                              INDUS SIDE AGAIN
                                                  June 27

Dear WILL SCARLET,

Today, near the edge of "Lhasa ke mulk," in this country where never a wheel is nor ever was, Iba pointed out what looked in the distance immensely like a colossal wheel track. He said it was the track of Kesar's chariot.

Here's more of that Saga.

KESAR AT KURULUGU'S CASTLE.

Then went the god-king forward. Nine gates he opened, one after the other. The innermost gate was of gold. As he opened it, he saw the Dzemo, the demon queen, sitting in a cage of iron. And thus she addressed him:—

"Foolish man, this is a giant's nest!
Foolish boy, this is a nest of giants!
How wilt thou escape?"

And Kesar made answer: "I am Kesar, god-king of Glingland. It is I will let thee out." So saying, he opened the cage of iron, and set free the Dzemo. Much gratitude, devotion and honour she showed him.

A fortnight long the god-king tarried in the demon's castle. Then came a great wind, and the castle shook and trembled. Kesar, affrighted, cried out: "What then is this? What is it I hear? Tell me, Dzemo." And the Dzemo made answer: "The demon-king is returning." "Where shall we hide then, man and beast?" asked Kesar. "He is far distant. Ten days must pass ere his coming. Fear not, thou," said the Dzemo.

Now, when ten days more had elapsed, came a wind stronger than that other, and the earth shook more than before. Again Kesar asked of the Dzemo what it portended. "The demon-king is half-way home," she made answer.

Then from her pocket she drew seven knuckle-bones and seven clam-shells. "Ha ha!" she said, "Hu hu! Hrum hrum!" And the seven knuckle-bones became seven stout lads, and the seven clam-shells as many buxom maidens.

At the Dzemo's bidding they dug two holes under the hearth, one eighteen fathoms deep and one nineteen fathoms. And the Dzemo in one hid Kesar and in the other, the foal,

Kyang-god-byerpa.   Now came the demon Kurulugu, back to
his house, and said to his spouse (back in her iron cage as he
had left her):—

> "I smell man flesh!
> I smell horse flesh!"

And the Dzemo made answer: "The king comes, bearing
on his right shoulder a hundred carcasses of horses and on
his left shoulder a hundred men's bodies, and gnaws an
eight-year-old child the while! How should I in my iron
cage smell one man and one horse only?"

Then said Kurulugu: "Fetch me my book here. Hold
it not under thy body, but bear it on thy head, and offer
incense."

The Dzemo went at his bidding, but she held the book under
her body, and for incense she burned dog dung, before she
brought the book to him.

And the book said: "The god-king of Gling has come, and
sits nine leagues deep under a lake and three mountains."
(That lake was the water in the great copper pot, and the
mountains were the three great hearthstones.)

"The book knows nothing," roared the giant, and flung it
into the fire. But the Dzemo drew its singed pages from the
flames, saying wisely: "Some day it may be of service."

Then shouted the giant: "Dzemo, I'm an-hungered. Food
I command thee!"

Then the Dzemo made ready a hundred measures of meal,
and the chopped flesh of a hundred horses, men and asses,
with a sauce, and served him.

"Dzemo," quoth he, "now is sleep come upon me."

"Good," replied the Dzemo, and placed pillow and rug
for his comfort.

"Shall I take only a cat nap, Dzemo, or shall I sleep properly?"

"When one is on a journey, one must sleep lightly like the
birds, but when one is at home again, it is right that one should
sleep properly." Thus answered the Dzemo.

"Dzemo, my Dzemo, how wise are thy sayings!" And he
fell into a deep slumber, lustily snoring.

Now, when Kurulugu slept properly, not till a year had passed
would he waken. When his sleep was secure, the Dzemo
drew from her pocket the seven knuckle-bones and the seven
clam-shells, and turned them into the seven youths and maidens.
Then they set the great copper pot to one side, and heaved up
the three great hearthstones, and fell a-digging.

Now, when King Kesar and his foal, Kyang-god-byerpa, came up from their hiding places, the mighty breath of the giant caught them and thrust them to the wall, and there held them. Then, in a long intake of his breath, he swept them up to his nostrils.

Kesar was sore afraid, and what to do he knew not. But the Dzemo bestrode the kyang, and like a hunter she rode upon Kurulugu's sleeping body, up and down, backward and forward, till Kesar took courage, and did likewise, while Kurulugu slept on, unheeding.

Nine lives had Kurulugu. Kesar cut them off, one after another. First the nose. Then he broke the great corner teeth off. Then the right hand. Then the left hand. Then he plucked out the eyes, and Kurulugu stirred in his sleep and murmured: "Who art thou? What dost thou?"

"I am Palle godpo," said Kesar.

"Oh, I shall not die at his hands," said the demon and turned on his other side and slept sounder.

Then Kesar cut out his tongue.

"Ouch! Who art thou?"

"I am Goni gonpo of Gling."

"O, he cannot kill me."

When both ears were cut off, the demon cried out:

"O woe! Who art thou?"

"I am Dongma Spyang of Gling."

"It is not he who will kill me," sighed Kurulugu, without waking.

Then prayed Kesar the god-king to the gods, his father and mother, for help in slaying the demon. Then he lifted the stone sword to smite the great head off, but Ane-kur-manmo stayed his hand, saying:—

"The wise one is without wisdom.
The prudent one has lost his prudence.

Thou hast lost thy wits. Slay him not with the stone sword. Quick! Draw thy knife, whose name is 'Three-Fingers-Long-for Sinners!'"

Then Kesar made haste, and did as she bade him, and as he drew his knife "Three-Fingers-Long-for-Sinners" from its sheath, Kurulugu woke and said clearly: "Thou art the god-king of Gling! At his hand I perish."

So he died. And Kesar cast the pieces of him into the water. The dust he gave to the winds. No trace left he, remaining.

Do you suppose there was a time when grown men and women sat around the fire and told each other the story of Jack the Giant Killer? Will your great great grandson's greatest grandchild listen in the nursery to Henry James or Meredith?

Yours,

LADY BA

Gypsy Davy
CAMP 82

ACROSS THE INDUS FROM NIMA

July 1

Dear ALBERT,

I wrote you in late October, from a camp on the Indus, near Skardu. I have never had an answer to that letter. I am wondering whether it is that you are not a writing man, or that my letter never reached you. It must have had a rather adventurous journey at that time of year.

I think it's time to try again, this time in midsummer, from a camp a good many hundred miles further upstream. We are about to make a long detour to get around a difficult canyon in the main valley, impassable for ponies at this time.

The water has begun to rise. (Just imagine the glaciers not seriously beginning to melt until July!) We were on the wrong side of the Indus, up near the Tibetan border. We had to cross, and that meant building a raft to cross on.

There isn't a stick of timber in the country, bigger than your little finger, or higher than your knee. But there are lots of goats. And it happened that a few sticks, half as big as your wrist and six feet long, had been packed up for the Lambardars of two tiny villages in nalas near where we were. Perhaps Iba had ordered them up.

Well, they killed a lot of goats and took them out through narrow slits in their rumps very carefully. They tied up the openings in the rumps, and the necks, and three of the legs, tightly. Then they blew up the skins like footballs through the fourth leg, and tied that. Then they listened all over very carefully for little leaks, and when they thought they had found that there was one, they hunted round for hours among the hairs to locate and mend it.

"They" were some twenty-five villagers, squatting on the river-bank. They had tea boiling in a big copper pot near the water's edge, and kept it boiling all day long. Every now and then a man would stop hunting for a leak and come and squat down by the pot, and pull a little woollen bag out of a big fold in his gown, and a wooden cup, and tip some sattu into the cup, and put in a little butter. Then he would take a big brass ladle from a stone near by and ladle in a little tea. He would knead the mixture with one finger very thoroughly into a stiff dough, and eat it in half a minute. Usually he began to talk before he got it well swallowed. One man always threw a little dry sattu into his mouth after filling his cup. Some of it went in, but most of it powdered his face. His face was always powdered like that.

There was a big huqa going, too, and every now and then a man would stop work and have a pull at that. You know they have to have a live coal on top when they draw on a huqa, so that the tobacco or tea leaves or wild rhubarb or whatever they happen to be smoking is well seasoned with wood smoke.

They were a grimy lot. That fold in their gowns was fat with things they stuffed into it. (I have seen a live lamb stuffed in there.) And the long blue sashes, yards and yards long, that belt in their dingy grey gowns and make the fold in them, the sashes had all sorts of things thrust through them. They all wore turquoise brooches near the roots of their pigtails.

A travelling lama happened by, laid down his scrip and set to work with the others.

There was no string, by the way, for tying that fourth leg, but everybody had a wad of wool in the fold in his gown, and spun string as he needed it.

Some of the men lashed the sticks together with hair rope into a square frame, and when the skins were ready, they lashed ten or eleven to each frame, the largest along one side.

Then half a dozen men held a raft up, skins down, and one man put butter and sattu and live coals into the brass ladle, and held it underneath and they all chanted a spell or a charm —broke a bottle of champagne over the prow, so to speak— and launched her.

They spent about half an hour, gingerly testing her, to see if she would really float. Then they loaded several sacks of barley, and a man-load of wood, on her, and a man sat down on either corner of the side where the big skins were, dangling his legs in the water. They paddled her with wooden shovels, wooden blades lashed to slender sticks. They started the stroke with the backs of their shovels together, in the middle of that side, and swept across the front, pulling against each other, round the corners, and about six inches down the sides. I should say the only part of the stroke that had any effect on the direction or progress of the raft was that six inches. It was chiefly the current which eventually landed them on a bar quite a way down the other side and quite a way from shore. There other men picked the freight up and carried it to higher ground.

The Mem-Sahib and I went across without any baggage and I carried her ashore. The milch goats (we have twenty of them) were hog-tied and laid on the rafts like sacks. The ponies swam, or appeared to swim. Some of them must have had their hind legs on the bottom, because none of them were strong enough swimmers to rise out of the water, as they did. Not one bag or box was spilled or wetted.

Here's hoping that this letter doesn't miss fire.

Yours,

GYPSY DAVY

P.S.—Of course they had to turn the rafts upside down at the end of every round trip and blow the skins up again.

Gypsy Davy   TIFFIN KE JAGAH
                                   INDUS SIDE
                                Noon, July 2

Dear PAT,

The old Indus has closed her gates against our further progress down valley. There's a wild gorge ahead. The only tributary we can see is foaming white with cataract and waterfall. This end of the gorge just below the Puga Nala where we have stopped for tiffin, is a noisy place.

Jim and Stuart have been taking a plunge in safe water up stream, absurdly white before all those black spectators. They report: "Coldest yet!"

We saw a mountain on the further bank at a sharp bend an hour or two back, of a lustrous pistachio-green like epidote, or, to be more precise, a big truncated spur like that,—a lovely thing.

Here come our spare mounts, turning up Puga Nala, cavorting under gay Lhasa rugs, and behind them an interminable string of laden ponies and yak and long-gowned men walking among them, and behind the last slow yak, Iba, riding, and behind him

the goats, grazing on flowers as they come.   There are
chickens in crates, riding, just ahead of Iba.

I made a lovely joke just now to Iba about the chickens, but
it won't seem to carry over into English (Rasul once described
to the Mem-Sahib how at a Chinese dinner, where he was
interpreter for me, I made a joke in English. "Then we two
men laugh.   Then I tell to the Amban's munshi into Turki.
Then we three men laugh.   Then he tell to Amban into Chinese.
Then all four men laugh.")

I suppose,—to get back to the important subject: chickens,
—I suppose an authority like yourself might hesitate to class
this adult mite as Gallinea.   But they are chickens for all that,
and they furnish juicy morsels, albeit morsels only, at our
banquets.   (The boys take turns at carving, and the carver
gets the rack!) And one hen lays a wren's egg daily, sometimes
on the march.

4 p.m.—We are camped on a low spur above a mess of
borax pans and sulphur mines, deserted at this time of year.
I wonder if they pack that borax out on sheep, the way they
pack the salt.   I imagine the sulphur goes up country into
Tibet to make powder for Tibetan matchlocks.

My Chinese guard near Koko-Nor at the other end of Tibet
used those muskets.   I believe they do literally touch a match
to them sometimes.   Of course, these men had no matches,
only flint and steel, but they kept big fires going all night at
either end of the line.   To furnish live coals?

My salams to the hens and the pheasants.

Yours,

GYPSY DAVY

Gypsy Davy   CAMP 86
                    JUST BELOW THE TAGALAUNG LA, RUPSHU
                                    July 9

Dear FAY,

I wonder, have you missed your vocation? Would a yak-
hair tent have appealed to you more than a tar-paper shack?

We shook the dust of the villages from our feet late in May,
and made our way with difficulty over a snow pass more than
eighteen thousand, into nomad country.

It was a late spring.   The nomads were as scarce as the feed
was on that part of their range.   We heard on every hand of

big bands of sheep and herds of yak starving to death. Three out of every five sheep died, they said. The yak lay down and let the wolves pull them to pieces. A headman sent to Iba begging for wolf poison. We sent messengers up country, where the best feed was, after yak to break trail for us over a snow pass to the north. Forty started, but seventeen gave out the first day, and of the few that reached our camp not one was fit for trail-breaking. We had to give up the Lingzi-thang we'd set our hearts on.

We had brought a lot of grain on Ladakhi yak for our own stock, but had been at our wits' end to find grass for some time. One day we found it along the margin of a bay on the salt Pangkong, scant, but in a manner of speaking, fresh and good. And we found a big spring near it. The boys, out foraging for better grass, found lean Tibetan sheep far back high up at the edge of the snow, in charge of a ragged man and woman. Poor enough feed, this of the sheep, and ours at the lakeside, but the wild ass and the wild sheep and the antelope and the Tibetan hare fatten on the steep hillsides all about, where you would take oath there was no feed. There isn't much, only small bunches, far apart, but it is wonderfully sweet and nourishing. If the horses would only hunt that, as my burros in the Sierras do, we should have them all fat. Some of them do manage to keep fairly fit, but the rest grow daily thinner and thinner.

We didn't meet with the nomads in any number till we left the great salt lake, and came into a broad grassy valley, fifteen to sixteen thousand feet above the sea. The margins of the little stream were green. I think there were a dozen widely scattered tents of black yak-hair. The sheep and yak were all out feeding high up the valley-sides in charge of herds.

Dingy black tents, woven of yak-hair and wool, the two mixed in each strand, the one for warmth, the other for strength and impermeability, I suppose; a wide slit in a mansard roof to let the smoke out; almost perpendicular walls; poles inside, at the ends of the slit, to hold the roof up; forked poles outside, one at each corner and one in the middle of each side, to hold the walls up; long guys of yak rope, passing through the forks. (Poles are precious. There is not a proper stick of wood anywhere to be seen, growing, for many miles down valley. There is only a bit of thorny, yellow-blossoming gorse, and sage.)

The people swarmed from their tents like bees, when they heard our bells. Silver and coral and turquoise; crimson and dingy grey; shiny black pig-tails; rosy swarthy Mongol faces; children clothed, and children naked, in arms, and under foot, clinging to crimson robes and hiding behind them, —one fast asleep in a pile of sheepskins outside a tent door, just visible, missing the show altogether; dogs innumerable.

The boys reported bags piled against the walls inside the tents, leather and yak-hair, full of barley and sattu and butter and milk, and coarse brick tea; sheepskin coats and pack saddles piled there, too; barley popping in hot sand over dung fires; sour milk being sloshed about in leather bags till butter should come. (There was strong drink brewed from the milk, but the boys didn't see that.) And always there is a little Buddhist shrine at the far end of the tent, a row of shiny brass cups before it, and a wick burning in a little bowl of butter.

It's a fine life in the open.   I think they move several hundred miles during the year, in two or three removes.   We passed families moving with their flocks and their herds and all their worldly goods.

In one lonely valley we met two jolly Lhasa beggars, gaily clothed, moving down toward Hindustan, months and months of travel before them.   They capered and sang for their supper, to the rat-a-tat-tat of loaded tassels, on little double drums, human skulls, crown to crown, and human skin for drum-heads.

In another lonely valley, there came two mounted men, to meet us, richly dressed and wearing swords, come a full month's journey from their camp down the Lhasa road, to see what manner of men we were, such wild rumours fly before us.

Yours,

GYPSY DAVY

Gypsy Davy   CAMP 87
                                                    GYA
                                              July 10

Dear ROSLYN,

We have been some time in the high nomad land, where the bottoms of the valleys are three miles up.   That almost virgin bit of Tibet, that Rupshu, is delightful open country after the gorges and savage mountain ranges,—that wreckage of the old plateau, where only narrow bands of sky show between stupendous mountain walls, all spiked with Matterhorns. Those Rupshu valleys lie open to the sky, broad, greening here and there; slopes gentle, for the most part, up to a smooth skyline. You can ride up almost anywhere, high, and look abroad.

But there day after day we, the Ri Sahib and the Ri Mem-Sahib, camped on valley bottoms, or at best some few hundred feet above them, rarely riding to the ridge tops. Tomar was so full of ginger that he was hard to hold. We were beginning to feel old. The littermen ceased singing on the trail up Polakonka La, not seventeen thousand feet. One man gave out. Angbo jumped into his place and the litter forged ahead, singing, but all the men, Angbo himself, came drooping down to camp on the far side. Iba said there was a noxious weed grew there that made all black men ill.

In this high country there has been generally less singing and less joie de vivre. But you should see the effect of a silver forehead bar! The litter comes to life. The men agree that Changpa women are homely creatures, not worth looking at, and yet, one silver bar above dark eyes in a black tent door-way!

We came on down into a broad basin, rimmed about with long lines of old abandoned beaches, stepping down the sides. A big lake there has shrunk and shrunk under the dry air, until it covers but half the bottom of the basin. Two fair green sheets of water now, cranes stalking up and down the reedy shores.

We passed a Changpa family on the move, a motley crowd of people amongst a swarm of sheep, goats, donkeys, yak— all, save the goats and the men, toiling under clumsy loads,— savage dogs dodging in and out, and, bringing up the rear, a jaunty beggar in a parti-coloured cap, cut like a rooster's comb, —badge of his profession, Iba says.

A little further on, a big encampment of those rusty black Changpa tents, and here and there a little white tent; one big black tent, a head-man's, weavers sitting in the sun before it making yak-hair cloth in very narrow strips on prototypal looms; ugly dogs prowling about; big piles of wool, and by them fine-featured dapper men in snow-white pugs, if you please, Kashmiris trading with the uncouth Mongols, hence the white tents.

Beyond all this, at the far end of the basin, we met big bands of those tall Tibetan sheep coming in, loaded with barley.

And then we climbed a long way up and made camp there, below a cliff. Next morning three yak cows, roped together by the horns, climbed slowly up the slope, two Changpa women goading them on. Three clumsy little humped black calves kept trying vainly to get at teats, always snatched away just as they found them through the long black fringes.

Iba got from the Changpa some tiny bulbs which we cooked and ate.   They tasted like chestnuts.   Save for these and a few delicate sweet wild carrots we were rather short of vegetables on those high pastures.   The boys say they saw the nomads boiling a kind of green, but what it was we did not discover, nor did Iba offer it.

We left the basin from our high camp, on a contour, saving a long climb down and up again, and came into the nala on the south of the Tagalaung La.

Angbo is always pointing out bands of invisible sheep high up valley sides, and far away bands of kyang on river flats. The kyang are bold and curious and venture fairly near.   They always interest the Aqboz.   The other day the Aqboz made off to join them.   It took the better part of a long day to get them back.

There was one high camp last night.   Jim and Stuart camped high above the Tagalaung La, hoping for a glimpse of K^2. They have made several unsuccessful attempts to see K^2.   They thought they had it this time, but when I got up there shortly after sunrise I failed to corroborate their findings.   They'd sketched a most lovely mountain, though, for a substitute. (Not that there is sketchable beauty to be looked for in K^2 at this distance.)

Tomar brought his Khush Qismat Mem-Sahib up to the boys' camp, and after she had told them what she thought of khaki shorts and purple knees in such a place, we all feasted our eyes awhile on the beauty to the northwestward.   That old plateau behind us has its charm, but it's in the wreckage that the thrilling beauty lies.

Here and there amongst those tumultuous skylines, from some peak you may have got under your feet, you'll see long, even lines,—still unravaged bits of Tibet.   And in that goal we failed of, the high Lingzi-thang; and in the Depsang, where Rasul says: "from north and south are both side big plain and east side very big plain and west a plain.   Myself was alone on that big plain"; and in the more moderately high Deosai, where we got our first real taste of the Himalaya, in all these you'll find great blocks of Tibet, still almost intact. And so I might lead you with giant strides to the Pamirs.

We watched the caravan toil slowly up the pass below us, and go hurrying down, loads rolling like boats in the trough, with the swing of the animals descending.

At length we started down ourselves, and shortly came on a small company of Balti coolies resting on the pass, wrapped in their shawls; en route to Simla, I suppose, with high loads of apricots topped by heavy bags of tsampa (scrip for the journey) standing beside them. My scale weighs a hundred kilos, but one of those loads drove the pointer past the 100 mark.

And now we're down among the villages, camped on a flowery terrace on the very edge of a deep gorge. Iba promises us "big red flowers" on the next march.

If the Lady Ba and I were only more sociable, we would have much more to tell you. The Chhota Sahib is the real traveller. I am enclosing a letter we have just received from him, on the Rupshu.

Yours,

GYPSY DAVY

Chhota Sahib

Dear SAHB AND MEM-SAHIB,

O, I like it,—this being on my own, going as fast or as slow as I want to.

I feel quite frisky now. I've just finished my first meal in two days, and my first meat since I left you. Apropos of that, I'm all for a vegetarian diet. Sattu for a week set me up finely for some of the stiffest work I've done in some time.

I left you at a good pace, about thirty miles a day, afoot. After several passes and valleys, and tea-parties with nomads, we finally got into the Indus valley and ended up one night at Nima.

We saw no more people for several days, until we had got well into Rupshu. It took a day to wheedle yak out of the nomads there for a shot across twelve or fifteen days of no man's land. We had counted on getting some sattu, butter and sugar at Shushal, Nima, and from these people. We did get a few sers of sugar from a lama on pilgrimage to Lhasa, but nothing at Nima, and these people wouldn't sell us a thing. The country has been pretty hard hit by the late spring snow. Over half the sheep are dead, and a large part of the yak, and the animals that did pull through are in rather weak shape.

We set out with four very poor yak and a feeble old greybeard and a boy to look after them. The first day was all right. We crossed a saddle, and made about eight miles. Saw several wolves at close range, and quite a few kyang. And a Lahul-wala, with fifty sheep, waiting the pleasure of the Lachalung La. He had stayed a little too late and got barred out for the winter. Blizzards, hunger and wolves had taken a hundred and fifty from his flock.

The second day was long,—mean icy fords. I was twice knocked off my feet by moving boulders in the torrent-beds. The third day we got on to snow. The yak moved slower and slower and began to get ugly and to lunge at us with their horns. Once while I was pushing one, he reared, lunged sideways, and we went through thin ice together into the stream, up to my waist. We managed to keep his feet so the loads didn't get wet. My clothes froze, even in bright sunshine. When I changed, it was ice armour I had to get out of. I even had to chip ice off my skin.

The yak-walas didn't like this trip at all. Yonton had overheard them the night before, planning to go back with the yak during the night, but he put the fear of God and Maharaja into them somehow, for they came on. He and I had to load the animals ourselves, though, as the men were much too weak to lift a hundred pounds. We had to load two hundred or jettison the difference, for more animals were not to be had.

About noon of the fourth day we got to the foot of the Lachalung with three-quarters of a mile of steep climbing ahead, and there the yak balked and lay down, and so did the yak-walas. Yonton went ahead to see what was what with the trail and I took the loads to the top.

Just as I got up with the last load, on rather wobbly legs, Yonton got back. Face as long as yours, Sahb, beard and all. And mine soon matched it. Nothing ahead but snow and ice and precipice and torrent. I had to see for myself, so we walked down a way together. It was pretty bad,—a deep gorge, steep icy slopes on both sides down to the brinks of precipices, impassable slopes; no way but wading in a half-frozen torrent in the bottom of the gorge; no surety of feed ahead, and the yak had had nothing for three days.

So, with a last look toward Lahul and Simla, and with a vivid mental picture of the south side of the Lachalung, we began taking the loads down again, and had all our things stacked near the yak by evening.

We had had no fire for several days, so I brought out a tin

of sterno I salvaged from your throw-away pile in Leh, and we melted enough snow to make tea for all four of us. Two cups of that hot strong tea in each of us put a different aspect on things, and our faces shortened up a bit. The yak-walas had only one ser of sattu left, either through malice or ignorance —hard to say which—so we had to share our five-day supply with them.

The next morning the yak were almost impossible. We had to throw large pieces of ice and rock at their heads to make them move at all. Sounds cruel, but it was a choice between that and their starving. We didn't get far that day, but the next day we got off the ice, and the yak found old horse-dung to eat.

One of them balked here. The nomads abandoned her. I tried my hand at persuading her. I put my best foot forward and held out my last Huntley Palmer biscuit, and called: "Nice little yakky-wakky!" She came—with head lowered and snorting! There was no dodging room, and she caught me fairly between her horns in the midriff. I jumped back at the last instant enough to ease the shock a little, and grabbed both horns. She kept to the path and so saved us a hundred-foot drop. She tossed me off presently and stood there, challenging. I collected my wind and my knapsack and left her.

The next morning Yonton and I set out, hoping to make the nomad encampment by night—we had no food left. We didn't make it. A little after noon we came upon a man and a young boy searching for the abandoned cargo of a large sheep pack-train, caught in a blizzard last fall. They had started for Lahul across the range, too late, and lost all they carried before they made the first pass. We could see nothing but skeletons pulled apart and spread out. No signs of the grain. They had brought little enough food for themselves, and had none to spare for us.

Toward evening we found a pinfold in a wide windy valley. We collected a large pile of sun-dried sheep dung with a stiff old skin we found there. It was well powdered. We spread some out for mattress and pillow, filled up some of the chinks in the wall with a bit of it, and lit the rest. It burned all night like punk. And stunk. I pulled my feet part way out of my boots. Yonton showed me how to keep my body warmer by pulling my arms out of the sleeves of my shirt, jacket and Burberry. I kept in touch with my feet by getting up several times during the night and stamping about.

As we lay there I recalled Sahb's picture of the jewelled mother bending over her naked babe in his cradle pit, his dusty cheeks furrowed by tears, and the song:—

> "Sleep, little babe, in your sheep-dung pit.
> Devils shall harm you never a whit.
>
> With a wee bit of butter and soot from the pot
> I've smeared on your forehead a charméd spot.
>
> Sleep little babe, in sheep-dung dry.
> Grand-dad with his prayer-wheel is sitting by.
>
> Sleep, little baby, in warm sheep-dung.
> I'll keep the devils off. *Padme Hung!*"

The night went, but not quickly, and with the first hint of dawn we were off again. We reached the nomads in the afternoon and sent two of them back to our men with food and fresh yak. The headman from a discreet distance sent us a goat, a peace-offering for the weak yak he had given us.

Tomorrow or the next day we start towards the Indus again by way of the Gya gorge.

We shall probably go out through Zaskar.

Yours,

CHOT

Rumours have reached us here that you are coming to Rupshu. I thought the yak I met near Shushal on their way to you would never be able to make the Marsimik La. I'll try to have this letter meet you.

Gypsy Davy   CAMP 87
                                              GYA
                                          July 10

Dear CHOT,

Yours of no date or place received by cleft stick in a black hand.

There are ravens enough in that impoverished land you travelled over, to warrant the fond trust you placed in them. Such asceticism as yours in these matters is as commendable as your attempt to pass through the eye of the needle with all that loot is "derogat'ry" as O'Casey would say. It seems to

me you must have had nearly half a ton.   Where did you get
it all? We haven't missed anything except Stieler's Iran-Turan
sheet.   Why did you cling to it so tenaciously?

Two hundred pounds is overweight for well-favoured yak
on such long stretches of bad going as you had ahead of you.
I don't think I should have tried over seventy-five, under the
circumstances.   But neither should I have trusted to the
ravens for my bread.   I should have gone out, holding adventure
at arms' length, as is the way with cautious men who travel
fatly, but bring home lean tales.

Yours,

مہر

Lady Ba   Camp 88
                                                Upshi
                                           July 11

Dear Will,

One of the daintiest of the thirty-four (?) varieties of wild
rose has a spirit of adventure out of character with its texture
and hue. We found it daring glaciers in the Braldoh valley last
year. And yesterday we saw it where nothing less ferocious than
a tiger lily, less coarse than a squash blossom, less morbid than
an orchid should have been.   Inside the skeleton thorax of
an interstellar dinotherium dropped upon the world's roof,
its ribs great purple slabs sticking up to the sky, a mountain
brook running down its backbone,—wild-rose trees, thick
from top to bottom with thousands of exquisite pale pink
blossoms!

Our jhus to your garden.

نذیق

Himis Monastery *July* 12

At all the shrines among the festival offerings of grain and
butter and water today lie wild-rose petals.

Gypsy Davy   Camp 89
                                                    Himis
                                                    July 12

Dear Ed,

I suppose that extraordinary power plant of yours at Cal Tech will smash the atom some day. Our little dynamo won't quite do that. Stu grinds out the juice and I apply it, not to your sort of atoms with regular habits, but to temperamental atoms rioting under human skull bones.

At Nima, Iba had been complaining of headache. We set up beside him on the ground among the chickens in the men's camp. There was a big appreciative black audience at our clinic there.

According to the directions of two frock-coated side-whiskered doctors, portrayed on the cover of our instruction-book by Cruikshanks, I applied one pole to the sole of Iba's foot, and holding the other myself, made passes over the ache with the fingers of my free hand. The ache retreated before me. I chased it about until it presently settled between his cheek-bone and his ear. While I was working there Iba suddenly called out: "Dekh sakta!" The doctors have not prescribed any treatment for blindness, and I didn't know that Iba's headache was blinding him. I was as much impressed as anybody.

Here at Himis, the big monastery in these parts, we set up again. The Abbot has been very friendly with us, and we have seen a good deal of him in his sumptuous little red den at the top of the monastery, a considerable climb from our garden up a long dark covered way, past the open kitchen door-way showing pots boiling, bigger than any ogre's, across a wide court, up long flights of stairs. Den isn't the word. Sanctum, I mean. We set up in the sanctum.

The Abbot sat on a sort of throne, above the rest of us, watching us intently through big spectacles,—a portly dark man robed in crimson, with bare shaven head and a bare arm. We sat on a low dais at one side, and in front there was a motley little crowd. Iba stood out, tall and stately in his crimson gown, and testified, as if he were in a revival meeting, or were a patent medicine vendor's accomplice: "The Sahb restored my sight!"

The Temporal Head of the monastery came up for treatment. His headache was quickly driven off. Another patient had an aching tooth. This is a rather delicate operation, involving a spoon. A handsome silver one was brought in by the Abbot's orders. Ache yielded promptly. The Abbot got so interested that he came down from his throne to a stool close by. From time to time someone slipped softly in for blessing. He reached out his hand without taking his eyes from me, and blessed the bowed head,—black greasy Mongol head, shaven to where the pigtail sprouted, head protruding from a mass of dingy grey, indicating a man hidden under all that wool. No other sign of him, not even a finger-tip.

At this juncture the King, a guest of the monastery during the festival, and an interested spectator, begged our services in his apartments.

We were led into a vast low-ceiled bare hall. The Dowager and the Queen and some ladies-in-waiting were sitting on the floor on the window side. We sat on the floor on the other side. The old Dowager studied us through a big reading-glass.

When refreshments had been offered, the patient was brought in, a young lady-in-waiting, much jewelled. It was explained to us that a little white animal was lodged inside one of her teeth, biting hard. We set up beside her, but had a most difficult time getting into her mouth—it was so very small.

When we got back to the sanctum we found the Abbot still keen. I presented the instrument to him after a dissertation on its virtues and its limitations. He was grateful and said it would enable him to be of service to humanity. It was a powerful little instrument, effective in many of the treatments the Cruikshanks doctors described. I think the Abbot may find it an efficient substitute for the scourge which hangs in the dukang where he holds services with all his monks.

Yours,

GYPSY DAVY

Lady Ba   CAMP 89
                                                                  HIMIS
                                                               July 12

Dear AUNT DELLE,

We have been out far beyond the reach of posts. I know when we come to Leh again in a few days we shall find for each week of our absence one of your dear letters. I must have at least one little note ready to send to you. I'm resting an hour in my tent after a call from the Temporal Head of the monastery.

Monastery! Yes, actually within the walls of a monastery we have a tent. And such a tent! Huge, yellow and blue, with so many guy ropes that I can't recall the number, and poles tall enough for the masts of a barque,—a tent with an ante-chamber, and little rope-latticed windows, put up in our honour in a garden, a walled grassy garden with wee wild flowers in the turf.

There's a kitchen at one end of the garden where our cook is installed. The Abbot wanted to feed us but Iba thought it best to decline. He sent us enough raw material for a long stay: plates of rice and fine flour and spices, and a great slab of butter, a big fat yellow disk with hairy edges of the goatskin in which it was packed,—and a live ram led by the horn straight into the tent!

The Temporal Head must be a busy man always, with all these lands and houses to see after,—it's like an old castle, this gompa,—and just now at festival time the place swarms with pilgrims. But he took time to come and chat with us pleasantly about all sorts of things,—a grave gentle person he is. He brought me a brick of real Lhasa tea, wrapped in the hand-made paper I covet, with a bit of gold leaf inside, on the tea itself.

I'm rather excited at the prospect of seeing the Abbot. He's supposed never to die, or rather never to stay dead, being reborn at once. He told Rasul once that a river had a habit of carrying off a certain bridge on the Simla road till they took one of his legs (he having just died) and buried it near by. That story loses by oratio obliqua!

In this particular life this man has spent at a stretch ten years in complete retirement from the world, seeing no one. Think what an ordeal that must be for a person who might not happen to have the "gift of meditation."

I'm supposed to be resting!

Next day July 13

Such days as yesterday and the day before! The monastery is full of treasures, paintings and statues, embroideries and jewels. My head aches with seeing the numbers of them. We have seen a kind of mystery play besides. And we have had several interviews with the Abbot. He is certainly friendliness incarnate whatever else incarnate he may be. He got up at dawn to bid us good-bye today. (I'm writing while

I wait for my horse. The Governor of the province fell ill here, and we lent him my litter to go home in.) The Abbot has given me an incredible wooden teapot,—a great big one, big enough for twenty cups apiece for a family. It's all cut out of one block, spout, handle, lid and body, very nice lines, and the most fascinating designs in brass applied to the wood,— motif fully developed on the lid, expanded on the sides, a slender spray of it running up the handle, and another, somewhat different, out along the spout. I shall copy it the first chance I get. Iba says it's an old pot. I imagine it is. There's an odour of ancient butter tea about it! But whatever its possible value, it is an enchanting thing.

Wait till I show it to you. I have a copper and silver teapot for you of the characteristic Ladakhi shape. It's pretty, but as Rasul would say: "beside my Himis teapot, yours nothing is!"

They're ready! I've got to give back to the old gardeneress the great key she gave me to carry at my belt all the while I was here;—the key to the inner rose garden.

I'm not romancing! It's all true. I cling to my great teapot as evidence I'm not dreaming.

Yours affectionately,
The Khush Qismat Ri Mem-Sahib

Gypsy Davy   CAMP 90
SHUSHOT
July 15

Dear Ned,

We had come down from high nomad country on the Tibetan marches, into the broad Indus valley,—a great desert of a valley sunk deep among the mountains. Bare cliffs, steep barren screes, low-lying fans,—wide swells of mountain waste spread out at every breach in the walls, crowding the river into bluff-bordered curves, lifting the trail continually from one to another of them.

A tawny waste for the most part, but at rare intervals on the broad stony backs of barren fans, green oases, flights of green terraces. Frowning across one, a tall crag that pierces the fan there, a village clustered at its foot, terrace on terrace of flat roofs on low walls, all grey; the crag itself half hidden under

lama masonry, massive grey walls battered like bridge abut-
ments, mounting in great steps up to the very top; barracks,
refectories, mews, libraries, granaries, treasuries, temples,
piled up the crag sides; upper storeys loopholed with windows;
long balconies drawn across; broad black lines up there, and
touches of red; parapets flaunting black yak tails.

We were on our way to Himis, in response to urgent notes,
brought a long way up country, in cleft sticks by messengers
from the Chagdso,—Iba's warm friend, temporal head of that
lamasery.

An imposing monk rode up to meet us as we struck our
tents at the last camp, and led us on our way. We looked in
vain for the high crag which should be crowned by Himis'
lamasery. The monk turned up a little side nala, and led
us up beside a big mani wall, interminably long, toward blank
red sandstone cliffs. We thought the trail must end abruptly
at the foot of those blank cliffs. But there it bent to the left,
and for us, following it, it was as if the monk had struck the
mountain open with a magic wand. We rode round the nose
of a great red wall of a spur, and shortly round the nose of
another overlapping that, and halted, as was meet, at the bridge
before the castle gate, in an enchanted valley, while our escort
rode forward to announce us. Immediately behind the castle
wall, red sandstone cliffs frowned down on us from great heights
under blue skies. The Chagdso came promptly down to meet
us and led us in, and up steep cobbled ways past white tents
shading merchants squatting amid festal wares, on up to a
narrow gateway in a high garden wall, beside a torrent
thundering among boulders.

Wild rose-trees in full blossom glowed on either bank,
and in clefts high up precipice sides. The gompa walls rose,
grey and dingy and high, behind us to where black yak-tails
waved against red cliffs. There was a streak of colour where
a balcony stretched across the Abbot's apartments, another
where one stretched across the royal guest-chambers, another
where visiting governors lodge.

This, as the gay merchants' tents forewarned you, was a
time of festival. It was not only wild rose-trees that adorned
the torrent's banks, but groups of pilgrims in their best. There
was rich crimson in the women's homespun, and turquoise
blue and coral red in the wide cobras on their heads. And
there were gay yellows and blues in stripes, and bits of scarlet
and gold brocade. There was a big copper pot boiling in the
centre of every group with Lhasa tea in it; and a large brass

ladle; and there was a silver-lined wooden cup, cut from a knot, in everyone's bosom, and a little leathern sack of parched barley ground fine, and another of yak butter. What more would you have? And there were lean donkeys and lean ponies and lean yak all about, for the wild roses are a month late this year.

We passed through the narrow gateway into the high walled garden. A gorgeous tent, such as maharajas use, was pitching for us there. An old woman curtseyed to the Lady Ba and handed her a ponderous key, which gave her the freedom of the adjoining garden where the Abbot's yellow roses and his vegetables grow.

Now you have the old monastery's setting, and incidentally, ours. The monastery may date back as far as the thirteenth century. It escaped looting at the time of the conquest, and retains much of its old splendour.

But all this apropos of a certain withered hand and arm, hand of an artisan, Iba and the Kalon said, dead some two hundred years, famous for the rich banners he wrought.

They led us by devious ways into the dukang, the gloomy, low-ceiled chapel of the place where a solemn ceremony was going forward, in heavy incense-laden air—the propitiation of a demon.

A big shaft in the centre, hung with rich cloths, lighted a large banner wrought in silks and pearls by that artist hand, depicting a terrific fellow mounted on a fiery black horse (Jim insists it was an elephant). There was raw flesh on the altar below. The Skusho sat, portly and cross-legged like a Buddha, on a great block of a throne near by. Crimson-robed monks, bare-headed, dark Mongol faces, squatted in long rows before him, chanting to an accompaniment of bells and cymbals, thigh-bone bugles, drums, oboes, long horns, and now and then a deep boom from a huge suspended drum. The music swelled to furious crescendoes, died away and swelled again.

Tiny wicks burning in butter deepened the gloom on all sides. Big Buddhas loomed before us as we groped our way about the walls, and their polished metal shone in the circle of our little light. We had to step delicately across a floor strewn with great three-eyed horned masks, hideously grimacing.

Iba thinks that the faithful performance of services such as these blinded the eyes of Maharaja's sipahis. Last year, I think it was, this particular ceremony was omitted and a flood destroyed the Court of Hells.

In the courtyard outside the dukang, a spirited black horse with splendid trappings, perhaps this demon's in the flesh,

was being held with difficulty by his keepers.   The chanting
ended and the dukang doors swung to.   The keepers stripped
the horse and let him go.   The crowd parted, and he was off
at top speed for far-away pastures.   We could hear him clatter
down the long cobbled way that led out beneath the buildings.
I wonder, was that demon off with him, or was he merely one of
the animals consecrated that day?   Or was he a scapegoat?

They led us then up to a balcony across the courtyard.
Two clowns came out upon the courtyard stage and played
with us awhile, until the doors of the dukang were set ajar.
A monk or two slipped out, descended the long broad flight
of steps there, and laid a prostrate figure modelled in red dough,
probably, on the pavement.   Iba said it was a devil.   Iba
and the Kalon are my only authorities for all the characters
we saw upon that stage, and we saw many.

The doors of the dukang at last swung wide.   Two elegant
little pages stepped out and stood, one on either side the dark
door-way.   There was a flourish of trumpets.   A brilliant
cortège issued from the darkness, passed between the pages, and
descended.   Gorgeously apparelled knights and scholars, and
hideously masked demons and demon soldiery circled about
the image on the pavement.   Iba and the Kalon said it was a
contest between the knights and scholars and that supine
devil and his demon allies.   The best efforts of knights and
scholars alike seemed unavailing until one of the scholars had
recourse to the withered hand.   (The gompa keeps it among
its treasures, in the flesh, or rather in the dried skin and bones.)
The scholar held it grasping a bunch of silken streamers in its
withered fingers, held it a moment over the prostrate figure.
The demons and their soldiery fled up the steps.   The knights
followed with less haste, and lastly went the lordly scholars.
Four hideous death's heads which I had not marked, remained,
eating the red figure, presumably now a corpse.

What wonderful fellows those scholars were!   Each man
looking in his full regalia the size of four!   What brocaded,
what embroidered robes, hundreds of years old, the work of
how many artists' hands, now withered and forgotten, perhaps
potent still!

I have given you but a faint hint of what was to be seen
in chapel and courtyard.   I don't imagine that there was any
relation between the service in the dukang and the play in
the courtyard.

Yours,

BA

P.S. LEH *Three days later*

You must not lay too much stress on Iba's and the Kalon's interpretations, or on my memory of them. I took no notes. The most interesting and authoritative writer on these matters that we have run across, Waddell, tells how this play in various dresses, but always, I think, centring round a supine dough figure, is performed once a year, from one end of Tibet to the other. Waddell says it has its origin in an ancient Tibetan play from cannibalistic times, which they called the Red Tiger Devil Dance. This was variously modified to nestle under the rather thin cloak of Buddhism that was thrown over the shoulders of these wild fellows. It is a terrific affair, I judge, when given at its best. What do you think, for instance, of stuffing a dough figure with dough organs and injecting it with a red fluid and then stabbing it with weapons and goring it with horns (on the heads of the demons!) until it is torn to fragments, and finally tossing the bits to the crowd to be eaten by them? Doesn't this savour of a rather spirited human sacrifice?

Lady Ba   CAMP 90
                          SHUSHOT, INDUS VALLEY
                                    July 15

Dear WILL SCARLET,

Where do you suppose Jim is to-night?

He and Stuart and the Bara Sahib are down at the men's camp, listening to two minstrels reciting the Kesar saga!

Two young men of this village are learning the saga from the old men, who have had the job of doing it at the feasts in the valley for years and years. It has to be passed on by word of mouth, of course. Iba has got them to come and recite as much of it as they have learned, to our men. You should have seen Angbo and I-she hurry with the dinner work! I was too tired after a long day's march, on top of the festival at Himis, so I shall go to bed as soon as I've tucked the next instalment of my translation into an envelope for you.

                                    Yours,

                                    LADY BA

P.S. *Next morning*

The Bara Sahib says the men were thrilled for hours last night. They sat in a half-circle around a camp-fire, while the bards sang and recited in turns. Iba, however, says they don't put nearly so much life into it as the old fellows did, and there is a rumour that your brother went to sleep. But he has been going to bed a little after sunset for some months now, getting up long before dawn, and doing twenty miles a day on foot, so it can't be set down against the minstrels if they didn't keep him awake. He doesn't know Ladakhi. If they'd recited in Urdu, they'd have had him listening.

The last letter was the end of Kurulugu, but I think you'll like the next chapter. Hor is Yarkand up north of our mountains, where Roger tried to go, on his way out. Gling-land, Iba says, is Ladakh. I should think it might be all of Tibet.

KESAR AND THE DZEMO.

Now when Kurulugu was dead, the Dzemo gave to Kesar the food and drink of forgetfulness, so that he forgot Gling-land, and the loving Bruguma, his castle and all his people. The livelong day he played at dice with Bruguma, or shot at targets, wielding the bow. Thus for three long years she held him.

Now in those years came the King of Hor to Gling-land, and broke down the nine towers of the castle of Kesar. Bruguma the Queen he carried away captive, and the son of the King he killed. Of all this Bruguma wrote tidings to Kesar, though she knew not where he tarried. In her blood she wrote the letter, and by the doves of the house she sent it.

Hither and yon flew the doves, but Kesar and his kyang they found not. Their eyes ached with looking, and their wings were lame with flying, and back to Gling-land they came still bearing the letter. Now was Bruguma afar, but Ane-kur-manmo the goddess received them. She bathed them in waters of heaven, and when they were refreshed, sent them forth again. And when they set out, she herself in the guise of a dove flew with them, guiding them to the demon-king's castle.

Kesar, the god-king, and the Dzemo were sitting at dice, when the song of the birds of Gling came to them. The Dzemo, hearing, sang loudly, that Kesar might notice nothing. But Kesar said: "Hark, Dzemo! I hear a sound like the songs of my birds of Gling-land!"

But the Dzemo said, scoffing: "How could'st thou hear the birds of Gling-land in this place?" And sang the louder. Then Kesar caught her by her long braids of hair, and forced her to silence. Then he spread two carpets, a white one and a black one. On each he laid meat, and thus he spake to the birds: "If the news that you bring me be good news, on the white carpet alight ye. If the news that you bring me be bad news, on the black carpet alight ye." Then all the birds fluttered down to the black carpet and began to eat the meat that was laid there. And the largest of them loosed from his neck the letter Bruguma had tied there, and gave it to Kesar.

So Kesar learned all the doleful things that had come to pass in his absence.

Now went Kesar in search of his Kyang-god-byerpa, but no trace of him found he. When he asked the Dzemo about him, she said only: "Who knows where he is? I know nothing about him."

Then Kesar went forth to seek him in earnest. Up three mountains went he, and into three valleys. At last on the edge of a glacier, standing on splintery rock he found him, bruised of back and his flanks sore wounded. Great sorrow filled Kesar's heart, and he called to the foal, and the foal came to him, thus reproaching his master:—

"O forgetful King Kesar!
Once dwelt I in the halls of Bruguma.
Mornings gave she meal and butter.
Evenings gave she cake and sugar.
When she went up, she stroked me in passing.
When she went down, she patted my forehead,
Saying, 'Ass, my ass, how thin thou art!'

"Three years long at the door of the Dzemo,
Mornings I found only splinters of wood to eat.
Evenings I found only measures of sand to eat.
When she went up, she hit me with her fist.
When she went down, she gave me a kick,
Saying, 'Ass, thou ass, that art far too fat!'
Then wept I, the kyang of Kesar."

Then Kesar made answer: "Thou dost speak what is true, Kyang-god-byerpa. Me, too, hath the woman betrayed and beguiled. We will go now to Gling-land. But alas! thy poor back! How canst thou travel?" Then the foal said: "In my right ear are good lotions which my mother Bruguma put there. In my left ear is a sharp little lancet. Lead me, O master, to a spring of nectar and milk, and there wash my wounds. Then cut with the knife and anoint with the lotions, and I shall be well."

And when Kesar had done as the foal advised him, Kyang-god-byerpa was full of fresh life and stronger than ever.

Now said Kesar to the Dzemo: "In a year's time I will return and fetch thee also to Gling-land." But the Dzemo was displeased and said only: "Now, even now, will I go with thee." Then gave the foal shrewd counsel. "Let her sit on my back," quoth he, "behind the god-king, my master. When we are far out in the stream I will heave her mightily backwards."

So Kesar put the Dzemo behind him on the kyang's broad back, and when they were well out in the river, the foal heaved mightily and flung the Dzemo back to the bank they had come from, and Kesar went forward, paying small heed to her angry reproaches.

And as he went, he sang this song of Bruguma, the crystal consort:—

"If she, taking the shape of a turquoise dove,
Should go to soar in the highest skies,
I, taking the shape of a white falcon,
Will go to take her home again.

"If she, taking the shape of a turquoise dove,
Should go to flee into the highest zenith,
I, taking the shape of a white falcon,
Will go to follow after her.

"If she, taking the shape of the fish 'Gold-eye,'
Should go to float in the deepest ocean,
I, taking the shape of a white-breasted otter,
Will go to take her home again.

"If she, taking the shape of the fish 'Gold-eye,'
Should go to flee into the widest ocean,
I, taking the shape of a white-breasted otter,
Will go to follow after her."

Francke Padre Sahib put that song into English himself. Gypsy Davy thinks I have emasculated the last part of the Dzemo episode for you. It was too raw and bloody. You will have to learn Tibetan or German if you want its full value.

There's a great deal more of the story Dr. Francke put into German, and more still, I think, that is only in Tibetan as yet. Kesar got Bruguma back—quite as good a story, that, as the part I've given you.

Lady Ba　　　　　　　　　　　　　　　Camp 91
　　　　　　　　　　　　　　　　　　Tsam Skang
　　　　　　　　　　　　　　　　　　　Midsummer

Dear Yeomans Orchestra,

Your love of music is giving Munshi Jim a lot of work this week.

He's had to get a carpenter to make wooden boxes in which to mail to you various instruments. The parcel-post regulations limit the size of box and consequent amount of instrument to be carried. He has had to cut the handles off the tall drums, and send them separately. The weight of the nails threw out his nice calculations in one instance. He doesn't know how to confess to silver and turquoise on the oboes without paying for the weight of the whole as precious. The P.O. babu is none too clear in his interpretation of the regulations, and Jim has to wrestle with Maharaja's instruction-book himself.

The twelve-foot trumpets we are afraid he'd balk at, so you will have to look in at the Peabody Museum at Harvard to see the pair that Mr. Dixon brought back.

We failed to get a human thigh-bone bugle.

I made a faux pas in Tankse by offering to buy a chased silver flageolet. All the farmers of the district had contributed to get it made, and it was distinctly not in the market.

We know you'll love the lama's bell, and the cymbals. But the nicest, I think, is the ling-pu, the little carved wooden pipe. Almost every man carries one in his girdle, and plays as he walks, or after his food, or at night beside the camp-fire. My big Sawang has double pipes, like Siamese twins. He plays on them to every lovely view.

He plays the four upper holes with his right hand, and the three lower with three left fingers, leaving the little finger free with a big silver and turquoise ring on it. (The one Edward bought of the Navajos would do nicely.) His left thumb takes care of the eighth hole on the under side. He raises each tone an octave by blowing harder, of course.

I don't know whether Edward can play "Good King Wenceslas" on it or not. They say the intervals are not like ours.

Strange sounds are buried in the instruments. I wonder if they'll come out for you.

　　　　　　　　　　　　　　　　　　　Yours,
　　　　　　　　　　　　　　　　　　Ri Mem-Sahib

P.S.—Jane Duncan gives some of the songs, as Dr. Francke noted them down, in her book: *A Summer Ride through Western Tibet*, quite the pleasantest book about these parts that we have seen, by the way.   You can find more of the music in an article Dr. Francke wrote for the *Zeitschrift der Deutschen Morgenländischen Gesellschaft*, *Band LX* or in a translation of it in Lavignac's *Encyclopédie de la Musique et Dictionnaire du Conservatoire*.   I'll copy off one for you.   They get harmonies by singing antiphonally, sometimes like a round.   Our printed music doesn't show the big crescendo in every line and the complete diminuendos between swells, as well as their written music, which looks like a series of waves incoming.

Gypsy Davy   TSAM SKANG AGAIN

July 20

Dear NORMAN,

We found three nice letters from you when we came in from our safar.

What a dreadfully uncomfortable bedfellow a Cold must be! I wouldn't get into bed with one, between chilly sheets set up on stilts in a cold draughty room,—no, not for anything. Our blankets and our woollen sheets hang in the sun all day, and Angbo folds in the sun's heat when he makes up the beds, and lays the nice warm bundle on the ground where there are no draughts.   If a Cold were to try to wriggle in with me, he would get the shock of his life.

All our meals are picnics, but we do not eat them among bluebells and primroses.   We have eaten them under wild rose-trees though, and near irises.   And now we're back in Leh in summer, we've a wide choice in the appointments at our picnics.   There's no sign of a bare brown terrace anywhere. The whole valley bottom is green with waving grain, and here and there's "pale charlock's cloth of gold." And all those tawny barren mountain sides are dotted with green bunches of tall grass waving in the breeze, bunches rather far apart to be sure. And there are big thistles, round-headed fellows, heads all spiked,—looked as if they couldn't blossom, but all of a sudden they did, big creamy and lavender crosses between the spikes all around the ball, not a bit like Scotch thistles.

What makes you think of African negroes when you write to me? Are those African negroes at the bottom of your letter? I think you have set their belly-buttons rather high for Africans. Are those skins or braided leaves about their middles? Why, I declare I believe you have drawn them right in the middle of a kiss, a very large kiss, with a big hug on either side! There's nothing African about these people here, though I must say you might mistake a baby for a pickaninny, when he'd been properly greased and sooted to keep off the evil eye. I wonder how a kiss would taste on all that grease and soot.

I must tell you about an adventure of the Lady Ba's white pony, Tomar. He is a very dignified pony, far from young, very sedate and deliberate in all his movements. He will not eat sugar. I think the Lady Ba is beginning to find him a good deal of a bore. She often resorts to her litter on the march.

It was on our last safar. We were climbing higher and higher up among the mountains every day. The bottoms of the valleys had got to be as high as the tops of some of the thunderheads you see in summer.

One day Tomar was feeding with a lot of other ponies in the mouth of a wild valley by the edge of the great Pangkong Lake. There were no trees in the valley, and only a few tiny bushes. And there was hardly any grass, except along the shore. There was no stream in the valley. It was a dreadful desert of a valley. There were wild animals all about, wolves and wild sheep and antelope and wild asses. On this particular day a band of wild asses came down to get some of the green grass by the Lake. They don't look a bit like Sevenoaks Neddy. They are much bigger and stronger and friskier. Their backs are brown and their bellies and their legs are white. And at that hungry time of year their heads looked like great blacksmiths' hammers.

Tomar went over to see them. I think perhaps he frightened them a little, he was so white. Anyway, they ran, and he ran with them. They ran over two "glaciers mountains" and across three valleys. Six of our pony-men pursued them. For three days they hunted and three nights they camped on

his trail.   They had their postins with them to keep them
warm at night, and some sattu to eat.

Iba gave Tomar up for lost.   He said the old pony must
surely burst a blood-vessel.

But early on the morning of the fourth day Tomar came
galloping into camp of his own accord, holding his head high.

After that, whenever the Lady Ba mounted him, he behaved
like a five-year-old, and kept her busy managing him.   And
whenever we sighted a band of kyang, I held her bridle-rein.

The higher we went, the friskier he got.   None of us could
keep up with him.   The Lady Ba lost all interest in her litter.

She wrote a song about Tomar's adventure, and Iba set it
to music, and the men all sing it.   These are the words:—

> Hamara Tomar shikar kiya.
> Kyang ke-sath chala gaya.
> Tin roz aur rat nahin dekha.
> Admion ke-waste taqlif diya.
> Phir wapas ekdam jaldi daura.
> Buddha ghora pahile tha.
> Abhi jewan, chalak, naya.

Yours,

GYPSY DAVY

Lady Ba   TSAM SKANG

July 22

Dear WILL SCARLET,

We're back on Tsam Skang.   On our crag the tents are up
once more, only Roger's lacking.

Leh's all green.   Welcoming gifts from gardens came to
greet us.

The Kalon and his lady sent cabbages and roses, and along
with them an exquisite slender silver vase such as they use
in Lhasa for libations.   When we visited the Kalon at his big
old house in the winter, I admired one he owns, so he had one
made for me just like it.

The boys went down today to make a ceremonial call, taking
our thanks and gifts.   My thank-you note took me an hour
to write!

And this is why I'm writing you.   The Kalon showed
them a book about Kesar!   The only one in Ladakh, they

understood. A proper Tibetan book, long narrow sheets beautifully written, placed between two heavy boards and wrapped in cloth, weighing fifteen pounds. We saw a whole library full of books like that in pigeon-holes in the monastery at Himis, in a room with pots of rice and grain, which had been blessed and then sealed, to stay sealed forever.

The Kalon's forefathers were hereditary prime ministers in the times when Ladakh had a king in more than title. One of them, on a journey to Lhasa, had his secretaries copy these two bookfuls from the many bookfuls of the story there are in the sacred city. (There is a Kesar temple there, the Kalon says, with statues of Kesar.) The old Kalon kept his secretaries working day and night to get as much copied as possible.

And Jim and Stuart have seen it. They say Sonam, our "literate litterman," who was along, (everybody who likes comes with any of us when we go anywhere) immediately began to read aloud when the Kalon opened the book. Everybody laughed. It was the part about Kurulugu's snoring!

Yours,

LADY BA

Lady Ba   *July 23*

Dear ALICE,

It seems strange to be back on Tsam Skang and not see Rasul. We miss him. I've been going over some of my notes of the stories he told us. I think you'll like this one.

"Was one man in Leh, John Sahib, one black man. Not his name, John Sahib, but not would speak if calling to any other name. If man say to him to own name, he say very big voice: 'My name John Sahib.'

"In Yarkand people speaking to him into Turki: 'Jah Sahib.' That mean 'cheat sahib.' He not know they joking to him.

"Was caravan bashi for sahibs. They think is good man. Not was good man. Was robber man. I working in my young time helping Qutedar at fort, giving grain and hay. John Sahib taking for his sahib many thing, not paying. Keeping Sahib's money for own pocket.

"One day I taking to him some grain. He say very angry: 'Not is enough. Is one sers too little.' I say: 'Sir, you weigh.'

He weigh. That come one sers too much. I taking back that one sers. I say: 'Now, I not bring any more grains until you paying to Qutedar all what you owing. You owing for so many sers barley grains so many rupees, for so many loads hay so many rupees.' That all I keeping in my head. He afraid to me. Why? I not afraid to him.

"After that time come John Sahib very much love on beautiful girl in Leh. That girl not wanted John Sahib. John Sahib sell everything, make presents for get that girl come in marriage with him. Last bring from Kashmir one very big glasses thing, like gate. One looking thing. Then come that girl very sweet in marriage. Come two three sisters also. Is custom in Ladakh two three brothers one girl marry. Two three sisters one man marry. Is custom.

"Very nice girls those girls and enough beautiful. Not more beautiful than other Ladakhi women. Now every day come little more beautiful. Everybody think that very interesting, how beautiful. When smiling, smiling very pretty. When make with hands some way, that way very beautiful. Everybody thinking very wonderful that all.

"I not go ever to John Sahib's house. One day Kalam Rasul go that house. After, he tell to me he see man in that house. He say salam. It is that glasses thing. It is Kalam Rasul he seeing.

"Then I thinking very hard in my head. One day I make some business. I go John Sahib's house. I come in door. Is nobody in big room. There I see long way off very ugly little one man. Pagri crooked.   I put straight my pagri. Ugly little one man put straight his pagri. I smiling very sweet. He smiling very sweet, same me.

"Then I go very quick my house. I telling to all people: 'Is that glasses thing making so beautiful those girl in John Sahib's house. What saying, what doing, that looking in glasses thing. That come very beautiful."

Is it a good year for the orchards?

Yours,

Lady Ba   Tsam Skang
                                         July 25

Dear JULIET,

I'm not so sure about the women.

I find in my notes on Rasul's conversations that though he said: "In Ladakh is custom two three brothers one wife take" (with all that implies of proper supremacy), he also said: "Is also custom two three wives one husband."

And even in the sect where women appear to hold trumps as evidenced by the Shamlegh woman in *Kim* and the wife of our melodious carpenter, it isn't quite proven.

One of our perfectly orthodox Buddhists married in the winter a woman who had a lot of turquoises and lived on the road between our camp and the village—sufficient reasons. Now he is back after a two months' safar, and the bride thinks it time he stayed at home a little.

He told Stuart about it. "Kis-waste baithega? Siraf aurat! What should I stay for? Only a woman! Work's easy. Sahb's temper's good. Good grub. New country. Jolly lot of fellows. Sab ham dost. What should I stay for? Only a woman!"

Yours,

Gypsy Davy   Tsam Skang
                                         July 25

Dear MARJORIE,

A crocus from California fell out of your letter yesterday.

There is a crocus in the Vale of Kashmir, from whose stigmas the precious saffron comes.

Rasul and I took saffron with us on a journey that we made together, as part of our stock in trade. We found the lamas in eastern Tibet very keen to get it. Rasul says they dip their pens in saffron dye, each time they write the name of Buddha.

Yours,

GYPSY DAVY

Lady Ba   TSAM SKANG
July 25

Dear DONALD,

I've been reading in Francke's *History of Western Tibet*, that the Dards along about the year 500, came up the Indus to fight the Baltis.   The two armies, as I understand it, marched along on opposite sides of the river and tried to throw things at each other, but it's pretty wide.   Jim and Stuart are always trying to get a rock across it, and I don't think they've succeeded yet.

They couldn't cross on the ice, for the river is so swift for a lot of the way that it doesn't freeze over.   Roger went down to see what birds he could find, about the last of February, and much of the river was quite open, and the places that were iced over would never have supported an army crossing.   Of course there probably are places where it freezes over solidly.

Well, the historian says that the Dards fastened several beams to the bank in such a way that they projected into the river.   After a short time (they were working in the night, of course) those beams were frozen in so solidly that it was possible to walk on them as far as the outer end.   Then they fastened several more beams to the first, and made them project farther still into the river.   When these were frozen in, another set of beams was brought, and so on, until the opposite bank was reached.   On such a bridge of ice and wood, the army crossed at night, surprising the Baltis who had not even posted sentinels.

And that's all I have to tell you about that kind of "water cross."

LADY BA

Gypsy Davy   TSAM SKANG AGAIN
July 26

Dear HEN-PARROT, (That's what your nickname means in Urdu)

We have two nice letters from you, mostly about letters that Jim has been writing you.   Jim has lost his pen, and there may be an interlude in which I hope you will find time to read one of my letters.   I expect, if I am to get you to read it, it will have to start about Jim.

R

He has a long beard now, like mine, but he isn't bald yet. His beard doesn't spread out quite as much as mine. It has a tendency to keep back toward his ears and under his chin.

Stuart's beard is heavier, but, of course, he's seventeen. He wears ear-rings, and a red bandanna instead of a hat, and a green sash with a knife in it. His ear-rings are big loops of seed pearl and turquoise and coral strung on silver wire. You would know him for a pirate anywhere. · He is practising against the time we hoist the Black Flag in the South Seas.

We don't have any hepaticas or apple-blossoms, and there are very few violets. But we have the loveliest wild rose-trees you ever saw.

There aren't many trees here, to cast shadows, but the mountains cast giant ones that creep for miles and miles across the valleys. And the old earth casts her shadow on the sky in the morning and the evening twilight. And the clouds cast shadows which go drifting over tawny crags and long scree slopes. And the ravens and the eagles cast shadows which skim over the long screes at high speed. Sometimes we see the shadows when we cannot see the birds.

GYPSY DAVY

Lady Ba   CAMP 92
                                                        NIMU
                                                     July 31

Dear CYNTHIA,

Gypsy Davy sketched my litter for Monica in pencil last summer. Now it would need your brush and full tubes of green and scarlet. Long poles green, short poles red, red seat-back, green canopy. Littermen in hot weather liveries designed by Iba for the amazement of Simla some two months hence, and worn this first march out of Leh (after a midsummer fortnight, spent on our old winter crag for re-organization): voluminous white Mussulman trousers, white blouses, little scarlet monkey waistcoats, and red Ladakhi horned hats sans fur for summer. They look under-dressed without their long robes, but very proud.

We made a rather late start, largely because we were so reluctant to be definitely leaving. The boys found last-minute errands, and we did not wait for them. Far ahead we could see what we took to be a funeral, a red object moving slowly, in the midst of a little company.

We came up with it where the trail was narrow. The red thing was a proper palanquin, and there was another of black and white ahead of it, both mysterious, private, with tiny close-latticed windows. I saw an eye at one! They were big and heavy and clumsy, and the bearers puffed and sweated. The pace was apparently too slow for the lord of the harem, as they were unattended. The Gypsy climbed a bit and passed the obstacles. My men, "neat and nimble O in every high degree" sauntered along behind the big palanquins, making rude comments, I fear, and appreciating, I hope, their sahib's inventiveness, as they watched the efforts of the bearers to get around curves with their burdens.

Now shift your point of view. You, say, escorted by your "afsar sahib" husband, trim, compact and self-contained, on hunting leave in Ladakh, riding up to Leh, miles ahead of your servants, meet upon the trail a singular company: stalking ahead a tall bearded sahib, wearing instead of shorts and topi, patched Shetlands and a raffish tam; behind, a palanquin, wide and heavy, suggestive of numerous occupants; behind that,—you drawn up in a widish place to let it pass,—another, scarlet, but quite as ponderous; behind that again a light gay litter exposing to view an immodest female in knickers and cowboy hat!

We, of our country, have a habit, you may remember, of saluting casual strangers on the road, not so much because we are more friendly than your countrymen, probably, as that our spaces are yet wide enough to make the custom practicable. But there was no "Good Morning" even from me on this occasion. Seeing them look down their noses, I hid meekly under my big sombrero, feeling myself justly snubbed by that monogamous young couple!

—But I hear Monica saying: "O mother! you'd never have passed by the Gypsy Davy so!"

Our love to her and to you and salams to your husband.

Your

"LADY BA"

Lady Ba   CAMP 95
                                  BEYOND KHALATSE
                                                August 5

Dear MONICA,

There's a valley I've been in today, that's like a deep crack
in the rind of the Earth. It's a secret sort of valley. It hides
from the sun till noon-time, and shoulders him off again about
half-past two. And away down in the bottom of that crack
I saw a little girl named Monica, just like you! Her hair's as
yellow as your hair, and her eyes are as blue as yours, and her
cheeks are even fairer than your cheeks, because the sun never
stays long enough to tan them. But though nobody thinks
anything about your being fair, people travel many days to
look at this Monica's fairness, and to beg her father and mother
for "medicine" to make their children look like her. You see,
all the other children in that crack and in the other cracks
for miles and miles about, have skins as brown as crusty whole
wheat bread and eyes as dark as currants in cake, and hair as
black as burnt toast. Monica looks like a meringue among
them. She plays with them and knows them apart, and loves
some and doesn't like others. And she can speak their funny
language (you should hear her say "dik-dik-dik" for "enough"
with her tongue going as fast as a humming-bird's wings)
and she can read it and write it and sing it!

When by and by she comes to England to school, I suppose
all the fair English children will look strange to her. She'll
feel as if the Monicas in dozens of mirrors had come out to
play with her. And if she says "dik-dik-dik" nobody will
understand her. I wonder if she won't be homesick sometimes
for the jolly little girls and boys of far Ladakh, in their long red
robes and their horned caps and their pointed yak-hair shoes.
What do you think?

                                              Yours,
                                              LADY BA

Lady Ba   CAMP 95
                              BEYOND KHALATSE
                                       August 5

DEAR HARLAN,

We are camped above the Indus, our last camp in sight of the River. The Indos of the Greeks,—their attempt at the Sanskrit "sindhu" meaning "river." *The* River! Like the Tibetans' Tsangpo,—The River.

Why don't you come over some day and shoot the Indus in a canoe, at least from the Tibetan border to the sea?

As far as we can hear, there's never been a boat on these upper Ladakh reaches, except the sectional one that Sven Hedin left here many years ago, on his way out of Tibet, and that hasn't been far. Maybe the Indus is too rough going, but as far as we have seen it, it looks feasible. We had to leave it at one gorge, and just below us here, there is another, and we know there is a superb one beyond Skardu. How would you like shooting rapids in such gorges as these? You might see stars in daytime in some of them,—if you could lift your eyes from the rushing blue-green water.

The best description I've ever come across of one of those gorges is quoted by Miss Duncan in her book, from Fa-hian, a Chinese traveller who journeyed down the Indus in the beginning of the fifth century, if you please, on his way to Afghanistan. "The way was difficult and rugged, running along a bank exceedingly precipitous which rose up there, a hill-like wall of rock ten thousand cubits from the base. When one approached the edge of it his eyes became unsteady, and if he wished to go forward in the same direction, there was no place in which he could place his foot, and beneath were the waters of the Indus. In former times men had chiselled paths along the rocks and distributed ladders on the face of them to the number altogether of seven hundred, at the bottom of which there was a suspension bridge of ropes by which the river was crossed, its banks being there eighty paces apart." There were dragons, too, he says, "which, when provoked, spit forth poisonous winds and cause showers of snow and storms of sand and gravel. Not one in ten thousand of those who encounter these dangers escapes with his life."

And then imagine the thrill of coming out—if you did come out—on the wide reaches down which Alexander took his ships—reaches not quite where he left them perhaps! The River is changing its lower course always.

Perhaps in a few years it won't be so hard to get permits to enter Tibet. We've had so many invitations, from merchants and the like, that it's hard to think of it as really "forbidden" land. Anyhow they might let you, and you might actually start at the Lion's Mouth, where the river starts. Iba says there are two great rocks which look like a mouth, but I think Iba is only trying to explain a symbol. Kunick Padre Sahib says that they say one of the other great rivers comes out of the elephant's mouth and another out of the peacock's. Even Rasul doesn't know where The River goes.

Some day some American or Canadian will pack in materials for building a canoe, build it, and show up at Karachi. I'd like the fun of grub-staking him. Iba says he would make all the band-o-basts.

Our thoughts are full of exploration to-night. The boys met an English hunter on the trail. He told them Odell saw Mallory and Irvine, on June ninth (when we were at the Pangkong) disappearing into mists on the back of Everest, very, very near the summit. He says Mallory, in his last dispatch, wrote: "We expect no mercy from Everest. . . . But here is the will, and perhaps the power, to conquer." I wonder if they acknowledged the mountain at last as "Goddess Mother of the Country." I suppose the Tibetan people will be surer than ever that the gods don't want their sacred height violated, now that the supreme sacrifice has been required. I think they actually got to the top. Such spirit as Mallory's must have carried him all the way. I wonder who will find their bodies there. You remember how Muir encouraged little Stickeen to cross the crevasse: "If we die, think what a glorious grave we'll be having!"

I'd have "liked fine to be their mother."

Yours,

RI MEM-SAHIB

Gypsy Davy

CAMP 97
HINISKUT

August 8

Dear JACK,

I agree, I have been using the word "Himalaya" much too loosely. The fact is, that southern range looms big enough in my imagination to need all this country for foundation.

I imagine the Indian plainsmen named it "the abode of snow," long before any man ventured in. I like the sound of it. I'm going to keep on using it, qualifying when I am driven to it, as "Kara-koram Himalaya," "Southern Range," and so on. Here's a sop for you. Why don't you call all this western wreckage of Tibet, all these fragments of the old plateau, as far west, north and south as an occasional level skyline still suggests the old surface, why don't you call all this Tibet, plus the proper suffix to indicate such origin? That ought to satisfy the physiographic urge in you. And while you're about it, why not adopt a similar nomenclature in your note-books for all mountain regions where you suspect such origins? To be sure, mountains which loom so very high above the more or less intact part of this plateau as the Nepal Himalaya do, may rumple somewhat for you, badly rupture perhaps, the neat block you'd carve up thus. Perhaps when you try to squeeze K^2 and the other giants of the Kara-koram into your Tibetan wreckage you'll have to add to the first suffix a second, meaning "cataclysmic," which might reduce your system to near absurdity. But why suppose the whole block ever neat? Why shouldn't parts of it be very rugged from the first?

But these are matters for you to wrestle with. I hold by Himalaya for the whole region. (And I'm trying to pronounce it Himah' as the fiat has gone forth from the R.G.S.)

I think, by the way, Iba's note-books and his map collection would interest you. Iba has never seen a railway or a ship, but he is a much travelled man, nevertheless. His little home-made note-books are full of valuable matter, set down clearly, in a very neat hand, Tibetan script, with here and there a plan or a sketch map. (He has a proper loose-leaf now with plenty of refills, and a fat red pen and a gold pencil!) He prizes his British maps, and although he can read no English, makes clever use of them.

Angbo can read nothing in any language. But I wish you

might have been by when Stuart first showed him a map. It was an old Indian Survey sheet. Stuart showed him Leh and his own village, Alchi, and pointed out a little of the Indus stream and the black ridges beside it. Angbo set out immediately to follow the Indus from Leh down to the edge of the sheet, going up all the side nalas and naming them and the villages in them, without hesitation, and without one mistake.

Later, when we were trying to give all the men an idea of Hindustan from Bartholomew's *Atlas*, Angbo pointed to the speck we told him was Leh, slapped his hand to his mouth to prevent too indecorous a laugh, and said: "Leh's no bigger than a louse!"

Rasul, oddly enough, never took much interest in maps, never owning any that I know of, though I once offered him some good ones,—and never took notes. He had an amazing memory for detail and a power of putting two and two together. He had an accurate picture of his mountains in his head, both in detail and in large. He once explored, and made a rough trail through a certain nala for Major Oliver, which he said the Major thought might make a dry route by the upper Shyok in the high water season, for caravans bound north. I believe it was the big tributary from the east to the Shyok north of the Chang-chenmo having an easy pass at the head. Rasul confidently expected that it would appear some day on the British map marked "Galwan Nala." He said one day: "Must to die, sir. If I am King, must to die, and become silt. But will live my name in the world."

Here's hoping you make Cabin and Trail.

Yours,

GYPSY DAVY

Gypsy Davy　　　　　　　　　　　　　CAMP 97
　　　　　　　　　　　　　　　　　　HINISKUT

August 8

Dear DAVE,

We are camped high up the side of the Indus valley in the little forester's, looking up a nala towards Zaskar. Or, to be more accurate, that thin-walled but stout little tent is backed up into a wind that shakes it rude y in cold wet gusts. We've had to lace the sheet across the front, and we're looking up the nala in our mind's eye.

It's a narrow nala, rather more like a crack than a valley. Nine blind men came down it all roped together a month ago, towed by a man who could see. They were much bruised with stumbling among the rocks of the way. It's a month's way, from Zaskar to Leh, where they hope to receive sight at the hands of the Mission Doctor.

My riding pony Nun Chun is a Zaskar pony. Nun Chun means "iron grey." I don't think he ever troubled himself much about trails till he met me. He doesn't need them. He was raised in very rough country between fourteen and fifteen thousand. The best of our Sierra donkeys would soon break his neck if he tried to follow Nun Chun's lead. You wouldn't believe your eyes to see the rocks he takes, with me on him. He takes them fast, without batting an eyelash. He likes bad fords. He's a strong swimmer. He takes bridges that sway and sag and have big holes in them and wobbly flat rocks for footing, and never loses his nerve or makes a mis-step.

He used to go straight up hills however steep they were, and have to stop to catch his breath pretty often when he had me with him. I taught him to zigzag, so that he could go all the way to the top without stopping. Now he goes out of his way to zigzag for fun when it isn't necessary.

Lady Ba has a Zaskar pony too, named Nunatuk. He's very clever, but he's not so clever as Nun Chun. The other day she fed Nunatuk with sugar when he was standing right beside Nun Chun. Nun Chun licked his chops all the while Nunatuk was eating the sugar, but otherwise he was very polite about it.

If you see one of our letters headed "Hiniskut" or "Kargil" don't think of us as down in the village, but high above it, on some spur or old moraine.

GYPSY DAVY

Gypsy Davy   CAMP 98
                    JUST BELOW NAMIKA LA

August 10

Dear RAY,

We had a mind to take the outfit up a certain canyon the other day, which led to where we would be. But the canyon was so confoundedly narrow, and the water so deuced quick, and there was so much crossing and re-crossing (except where you were going straight up the stream-bed, in places where there were no banks at all!), and the footing was so precarious among big slippery boulders hidden by water, dirty as well as quick, and the volume of water varied so erratically, rising in bright sunshine from melting ice (glaciers at the stream's head) and rising in sudden little rains, and the places where you could escape a flood were so small and comparatively few, at the foot of those rock walls, and all under fire from falling rocks when it rained, that—take it all in all—we came to the conclusion that it was no place, in this month, for the Lady Ba, not to mention twenty odd men and some fifty or sixty ponies.

Even the dry nalas hereabouts are not always dry. Bearing this fact in mind, we encamped yesterday at a respectful distance above the bottom of one which carries tomorrow's trail up to a little divide,—a narrow winding nala with just a trickle of water in it, a blind sort of nala, so well camouflaged that I didn't suspect it of having any drainage basin at all. It seemed just a little wrinkle in the bare hillside.

It began to rain. We went into the tent. It must have rained rather hard for half an hour or so. Presently we heard a loud roar, a continuous roar, and stepped out to see what was up. The roar seemed to come from the direction of that pass, but there was nothing noisy-looking to be seen in that direction or in any other.

The roar grew louder. Our men came pouring out of their tents below us. They began yelling across the nala. There was a little cobble-stone hut over there. Suddenly a lot of men burst out of the hut and made for higher ground, just in the nick of time. The last one was not well clear of the hut when a barrage of muddy water tore through the camouflage. You might have thought the earth had opened and let loose that tumbling sinister black wall.

We've plenty of lively water ahead, beyond the last high pass, and I expect it's lively dirty water, with nasty bottoms, and I expect it's many a pony that will go down and get carried beyond his depth, and get water into his ears and have to be fished out.

Tundup has made a boot for the litter, a kind of poncho with a slit for Milady's head.

Yours,

GYPSY DAVY

Lady Ba   CAMP 100
                                               KARGIL
                                          August 13

Dear WILLIAM,

You want to know what "Year of the Wood Mouse" means?
To explain it would make my head swim.   But I can give you
a table, and let you figure it out for yourself.   I copied the table
out of one of Waddell's books.   The Skusho of Himis, by the
way, tells us Waddell Sahib's book: *The Buddhism of Tibet*,
is half true, a big proportion of truth, we think, for the Skusho
to credit any foreigner with.

1862	Water Dog	1922
1863	Water Hog	1923
1864	Wood Mouse	1924
1865	Wood Ox	1925
1866	Fire Tiger	1926
1867	Fire Hare	1927
1868	Earth Dragon	1928
1869	Earth Serpent	1929
1870	Iron Horse	1930
1871	Iron Sheep	1931
1872	Water Ape	1932
1873	Water Bird	1933

The next year, 1874 or 1934 you can see, would be Wood Dog.
What is your class year? I'm afraid I was born in the year of
the Earth Hare.   What an unadventurous life one would
expect me to live! Suppose one were born in the year of the
Fire Dragon, for example!

                                          Yours,

                                          LADY BA

P.S.—Gypsy Davy says that a rabbit's life is more full of
adventure than a dragon's. To be always scampering to
save your tuft must be much more exciting than calmly to
go about breathing fire.

Gypsy Davy   CAMP 103
                                            SURU

                                            August 18

Dear ALBERT,

Are you never going to train your guns on us again? It's a long time between shots. You'll have to use a high trajectory to get us now, we're down so low behind the outer wall,. the big southern barrier, and so close to it.

You know these walls are very massive and very high. The battlements scrape star-dust off the stars they ride beneath. But for all that, they're nothing but young ruins that will crumble down into as flat a heap as any old Prussian castle gate before Lazy Peg. Or any of those ancient cities they dig down through, heaped one upon another in such thin layers that it is no great matter to miss one altogether.

The Lady Ba felt something of a shock when I set out to raze these mountains for her. Heaven knows I've had trouble enough leading her up to them while she thought them substantial things. She was a plains-girl, you know. She didn't exactly shy at her first mountains, those little Sierra Madre, the way the horses used to at the hill the New Englanders in Chicago built long ago to comfort them, but she stamped her foot with rage when I told her they were nothing, that we must be off to real mountains. She stamped harder when she had come to love the Sierra Nevada, and I told her they were nothing, and we must be off to the real mountains. These are the real mountains, and it's a shame to talk of them to her as ruins. But ruins they are, and worse than that, they're not so very old.

Odell found fossils near the top of Chomo Lungmo on that glorious climb, you know, and that means that the rock he dug his fossils out of has lain out flat as any pancake under the sea.

There was once sea here, where these mountains are, where Tibet is, a long arm of the Pacific, reaching to the Midland Sea. They call it Tethys. There were mountains, high ones, to the north of it, and to the south. I am not so clear in my head as to how they know there were mountains to the north, but the roots of the old mountains to the south still range through Hindustan.

Those ancient mountains on the shores of Tethys crumbled to ruin as these young ones are now doing. Long cloaks of wasted rock crept slowly down their slopes. Wild mountain streams tore at the hems, and swept away rocks innumerable, tumbling and tumbling over each other with a deafening roar, down toward the sea. And when the mountain water reached Tethys, flowing demurely at the last in broad rivers, the currents carried only mud, and now and then, in flood, sand, along with a museumful of things the water had dissolved and held. This mountain essence spread out there on the sea-bottom, layer on layer, until there came to be a mighty thickness of it.

All this was long ago when those horrible monsters haunted the planet, and if there were any men about, they must have kept close to their holes like rabbits. You can see the wraith of one of the sea monsters today if you watch from some high spur of the Himalaya plunging down into a troubled cloudy ocean over Bengal; if you watch in December, say, from the highest hut where the Singalila spur from Kinchinjanga pricks through the cloud, if, riding thus on the back of Meredith's "solitary monster of old seas crossing the Deluge," you keep awake till midnight, you'll see Hydra rear up out of Tethys. But that would be observing from mountains that are themselves not yet risen out of Tethys, wouldn't it? Let's get on.

When those old mountains had been pretty effectually laid in their grave in Tethys' bottom, "wave-drifted mica flakes, down there in the diluvial darkness," they came to life again after the manner of the Dalai Lama and the Skushos and the Raja of Stok and in fact about everybody in the high Himalaya. The bottom of Tethys began to buckle. I suppose there came a thrust from the north against the solid roots of that old range to the south. And in the course of time, with many such bucklings and the slow jerky heaving up of Tibet in one big somewhat crumpled block, with quakes that racked the planet and a devastating hubbub, after a very long while, they got the roof on the world. The wild geese, if there were any in those days, must have had an easy flight southward over the lowland before building operations started. But each year thereafter they'd have to circle higher and higher until, when the battlements went up, they'd have to begin hunting passes between them.

The mountains are none too steady yet. We felt a tremor in the rock platform on Tsam Skang under us one night. The stove in the pit between us rattled, and there was a sound like distant thunder. Perhaps some mountain near us was taking a step up or a step down. Perhaps the tremor came from far away: the bottom of the Persian Gulf buckling a little?

Anyway Tethys seems very real to us while Munshi Jim is writing down this letter in the early morning.   Here at Suru in August Jim's fingers are not numb like Chot's on Tsam Skang in the winter.   But his wits are numb, or else mine are.   He's yawning!

Yours,

Gypsy Davy

Lady Ba   Camp 103
                                     Suru
                                  August 18

Dear Ellen,

I wonder if your southern darkies are as much fun as these black pigtails of ours! I have always imagined that, though it might be as much work to be served by a lot of children whom you in turn would have to look after, as it would be to do your own work, it would also be much more entertaining.   Now I know it.

Gypsy Davy and the boys are off, for two days and a night, to see the Nun Kun glacier.   I am dwelling "alone" in Suru. The cook-tent is about two minutes' fast run from my tent. Angbo never goes at any other pace except when he's carrying a dinner tray loaded.   Return trips he makes at top speed, swinging the empty tray over his head and singing! He has served my meals, swept the tent, aired and made my bed, pausing on each visit for a bit of chat.   Angbo is very fond of talk and finds it an inconvenience, that I know no Ladakhi and he only four hundred words of Urdu.

Iba's tent is just in sight beyond the cook-tent.   He has called half a dozen times since the men left, on various pretexts, but really to be sure that I am all right.   The men call him "Baba Iba"—Father Iba.   He does take care of every one of us.

As night fell, eight big fellows appeared with their beds and stretched themselves at the four cardinal points and the four intermediate about my tent.

Today they've taken turns sitting a little way off to make any villagers who may start this way fetch a long detour to preserve my privacy. I wanted a messenger a few minutes ago.   Mota Sering (that means Fatty Sering) was on guard. I called and called and called again.   Angbo came running, woke up my guard and sent him packing.   Gentle Norpel has just brought the laundry.   How he gets our dirty things so beautifully clean in cold water I can't imagine.   He puts little black threads in before washing, to indicate places that will need extra scrubbing.   He folds things very neatly.   I imagine he'd even iron them if we provided means and showed him how.   Here comes Joldan to go on guard.   He's a dignified person, given to strolling by himself and picking flowers to wear. All the littermen pick flowers for my sketch-books.   They used to bring tight bunches of stemless blossoms at first, but now they are careful about stems and leaves.   I have sketched over two hundred this summer, and they have all watched the number grow.   They are always looking out for new flowers. They actually know which I have had.   They'll scramble away up a cliff face or down to the brook edge or over a stone wall through an abatis of thorns to get me one they think is new. And if somebody says scornfully: "Purana! Old!" the face of the giver falls dolefully, and I have to take the flower to wear, even if I don't need it for sketching.

We simply can't bear to make them feel badly.   Once I criticized one detail in a perfect four-course dinner, and Angbo's face filled with sorrow, and he murmured: "Khana accha ni!" —"Dinner's no good"—in a tone that broke my heart.   Iba thinks my heart breaks too easily, and that I spoiled my room-boy I-she.   He says a sensible servant is not spoiled by praise, —rather stimulated by it,—but a foolish one is, or one who is only a little sensible.   He says his job would be easier if the Sahib swore more, and I praised less.   So I'm trying. But it's hard not to praise them.   They work such hours and hours so cheerfully.

I watch their hats as indicators of their states of mind.   They are the drollest hats!

> Two horns turned up: normal, all channels open.
> One horn over eyes: absorbed in work, don't interrupt.
> Both horns down: ear-ache or megrims.
> Only one horn up: feeling jaunty.
> Back in front, like a poke-bonnet: mood of meditation.

The hats looked very nice and fresh when we left for the summer safar, but now they are thoroughly seasoned, a bit faded, a bit greasy, comfortably squashed out of shape, two or three charms sewed on one, a yellow rag, blessed doubtless on another, needles stuck in all of them, home-made or black-smith-made rather, wound round with thread.

They can all sew, some of them very well indeed.   Tundup

the tailor, does really good canvas sewing, and has carried out
several ingenious and extensive operations on the tent.   I
haven't done a bit of mending for ages.   I simply shout
"Tundup mangti!" and if he is too busy for my little job he
turns it over to one of the others, and patches and darns of the
neatest sort are soon forthcoming.

At present they are all working on headnets for themselves
against the time when we shall get into mosquito-land. We have
been lately trying to teach them to drink only boiled water,
telling them that when they have crossed the pass into Hindustan
anything else might be fatal.   Their habit is to drop on their
knees beside any ditch and drink deep.   I suppose they think
that it is some kind of religious pollution they'd get from
drinking Hindu water.   In Leh they know the few Hindus
have to pass the convenient ditch whence the Buddhists and
Mussulmans get their water, pass again the one pipe which
takes water to the Christians, and go away off to an open stag-
nant pool, technically unpolluted.

They are such a lot of old dears we couldn't bear to have
them come to grief in our service.   Wasn't it sporting of them
to want to travel so far? Iba has written a kind of hymn of praise
which they sing very solemnly, about how good we are to take
them to see strange countries.   He says: "Eye hath not seen
nor ear heard" of such kindness.

Interrupted by the cook with a stomach-ache. The cook
is of high rank.   He is travelling with us, somewhat as young
lords are sometimes sent on far journeys to break off a drink
habit.   Most of these men of ours are comfortable zamindars'
sons, improving this opportunity to travel.   They all use
the "respect language" in speaking to Longpa.   He is of
higher birth than Iba, but as Iba is headman and technically
his superior, they address each other ceremonially.   Longpa is
a good cook too,—"prince de race et de cuisine," as an Indian
we used to know called himself.   Longpa is usually very
jolly, and inclined to look upon the making of soup and cakes
and the roasting of meat as mere incidents in his day of singing
and joking and smoking.   But to-day he was properly gloomy.
I've given him our two striking pills, a white soda tablet and
a black charcoal one, and I imagine he'll recover.   If he doesn't
I may have to try the even more spectacular remedy of an
ammonia vaporole broken at his nostril! Apparently the pills
or his faith in them had effect, for I can see him braiding
Angbo's pigtail.   Those pigtails take a fearful amount of
dressing.   Our men delight in being clean now that they

have soap. They're always washing their hair and tidying up. The loose hairs that look so harum-scarum in their pigtails are really in the design, and the braid itself is much more elaborate than the simple braid of our childhood. Angbo particularly likes to weave a red rag into the end of his.

Nice Angbo! He started out as a litterman, became leader of the littermen, then Iba's help in the serai, then room-boy, and now he is assistant cook, quite as good as H.R.H. Longpa. Rasul considered Iba as his pupil in the honourable art of serving sahibs, and Iba does him credit. Now Iba is training Angbo to be a caravan bashi some day, teaching him traditions which date back probably to Rasul's wise old mother. When she sent her boy out on his first journey she sewed three rupees into his clothes, telling him to show them to the Sahib, so that if he should lose or break anything of the Sahib's, he could pay for the thing with his own money. She also supplied him with peppers, needles and thread, and, in case the Sahib's allowance for servants shouldn't be adequate for a growing boy, "barley wheat" and a lot of kulchas, thick round cookies of shortbread. She told him to give some of the kulchas to his master. Her rules were these:—

"1. If Sahib getting up early in morning, get you little more early up. If going late to bed, go you little more late.

2. If Sahib abuse to you, don't you fall into sorrow. If Sahib be glad with your work, don't you be happy. You be always same.

3. Eating what wanted for stomach, but Sahib telling. Taking no thing of Sahib, by hiding.

4. Obey to Sahib more than me.

5. For own fault must tell it is your fault. Must not tell it is to other man. If be any fault, tell quickly 'is my fault.' "

Sonam Sering has come to guard. He's playing a game, picking up and dropping little stones or dung pellets and reciting a verse. His fate depends on which line he is singing when a certain marked one falls, something like the "doctor, lawyer, merchant, chief" game we used to play on buttons.

I have wanted to buy you various quaint or pretty things, but Iba is a severe purchasing agent. He comes to my tent with a man carrying articles I have expressed a desire to buy. I select. The articles are taken away. I inquire later. Iba says: "The man is a robber. He wants forty rupees. I have offered fifteen!" He's quite right. If I were to do my own buying of knicknacks all the prices for grain and the rest of our supplies would mount, but I sigh for a few of the darling things I've almost had!

It really costs amazingly little to run this big caravan; at least fifteen menservants for the price of a Little Rock cook. They don't care about the money. They think much more of their nice clothes—so much, in fact, that when we got into a region where there were very few people, one of my littermen appeared in rags and tags. I thought he must have been robbed, or have let his "velvet gown" get too close to the campfire. But Iba said he was saving his fine apparel for country where there'd be someone to appreciate it.

They are very scornful of all the girls they see outside their own district though I notice they burst suddenly into louder song whenever they catch sight of one. They think our boys, aged sixteen and seventeen and twenty, must be fooling when they deny being married. All three have seriously undertaken to bring their wives to Ladakh on their honeymoons, and the whole litter-crew has volunteered service. I wonder if some girl of ten or twelve or fourteen is seeing prophetic dreams of a strange red-and-green litter and a row of smiling, white-toothed, dark-faced fellows giving her salam. She's a lucky child if she has. I do hate the thought of ever leaving them, Ellen! And in a few days we'll be over the pass, in the Wardwan valley leading down to Hindustan. And Hindustan, fascinating and wonderful though it will be, I suppose, with jungle and monkeys and parakeets and marvellous ruins, won't be, can't be this land of our heart's desire and temporary attainment.

My love to you all three. Has Charles received his little red coat?

Yours,

نذق

Lady Ba   THE CAMP BEFORE THE SPANG LA
CAMP 104

August 20

Dear MOTHER,

We marched today up a wild valley, in whose bed a grey stream roared—swirling grey water, shining stuff in feathery patterns.   I met a barefoot boy whose feet sparkled. Yesterday, reading Vergil, I found that "mica" means "sparkle." I read Vergil in school without a quiver, and now, at three times school age, I'm reading it with delight. Why, the Trojans, cast up on the African shore, got fire with flint, just as our Ladakhis do! Do you suppose they wore pouches at their belts, to carry the flint and the tinder, with an edge of steel and ornaments of brass? And they roasted grain over a hot fire and ground it on stones, exactly as our men make sattu!

But this letter is about flowers.

The whole day's march lay through a wild-flower garden. In this valley there's not a village and no one has tried to shape him even a terrace.   All up and down the slopes to the very base of precipitous crags, by the edges of dirty snow-banks, grow flowers, flowers, flowers.   Tall fireweed like that that's making our hill in Cornish a pink glory today, wild geranium, deeper blue than you know it, a purple blue, quantities of it bowing in the breeze, magenta heads of wild onion, and pink and white spires of smartweed or knotgrass, that we used to call "kiss-me-over-the-garden-gate."   Clear streamlets tumble tumultuously down to join the silvery river, and by their sides a cousin of marsh marigold lifts glossy leaves and big creamy blossoms.   One clump was reflected perfectly in a pool, and Sawang ran around the pool to pluck some for me, to the great amusement of the rest, who watched his reflection in the water, and pretended he was drowning.   They are just like children, and love to prink over a water mirror like Narcissus himself.

In one place while they were putting on their sandals after carrying me across a ford, I saw the bank above me all lustrous with gentian, the square-cupped, dark silken kind, with fringes. I picked one long-stemmed one for each of the littermen, and they all said: "Beautiful, Highness!" and Norpel ran a long way ahead to carry his to Gypsy Davy. I put out my hand to a wee, bright blue thing in the grasses not long after, and it was another kind of gentian, the fourth variety I've

found this summer. One, pale blue, five-petalled, is very
lovely by field margins: and another, with a tiny extra bract
alongside each petal, Gypsy Davy brought down from a high
spur above Suru where he and the boys bivouacked the night,
to watch the old moon and the mists on the Nun Kun massif.

You know the bluebell that isn't the Scotch bluebell, nor
the Jacob's ladder bluebell, nor the hyacinth bluebell that
makes Kent woods a heaven in May—the sapphire bluebell,
pink in budding and in withering, thick clusters with long
leaves, rather coarse. It's here—or so close a kinsman that it
deceives me. Up the slopes it goes to-day—slopes gilt with
the first yellow daisies. There were real Vassar daisy-chain
daisies too, earlier in the day. A purple aster. A white lily.
Lupins, the small purple downy, and the big spreading yellow.
And there were masses of tall elephant's heads. I have seen
that droll flower rather high in the Sierras—a little pair of
pink and white ears, with a curled pink trunk between. Here
there are varieties: bright pink and clean white, like the cloth
we used to call "print"; all lavender; pink faintly veining
white; a bright, bright yellow; and a lemon yellow,—all
with the elephant's trunk, though in some, the ears are like
curving shells. And Queen Anne's lace, fine as rose point
and yellow as old gold.

We had tiffin by the way: creamed potatoes, and rice with
raisins, and a great heap of chapatis with good butter, and
Skardu apricots, and scrambled eggs, and chocolate. And
while we ate, and I sketched my new flowers (two hundred and
thirty-eight this summer, so far) Iba and the caravan went on
ahead, loads on big black dzo with big wooden rings in their
noses, our own ponies travelling light, because tomorrow we
cross the pass over the southern chain of the Himalaya.

After tiffin we went on, and soon came upon the camp all
ready for us: green tents pitched on a grassy mead, pied with
forget-me-not and buttercup, cinquefoil and edelweiss. Cliffs
steep behind us; water roaring by, emerging from a tunnel
under a huge mass of snow that bridges the river for us;
beyond the snow, a group of sharp pinnacles of tawny marble,
rising from level bands of marble, streaming out like the manes
of wild sea-horses like those Walter Crane drew.

It's a dangerous camp. Flood may beset us, and avalanche,
and the littermen have industriously dug what they call a
"nala" (that's a valley) for draining, and directed it straight
into the tent!

If Allah wills, however, our one night here will be fortunate, and we shall survive to move on to the Pass tomorrow morning, starting by the light of a dim old moon.   Allah sends floods to drown the wicked, and drought to starve them out.   But we, though unbelievers, are Iba's friends, and Iba has been smiled on of late by that same great Maulvi who came to his assistance in the Shigar valley last year.   The Maulvi is on tour in the region, and pilgrims have gathered by the thousand to bring him gifts and receive his blessing.   Iba was given a private audience, and after that he had but to express a desire to anyone, and it was at once fulfilled.   He says that by this grace a pass has been revealed to us, less arduous than the glacier-covered Bat Kol by which we had expected to cross the range.

The Pass tomorrow!   Always in these mountain journeys we are moving towards the Pass, or crossing it, or are just over, and moving towards the next one.

There was the Zoji, our first one, a wide well-kept trail, with no hint in our August crossing of the kind of storm that could keep Roger hiding for five days in November, or again in March give him an adventure; then, the Marpo, above which we kept vigil for Nanga Parbat; the Burji, leading out of the Deosai into the Skardu country, long steep zigzags— a dead pony stiffly lying across the stone wall of a little shelter in which he had died in the snows; the nine hours on yak- back up the glacier of the Khardung, slow, weary, difficult plodding; and this spring the snow-bound Chang La which Iba got us over, in spite of the pessimists.   There were passes south of the Indus, too, when we dipped into Rupshu, and little passes again between tributaries of the Indus, on that bit of the Treaty Road on which we travelled from Leh to Kargil, each with its individual character, and, unless glacier-bound, each with its flowers.   Always as we approach a pass there are more flowers, and more beautiful.   The most delicate dwell in the most austere places.

The old Kesar saga has a song Francke Padre Sahib translates:

"A flower, blooming on the pass,
  Oh, a pure flower is in bloom!

"On all the high passes
  A flower of fine shape is in bloom!

"Thou art but half opened,
  O Lord, who art like a flower of the morning!

"Thou art but half opened,
  O Lord, who art like a Kaliman flower!"

What lovely flowers will we be finding on tomorrow's Pass and beyond it? Over there the mountains have moisture in plenty and over there the forests begin.

I wish you could see them, too.   I always wish that!

Yours,

Gypsy Davy   CAMP 105
                                                 August 22

Dear CHOT,

We're camped on the India slope of the Himalaya. We've come a long way and been a long time about it. We tried the Simla road after you, but the snow was still too deep. The Mem-Sahib and I both began to feel the altitude, and the boys' appetites had dropped from twenty chapatis to seventeen.

Later we tried the Zaskar road. Water too high. Then we came on to Suru and collected dzo for the Spang La. Did they tell you about the Spang La? It isn't on our map. Lies a little north-west of your Bat Kol. We have a mind to make Simla up the Chandra.

We found Allah's snow bridges in the Chilung better built than the human substitutes over Suru tributaries. Iba camped us in the hands of Allah on a flat where the stream from the Bat Kol joins the Chilung.

We awoke while the valley still lay enchanted in the night. There was a vague feeling of stir in the air. Quite suddenly a bright flame leaped up where the Suru men lay hidden among their shadowy dzo, and in the circle of firelight there, there was bustle, and multiplicity of little things.

The Mem-Sahib didn't much like the grinding of the boulders in the stream-bed while we waited. I was glad enough myself to be safely under way, crossing a solid snow bridge with all the caravan to higher ground.

How consistently these difficult gorges, in the lower parts of valleys which have had big glaciers in them, give place to wide flats in the upper reaches,—grey streams braiding patterns in deep gravel! This valley ended shortly, blind; walled in by high black cliffs, and snouts of glaciers reaching down between them, spouting dirty water. There was some steep grey moraine piled up against cliffs on the south, and for this we made, crossing one shallow grey stream after another.

Angbo pointed out sheep, many hundreds of them, hard to see, feeding among rocks on high, craggy slopes behind us. And presently we came upon two tall black pugs. They seemed half-naked after our fellows. They were very polite to Iba, and told him they were in charge of all those Punjabi sheep. I wonder if it takes them longer to come in here from the Punjab with sheep than to make the Deosai. In either case it must take a fair part of the grazing season. You remember there wasn't a sheep left on the Deosai at this time last year.

We stopped for tiffin when we had crossed the last grey braid, and let the caravan go by. Longpa made chocolate from Punjabi goat's milk. The loaded dzo and empty ponies toiled up coils and coils of trail on the grey moraine. Some dzo or other seemed to be standing, every time we looked, having his load adjusted. And now and then there were long waits as if the caravan had found its way barred. At length the last dzo disappeared. The last stone came rattling down. And we set out.

The Lady Ba was a handful on that trail. I missed you sorely. Tomar took to stumbling, and Nunatuk had to be substituted. Nunatuk, as you know, is very clever with his feet, but there were stretches where I couldn't trust him. At such we put the Mem-Sahib into her Braldoh harness and dragged her up. We had a fool of a chaprasi from the Kargil Tehsildar, who kept trying to butt in and show Nunatuk what to do. I'll wager that fellow sees me in nightmares yet.

We crossed a nasty little stream, so dirty that Nunatuk had to feel his way among the boulders. The moraine began to groan beneath us. We saw little slips on steep gully sides, often repeated in the same spot. Presently it dawned upon us that we had left the moraine and were travelling on glacier.

At last we came out on easy snow slopes. It was a long, wide, shallow pass, covered deep with snow and ice. We kept to a steepish slope of hard old snow on ice. The footing was good except at places where snow water was ponded back by slush. The Mem-Sahib was in her litter on this slope, and her men were going barefoot to save their chapli. When men fell in such places, they broke dams, and violent little floods threatened the litter. It must have been cold work. The tiffin coolie and the dzo men had no footgear. Jim and I have had them all in our clinic at this camp, patching stubbed toes with burn-wax, and bandaging them. What pitiably cracked heels most of these poor fellows have, old and young alike!

We got off the snow at last at the far end of the pass, and looked down into the Morsekhol (we think it was) blind like the Chilung, only its head was all precipice, rock below and ice above. There was a big, dirty glacier down in the valley bottom, starting at the foot of the rock cliffs. No connection with the glaciers above, except by avalanche.

None of us knew exactly where the India side of the Bat Kol La lay. We thought it might be here in this impossible place, at the head of the Morsekhol. We wondered how you had made it without a parachute. I took a chance, and told the men that you had made it somehow, and they gave their cheer: "Hip hip hoorah! Hamara Chhota Sahib!"

It was a long, steep, muddy, slippery way, zigzagging down loose moraine to the old second-hand glacier in the bottom, and thence down and interminably down side moraines, until we got past his ugly snout and left him growling there behind us.

The valley below was all green as far as we could see, from the river-bluffs almost up to the ridge-tops. We found the ponies and the dzo up to their bellies in rich flowery grass, half of them lying down and eating like camels, where they lay. Iba said our ponies were "hairan." The men are excited. I wonder what they are thinking. There are no people here and no ditches. There is a wet sky, but it isn't raining. Did Yonton have to take more than one all-day soaking before he twigged to the possibility of this substitute for ditches?

Yours,

Lady Ba   CAMP 105
                    OVER THE CREST OF THE SOUTHERN RANGE
                                          August 23

Dear LETTICE,

Haven't you wondered how a butterfly must feel when it first realizes it is a butterfly, it that went to sleep a grub?

We've left the high places. There's a month of mountain travel before us yet, but behind us is the region of the gods. I'm looking back, and I find it hard to trace the thin thread of continuity that links me with the me who went in over the Zoji La, only fifteen months ago by your calendar.   But what is Time, past or coming, to a new-waked butterfly?—wings very new and somewhat wobbly, but wings for all that.   My Earth is round.   The East is within me.

We were startled out of our sleep this morning before dawn by the roar of avalanche.   We are always glad to be awakened in these mountain nights.   We feel we're missing something precious while we sleep, and yet our sleep is of a finer quality than any housed-in sort.

From our beds we could see the misty valley head, the skyline peaks now hid and now discovered by the clouds.   A high cloud caught the sun.   The peaks showed black.   Suddenly, behind the black peaks, we saw a remoter peak, white, but ghostly white.   Little lighted clouds played delicately about it.

Then, between the ghostly peak and the black one came a thread of light.   Lighted cloudlets drifted over the ghostly one, and we knew it for what it was: the shadow of the black peak on the sky! It vanished, and the black peak showed white, as we knew it must be, thick with a great ice-cap as we saw it yesterday.

Then another peak cast its shadow, and another, and another, on the sky, the whole ridge at the valley-head showing.   The sun was still out of sight, and had not touched one of the peaks on the face toward us, but for each point or depression or long sweep or little jog, there was a mate out on the sky. Now one would disappear, and another come.   Then, after twenty minutes, the first one showed at a new angle.   By and by one peak showed us an illuminated face and its shadow on the sky at the same time.   Then the lighted cloud hid the peak, but the shadow's shape was still clear out there.

Gypsy Davy has told me, before, that he has seen the shadows of peaks on the sky, but in all my mountain years, I have never seen them: "Planet-pacing shadows at Earth-coeval rate."

I feel my wings spread out, full.

We salute your East Windows.

A Fortunate Woman

Gypsy Davy   PATHANKOT

October 1

Dear NED,

We have left the naked mountains and the blessed sunshine and the merry rosy people. We have come a month's way down. We breathe a heavy lowland air.

The first of the way lay in the deep Marau-Wardwan Nala, a green way under a misty low-hung dripping roof, hiding what snow-crowned bald pates there was no telling, setting a hundred torrent-beds awash with foaming water tumbling from half-veiled cragged heights, down steep slopes and ledges dark with forest, down slopes less steep where green waves run through tall grass stained with blue and gold and rose of flowers; a way loud with the roar of impetuous water, thunderous by the wild flood in the valley bottom.

The upper reaches are empty of men or cattle, though the richest grass grows there, luxuriant, unvexed by any tree or bush. Down lower, where the birch begins timorously, on down to the firs, Punjabi cattle range, bullock and naked buffalo, herded by ragged lowlanders, whole families of them living damply under leaky cotton sheets, come a long wet journey up from their parched plains. In the middle reaches, among pines, a scant drab sullen population half-heartedly tills a fertile soil. The lower reaches, down toward Kishtwar, are more populous, shorn of forest, and better tilled, but the valley is as damp and dismal, and the people as morose and sullen. It seemed to me that the people in the Hindu villages were less morose and less unfriendly than those in the Mussulman villages.

There was a vague sense of danger hanging over us all our slow journey down. There was no certainty about the trail ahead. We could never be quite sure a bridge was there until we came to it, and there was no alternative crossing of the turbulent river possible by ford or ferry at any of the places where we had to cross. The thought of unsafe scaffolds ahead along cliff faces wetted with spray tossed by the river—that long caravan always at my back—was not an easy thought. The mending of trail on solid ground is a simple matter, but not so rebuilding broken scaffold. As it was, two of our ponies were crowded off narrow ledge and drowned, but those accidents were the fault of our own men, and no fault of the trail-makers.

There was less certainty about our relations with the people.

In all the long safar before, we had been on ground where Iba knew his men, but here they were strange to him, and he distrusted them in proportion. There were rumours of unrest in Hindustan, of riots in Kashmir, and every now and then one of those ominous black pagris would cross our path.

The village headmen talked of tigers. One showed us a mauled villager by way of warning against forest camps. But mountain jungle, mildly tiger-haunted, is to be preferred above the best village, even among friendly people. Iba put the horses at the pickets in the night-time and built big fires and set guards about at such camps. But the guards were village men as sleepy as our own, and I have found, at midnight, fires low, guard fast asleep, whole picket lines adrift. I was not however, forced to dispute any matter with a tiger or other beast of prey.

The thought of venomous snakes and insects put us up on cots for the first time in all these months, and the archfiend Anopheles brought out the nets and saw to it that they were carefully gone over every day with thread and needle. I put the men into headnets and cotton bags, for they sleep naked on the ground with only their coats thrown over them, and carelessly expose wide vulnerable areas. Even in the bags they had to be repeatedly kicked awake and bid tuck themselves in. The ban of altitude was presently lifted from one after another of the hostile microbes after Anopheles' nursling came among us, and they were hungrily at large in unfamiliar guises, so that none of our company were well able to do battle with them, and we went about to dodge them.

But none of all this damped the ardours of our young zamindars. They played with their reflections in wayside pools, and were stayed from drinking fatal draughts therefrom only by my order wrathfully enforced. They hunted wild flowers for the Lady Ba in tall grass, having continually to be admonished to feel before them with khud sticks for ambushed venom. (The Lady Ba closed her list at four hundred, long before the end.)

Docile coolies (Brahmins, some of them, Iba boasted) gave place to rough Punjabi muleteers, black-pagri-walas, a half-dozen stalwart handsome fellows, with a band of forty mules bound homeward. These pillaged and clubbed their way among a timid peasantry,—I had the bandaging of one head of their breaking. They led the till now all-powerful Ibrahim, fuming, by a ring in his nose. He presently came to see that it was they who chose him, not he them, and submitted to their extortions, after which they were most amiable to all of us. I made a fever-smitten one of them my friend by quinine hydrochloride tablets.

For the men, each day brought new wonder. Old wives' tales, dismissed in the bazars of their villages as moonshine, now showed credible appearances: huge naked beasts; calves big as full-grown Ladakhi cattle; trees, beside which the tallest poplar of the Leh Residency compound would be as a sapling; stranger and stranger trees; wooden fruit hanging; ceaseless metallic sounds in the branches made by a janwar tantalizingly difficult to see; logs on the fire, dripping butter; whole villages of wooden houses, riven slabs, more timber in one village than in all Ladakh, and better; bridges with no sag or sway; the cloudy roof, hardly to be seen through roofs of foliage, suddenly letting down as much water as when a glacial dam breaks and floods a valley; mosses; ferns; paroquets flashing green overhead; fat slimy snails underfoot; monkeys, admion ke muafik, chattering and sporting in the forest, squatting on village roofs, fifty storming Angbo's kitchen on a green hilltop what time he slept; roadside shrines, monoliths too great for any number of men's lifting; uncouth carvings; huge stone tanks of green-filmed water where slender men and women of great beauty go down to bathe devoutly in their respective corners,—nakedness and bathing hardly known in cool dry Ladakh; a tall ruined palace by such a tank, rarely frescoed, monkey-haunted; weird holy men, ash-besmeared; a barge on the Ravi for the crossing of it, which Big Tashi tried to push off by shouldering the side from within, desisting for a moment to watch a man shoot by on a small buffalo hide, and appear shortly as a headless buffalo erect on human legs walking up the farther bank: a host of strange impressions made on fresh minds, and always Sonam the chronicler writing, and drawing rude pictures on strong Lhasa paper stowed in his bosom,—overmuch space perhaps given to price of sheep and butter and wheat and coolie hire, but other matters of moment recorded.

Angbo chose the last camp, as high as the low hills permitted, arid hills thereabout, rocky and thorny.

Tents were struck at the next sundown for the last march: after nightfall, the trail giving place to a most unfamiliar surface, hard and smooth without rock or wrinkle, wide like a river, disconcertingly wide, so that men and ponies, hairan, drifted from side to side upon it; a tiny light by the roadside, all the men bending down to examine the strange appearance; then many dancing lights over a swamp; loud creaking ahead; looming out of the dark, tall as three yak, a huge bullock, and behind him, between two rundles of just proportions, a mountainous Cart,—their first.

Hours of following the strange empty highway through forest and swamp by great stone bridges, down and down on easy grades with many windings, so that the Lady Ba, lying in her litter for her last sweet night ride, saw now Cassiopeia before her, and again the Archer; the singing and piping of familiar places hushed in all this strangeness, in this great swamp at the foot of the Himalaya, where mountain water oozes out at the edge of the lowland, this terai.

After midnight, there came a tumultuous sound of cattle lowing and men calling, and suddenly we found ourselves in the midst of a wide stream of mountainous carts and loaded cattle, long linked camel-trains among them, all moving slowly out along a great level dusty way against us.

And then, while sahib log sought low stars to the south, where only low trees instead of mountains hid the horizon there, a shower of sparks shot up above the tree-tops, and we heard loud pantings as of some monster near at hand. But the Sahib held on his way, regardless. And shortly there was unceremonious dumping of loads in the dak bangla compound, and all hands were off for the railhead to watch and listen, drunken with wonder and excitement.

Today we have formally paid them off, all save two most intrepid who have cast in their lot with us for better or worse,—Baba Iba to shepherd the others with his ponies homeward. To us in the dak bangla room each came, alone, to make his salam, receive his chit, his money and our address for news of his safe arrival in his own country. They took the dust of our feet, they hailed us as their father and mother, they prayed blessing upon us, and often forgot their money, bowing themselves out, half tear-blinded.

And now Sawang pipes at our door while two of the littermen in the verandah jerkily ply the pankha over our last meal of Angbo's serving.

They will have a week or so of tamasha, invest some of their earnings in bazar treasures, see many strange and ajib sights and customs, but for them as for us this khush qismat safar is ended. We are all sorry.

Yours,

Gypsy Davy

THE CARAVAN VOCABULARY

THESE are the Urdu words we taught our village men, with a few Ladakhi and Turki words which we all used commonly. The Urdu words are transliterated from Forbes' *Hindustani Dictionary*, in accordance with the R.G.S. Technical Series, No. 2, *Alphabets of Foreign Languages Transcribed into English*. The Ladakhi and Turki I have set down as they sounded to an ear not sensitive to their finer shades. The letter to Stuart on page 107 gives as much grammar as the boys needed at the outset.

Pronunciation is indicated according to the R.G.S. rules:—

Vowels :

> ā and a, as the two a's in lava
> ai, as in aisle
> au, as ou in out
> e, as in eh
> ī and i, as in marine, piano
> ō and o, as in both, rotund
> ū and u, as in rude, pull

Consonants:

as in English except—

> g always hard
> ḥ not sounded after a or t; making k or g before it guttural;
>   sounded after b or d, as in cab-horse, wood-house.
> q a deep guttural k
> s always as in so
> The little inverted comma represents a guttural sound "impossible
>   for a European throat to pronounce."

Of course, one can get a proper accent only by association with cultivated people, but this rough and ready sort is practicable for communication with servants and village officials.

A

ab	now	āj	today
ab-hī'	immediately	ajib'	wonder
ach'hā	good	āmbān'	Chinese official
ād'hā	half	ā'nā	to come
ād'mī, (ādmiōn')	man, men (as object of postposition)	an'dā	egg
		an'dar	inside
af'sar	officer	and'hā	dark
af'sōs	sorry	angre'zī	English
āg	fire	ānkh	eye
ag'ar	if	ān'nā	one-sixteenth of a rupee
ag'archi	although	āp	you (in respect language)
		āq'bōz	light grey
ā'ge	ahead (ke-age placed after object=ahead of)	āqsaqāl'	"white-beard" (in Leh, official in charge of traders)
āh'sta	slow		

271

ā'rā	saw
ārām'	rest
Argūn'	half breed
āsān'	easy
as'bāb	luggage
ās'mān	sky
ā'tā	flour
āth	eight
aur	and
'au'rat	woman
ā'wāz	voice, noise

B

bā'bā	father, daddy
bābū'	official or clerk
ba'd	after
bad'alnā	to change
bād'shāh	king
bāgh	garden
bahā'dur	brave (honorary title)
bā'har	outside (ke-bahar, placed after object=outside of)
bahut'	very (usually pronounced like boat)
bai'thnā	sit, stay
ba'je	o'clock
bakh'shish	tip
bak'rī	goat
banā'nā	to make, prepare
band	shut
bānd'hnā	to tie
band'-o-bast	arrangement
bandūq'	gun
bang'lā	house (dak bangla=rest house maintained by Government for travellers)
bāp	father
ba'rā	big, elder, superior
barā'bar	equal
bā'rah	twelve
barf	snow, ice
barha'ī	carpenter
barsā'tī	canvas, waterproof
bas	enough
bāt	matter, speech
bat'tī	candle, light
bāwar'chi	cook
bāwar'chī-khā'nā	kitchen, cook-tent
bā'yān	left (hand)
bazār'	market
bech'nā	to sell
be'gam	queen
bel'chā	shovel
be-wu'qūf	foolish
bhā'ī	brother
bhar'al	"blue sheep" (ovis nahura)
bhā'rī	heavy
bhe'rī	sheep
bhū'kā	hungry
bhūl-jā'nā	to forget
bhū'sā	straw, hay
bīmār'	ill
bip	raft of poles

Bod	Tibetan, or Ladakhi, equivalent to Buddhist
bojh	load
bol'nā	to speak
bud'dhā	old (of people)
burt'sa	sage-bush

C

chā	tea
chābi'	key
chābuk'	whip
chad'dar	shawl, sheet
Chag'dso	temporal head of monastery
chakor'	partridge
chak'wā	duck, m.
chak'wī	duck, f.
chālāk'	lively
chal'nā (chal'o jā'o)	to go (get out)
cham'chā	spoon
cham'rā	leather
chang	beer
chang	north
Chang'pa	nomads
chapā'tī	a thin crisp sheet of unleavened bread
chaplī'	sandals
chaprā'sī	messenger, attendant
chār	four
chā'ras	hashish
charoq'	Yarkandi soft-soled boot
chauki-dār'	watchman
chā'wal	rice
chha	six
chhor'nā	to leave
chho'tā	small, young, minor, short
chhu'rī	knife
chinār'	plane-tree
chī'nī	sugar
chit'thī (short, chit)	letter, recommendation
chorten'	Buddhist monument
chup ra'ho	keep still

D

da'f'a	time, once, twice, etc.
dā'hinā	right (hand)
dāk	post, distance of about four miles
Dā'lai Lā'ma	Chief Lama
dā'lī	present of fruit, etc.
dān	container (chā-dān, teapot; yak-dān, box for yak to carry)
dā'nā	grain
dānt	tooth
dar'akht	tree
dard	pain
dar'nā	to fear
darwā'za	door
dar'zi	tailor
das	ten
dastūr'	custom
daur'nā	to run
da'wā	medicine

deg'chĭ	pot
dekh'nā	to see
de'nā (dĭ'yā)	to give (gave)
der	late
dhĭ'lā	loose
dho'bĭ	washerman
dho'nā	to wash
dhŭp	sunlight
dil	heart
dil-chasp'	interesting, pleasant
din	day
do	two
dost	friend
dūdh	milk
dukān'	shop
dukāng'	monks' assembly hall
dūr	far
dush'man	enemy
dzo	cross between yak and bullock

E

ek	one
ek-dam'	"one breath," at once

F

fakĭr'	holy man vowed to poverty

G

gad'hā	ass
garm	warm
ghar	house
gharĭb'	poor
gho'rā	horse
ghusl	bath
gĭ'lā	wet
gol	round
gom'pa	monastery
gosht	meat
gyā'rah	eleven

H

hai	is
hain	are
hairān'	astonished
hā'jĭ	pilgrim
halāl'	Mohammedan way of cutting animals' throats
hal'kā	light
ham	we, us (commonly used for I, me)
hamā'rā	our (mine)
hān	yes
hāth	hand
ha'wā	air, wind
hawāl-dār'	sergeant
hāz'rĭ	breakfast (chhota hazri, early morning tea)
Hindūstān'	India proper
ho'nā	to be
hukm	order
hŭng	interjection at end of Buddhist prayer formula

hu'qa	pipe by which tobacco is smoked through water (usually transliterated hookah)
huzūr'	The Presence, sir

I

id'har	here, hither
is'-pās	on this side
is-wās'te	therefore
ĭt'nā	so much

J

jab	when
jadū'	enchantment
jag'ah	place
jag'nā	to wake
jaldĭ'	quick
jā'nā (ga'yā)	to go (went)
jān'war	animal
jan'ga	forest
jawān'	young
jhū (jhū'le)	Ladakhi greetings (respect language)
jinn	devil
Jongpen'	Tibetan district officer
Josh-khā'nā	to boil

K

kab	when?
kab'hĭ	ever
kab'hĭ kab'hĭ	sometimes
kab'hĭ nahĭn'	never
kāgh'az	paper
kā	of (placed after its object)
kal	yesterday, tomorrow
kā'lā	black
Ka'lon	Minister of Raja
kam	less
kām	work
kam'arā	room
kam'mal	blanket
kam'tĭ	deficiency
kam-zor'	weak
kān	ear
kān'gri	hand brazier
kān'tā	fork, hook
kap'rā, kapre	cloth, clothes
kār'awān bā'shi	headman of caravan,—Iba
kārind'a	steward
kar'nā (kĭyā)	to do, make (did)
kāt'nā	to cut
ke	of (placed after its object)
ke-bā'bat	about (placed after its object)
ke-sāth'	with (placed after its object)
ke-wās'te	for (placed after its object)
khabar-dār'	careful
khā'nā	to eat; dinner; house
kharāb'	bad, evil
kharĭ'dnā	to buy
khiyāl'	thought (hamko khiyāl hai = I think)
khūbān'ĭ	apricot

T

khu'lā — open
khurjīn' — saddle-bags
khush — happy
kī — that, conj.
kid'har — whither?
kis-wās'te — what for?
kitāb' — book
kit'nā — how much?
ko — to (placed after object)
kuchh — something
kuchh nahīn' — nothing
kul'cha — cake
kyā — what?
kyang' — wild ass
kyūn'ki — because

L

lā — pass
lagām' — bridle
lākh — 100,000
lāl — red
lā'ma — Buddhist priest
lam'bā — long
Lambar-dār' — village headman
lā'nā — to bring
lar'kā — child
le-jā'nā — to carry
le'nā — to take
ling'-pū — flute
log — people
lo'hā — iron
lo'hār — blacksmith
lokrī' — wood
lum'ba — valley
lung'ma — valley

M

mā'bāp — parents
madad' — help (madad dena, to help)
ma'gar — but
Māhārā'jā — a great king
Māhārā'nī — a great queen
mai'lā — dirty
mak'han — butter
ma'lūm' — knowledge (hamko malum hai=I know)
māng'nā — to want
mā'nī — jewel, word in prayer-formula
mār-dāl'nā — to kill
mar-jā'nā — to die
mār'khŏr — wild goat
martŏl' — hammer (Portuguese)
masjid' — mosque
maul'vī — learned Mussulman teacher
maund — about eighty pounds weight
maus'am — weather
mazbūt' — strong, secure, tight
mekh — nail, tent-peg
mem'-sāhib — European woman
men — in (placed after its object)
mihr-bā'nī — kindness, please, thank you
mil'nā — to get
mit'tī — earth
mo'tā — fat, thick

muā'fik — like, according (ke-muafik after object=like)
muez'zin — he who calls the Mussulman folk to prayer
mulk — country
mulla — learned man, Mohammedan priest
mun'shī — clerk, secretary
mur'ghī — hen
mushkil' — difficult

N

nahīn' — no, not
nā'ib — assistant
nā'lā — valley, ravine
namāz' — prayer
nam'da — felt
nan'gā — naked
nau — nine
nau'kar — servant
na'yā — new
nazdīk' — near
nī — no, nor
nī'che — low (ke-niche, following its object=under)
nī'lā — blue

O

om — interjection opening Buddhist prayer formula

P

pābū' — Ladakhi shoes, felt and yak-hair
pād'me — lotus, word in Buddhist prayer formula
pag'rī — turban
pahār' — mountain
pa'hile — before (time)
pahunch'nā — to arrive
pai'sā — quarter of an anna
pak-dan'dī — foot path
pānch — five
pan'dit — learned Hindu
pank'hā — fan
pā'nī — water
par — on (placed after its object)
pār — scaffold
parā'o — camp, march
par'bat — mountain
pashmī'na — fine wool under goat's hair
pathar' — stone
pattī' — bandage, puttee
pāyāb' — ford
perāg' — Ladakhi woman's head-dress
phir — again
pīch'he — back (ke pichhe after object =behind)
pilāv' — rice cooked in butter, with meat or fruit or vegetable
piyā'sā ho'nā — to be hungry
pon'ga — pack-saddle
ponpo' — lord
postīn' — fur coat
purā'nā — old (of things)

Q

qabr'stān	graveyard
qain'chī	scissors
qis'mat	luck
Qorān'	sacred book of Mohammedans
qu'lī	coolie (too thoroughly established in English for challenge)
Qutē-dār'	official who distributes grain and wood

R

Rā'jā	King
Ramzān'	Mohammedan month of fasting
Rā'nī	Queen
ras'sī	rope
rās'tā	road, trail
rāt	night
rī	mountain
ro'tī	bread
roz	day
rū'pī	rupee, coin worth about one shilling and fourpence, or thirty cents.

S

sab	all
sāf	clean
safar'	journey
safed'	white
sā'hib	lord, master, Mr.
sā'īs	groom
sak'nā	to be able
salām'	Mohammedan greeting and farewell, salaam
samajh'nā	to understand
sandūq'	box
sard	cold
sā'rī	Indian woman's veil-robe
sar'sing	a Baltistan tree
sāt	seven
sattū'	barley parched and ground
sau	one hundred
sawār' ho'nā	to ride
sawe're	early
se	than
ser	two pounds weight
serā'ī	an inn for man and beast
shā'bāsh	bravo
shaitān'	wicked
shā'pū	wild sheep (ovis vignei)
shā'yād	perhaps
shikār'	game (shikar karna, to hunt)
shor'ba	soup
sikh'nā	to learn
sipā'hī	soldier (usually transliterated sepoy)
sirf	only
Skū'sho	re-incarnation
so'nā	to sleep

stor'ma	effigy or emblem
sub'ah	morning
suk'hā	dry
sust	lazy

T

tamā'shā	show, party
tambū'	tent
tām'tām	drum
taqlīf'	trouble
tarkā'rī	vegetables
Tehsīl-dār'	Revenue-Officer, representative of Governor
ter'ah	thirteen
thā	was
thai'lā	bag
tha'kā	tired
thīk	right
tho'rā	small
tif'fin	lunch
tīn	three
tok'rā	basket
to'pī	hat
tsām'pa	barley
tum	you (to servants or intimate friends)
tumhā'rā	your

U

ud'har	there
u'mīd	hope (hamko umid hai-= I hope)
un'chā	high
ū'par	up
us'-pās	on that side

W

wā'lā	one who (bakri-wala=goatherd, das-wala= a ten-rupee note)
wā'pas	back, adv.
waqt	time
Wazā'rat	the Governor's post
Wazīr'	Governor
Wilā'yat	England
wuh	that

Y

yā	or
yād	memory (hamko yad hai= I remember)
yih	this

Z

zak	goatskin raft
zāmin'	field
zāmindār'	farmer
zarū'rī	necessary
zel'chā	saddle rug
Zil'dār'	an official between Tehsil-dar and Lambardar
zīn	riding saddle

INDEX

PLACE names are spelled according to the rules of the Royal Geographical Society's Permanent Committee on Place Names, which follows the usage of the Indian Survey for all Indian Empire names. Specifically, most of these names have been taken from Major Mason's *Routes in the Western Himalaya*.

Pronunciation is indicated according to the rules given at the head of the Caravan Vocabulary, page 271.

Places which appear on The Map are indicated by references showing the latitude and longitude square in which they are located, e.g. Nanga Parbat (35°, 75°) means that Nanga Parbat is to be found on The Map in the region bounded on the south by the 35th parallel of latitude, and on the east by the 75th meridian.